BESTSELLING BOOK SERIES

Renting Out Your Property For Dummies®, 2nd Edition

Handling a Telephone Call f… …nant

- Have near your phone a pen or pencil, a blank no… …ental property and the area.
- Answer the telephone professionally with a business-like greeting (such as 'Chris Jones, how may I help you?') within the first three rings.
- Provide basic information about the rental property while obtaining information about the prospective tenant.
- Use open-ended questions and try to build up a rapport with the prospective tenant.
- Ensure the prospective tenant is suitable by outlining your rental selection criteria.
- If the tenant is suitable, convince him of the benefits of renting your property.
- Anticipate and be prepared for objections – these are a sign of the prospective tenant's interest.
- Convert phone calls to a viewing, because even the best rental properties can't be rented over the phone.

Avoiding Problems upon Move-Out

- **Know exactly when the tenant is moving out.**
- **Don't allow the tenants to use any portion of their deposit as their last month's rent.** This way, if the tenants leave the property in a poor condition, you can use the deposit for what it was intended.
- **Get a forwarding address for your tenants.**
- **Provide tenants with a letter that clearly communicates your expectations regarding the condition of the rental property and the return of the deposit.**
- **Immediately conduct an inspection of the property with the tenant when she moves out.** Compare the condition of the property to the checklist you made when the tenant moved in.
- **Take photos and have contractors or suppliers provide detailed invoices for any work required in order to repair damages.**
- **Promptly schedule the necessary repairs to make the property ready to rent again while looking for any other damage done by the vacating tenant.**
- **Within legal requirements, account for and return the unused portion of the tenant's deposit to the tenant's last known address.**
- **If the deposit itemisation form and refund cheque are returned, keep the envelope.** They can serve as proof if your former tenant ever alleges that you did not attempt to return the deposit.
- **Always look out for signs that the tenant has abandoned your property, particularly if the current rent is late and/or you are pursuing legal action against the tenant.**

For Dummies: Bestselling Book Series for Beginners

Renting Out Your Property For Dummies®, 2nd Edition

Preparing to Show a Rental Property

- **After you have legal possession, remove all of the prior tenant's personal possessions and any rubbish.**
- **Check all plumbing (toilets, taps, and pipes) to ensure they are working properly.** Make sure that there are no leaks, that the plumbing has the proper pressure, and that there is adequate drainage.
- **Check all appliances to ensure they are working properly.** Run the dishwasher through a full cycle. Be sure that all the racks are in the oven.
- **Check all hardware.** Change the locks and ensure they are operational. Pay attention to all catches and latches.
- **Check all windows, curtains, and blinds.** They should be clean, unbroken, secure, and operate properly. All window locks should be working.
- **Check all walls, ceilings, and skirting boards.** The paint and/or wallpaper should provide proper coverage, without holes, cuts, scratches, nails, or bad seams.
- **Check all carpets, rugs, lino, and wooden floors.** They should be clean and in good condition. The flooring should be properly installed, with no bad seams.
- **Check bathrooms.** Thoroughly clean the toilet, bath, shower, sink, mirrors, and cabinets. Check the toilet roll holder and towel rail to ensure they are clean. Put a new toilet roll in each bathroom.
- **Check all cupboards, wardrobes, and storage areas.** Rails, hooks, shelves, lights, floors, and walls should be clean.
- **Check all counters, cabinets, and doors.** They should be clean and fully operational, presenting no hazards.
- **Check smoke detectors and all lighting for proper operation.**
- **Check all patios, balconies, and hallways.** They should be clean and railings should be secure.
- **Check the heating to make sure it is working properly.**
- **Check the rental property's kerb appeal, including the front and back gardens, drive, and path up to the front door.** Keep them as neat and tidy as possible.
- **Perform a final inspection of the entire rental property for appearance and cleanliness.** Be sure to recheck the property every few days that it lies empty.

Item 2921-8.
For more information about John Wiley & Sons, call (+44) 1243 779777.

For Dummies: Bestselling Book Series for Beginners

Renting Out Your Property FOR DUMMIES®

2ND EDITION

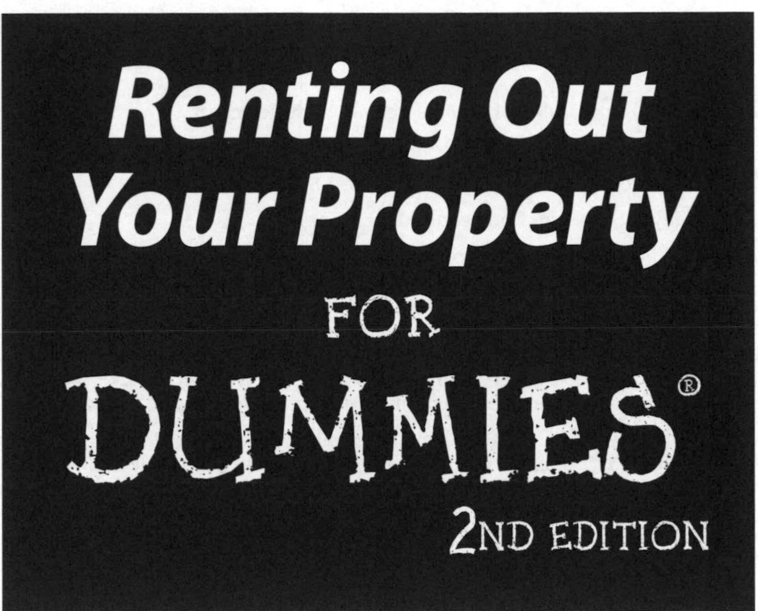

by Melanie Bien
and Robert Griswold

John Wiley & Sons, Ltd

Renting Out Your Property For Dummies®, 2nd Edition

Published by
John Wiley & Sons, Ltd
The Atrium
Southern Gate
Chichester
West Sussex
PO19 8SQ
England

E-mail (for orders and customer service enquires): cs-books@wiley.co.uk

Visit our Home Page on www.wiley.com

Published by John Wiley & Sons, Ltd, Chichester, West Sussex

For general information on our other products and services, please contact our Customer Care Department within the U.S. at 800-762-2974, outside the U.S. at 317-572-3993, or fax 317-572-4002.

For technical support, please visit www.wiley.com/techsupport.

Wiley also publishes its books in a variety of electronic formats. Some content that appears in print may not be available in electronic books.

British Library Cataloguing in Publication Data: A catalogue record for this book is available from the British Library

ISBN-13: 978-0-470-02921-3

ISBN-10: 0-470-02921-8

Printed and bound in Great Britain by Bell & Bain Ltd, Glasgow

10 9 8 7 6 5 4 3 2 1

About the Authors

Melanie Bien is associate director at independent mortgage broker Savills Private Finance. Before joining SPF at the end of 2004, she was personal finance editor and property writer on the *Independent on Sunday.* She has written about buy-to-let for a variety of national newspapers, magazines, and Web sites, and written several books and pamphlets to accompany television programmes on property makeovers and design, buying, renovating, and selling property.

Melanie also has first-hand experience of renting out property, owning, and managing six buy-to-let properties in conjunction with her brother and parents. She lives in East London.

Robert Griswold earned a Bachelors degree and two Masters degrees in real estate and related fields from the University of Southern California's School of Business.

Robert is a hands-on property manager with more than 20 years of practical experience, running Griswold Real Estate Management. He hosts a weekly radio show, and has written for the *Los Angeles Times, San Diego Union-Tribune,* and *San Francisco Chronicle.* He has twice been named the #1 Radio or Television Real Estate Journalist in the Country by the National Association of Real Estate Editors in the US.

Dedication

This book is dedicated to my brother JB and my parents, Helena and William. Their enthusiasm and encouragement helped to make writing this book a real pleasure.

— Melanie Bien

Author's Acknowledgements

I would like to thank Jason Dunne and Daniel Mersey at Wiley for the opportunity to write this book and for their help, direction, feedback, and constructive criticism during the process. Also, many thanks to everyone who works behind the scenes at Wiley for their efforts in making this book possible.

A special thanks to Malcolm Tarling at the Association of Residential Letting Agents for his help during the research of this book and expertise on this topic. I would also like to thank David Hollingworth, Ray Boulger, and Mark Harris – mortgage brokers who know more about the market than one could ever really need to and proved invaluable to me during the research process.

A special mention to Robert Cole who was the inspiration and encouragement behind me choosing personal finance, and hence, property writing, in the first instance. The lessons in the pub were inspired!

Thanks also to those friends I had to cancel at the last minute for being not only understanding but encouraging: it was more to do with deadlines looming than the allure of assured shorthold tenancies, honest.

And finally, thanks to my family for their untiring support and encouragement. To my mother for the wonderful reflexology treatments which helped me relax, my father for his knowledge and sound advice, and my brother for getting me away from it all to the Arsenal every now and again.

— Melanie Bien

Publisher's Acknowledgements

We're proud of this book; please send us your comments through our Dummies online registration form located at www.dummies.com/register/.

Some of the people who helped bring this book to market include the following:

Acquisitions, Editorial, and Media Development

Project Editor: Daniel Mersey

Content Editor: Steve Edwards

Executive Editor: Jason Dunne

Executive Project Editor: Martin Tribe

Cover Photo: © Peter M. Wilson/CORBIS

Cartoons: Ed McLachlan

Composition Services

Project Coordinator: Jennifer Theriot

Layout and Graphics: Carl Byers, Andrea Dahl, Denny Hager, Barry Offringa, Lynsey Osborn, Alicia South

Proofreader: Laura Albert

Indexer: Techbooks

Publishing and Editorial for Consumer Dummies

Diane Graves Steele, Vice President and Publisher, Consumer Dummies

Joyce Pepple, Acquisitions Director, Consumer Dummies

Kristin A. Cocks, Product Development Director, Consumer Dummies

Michael Spring, Vice President and Publisher, Travel

Kelly Regan, Editorial Director, Travel

Publishing for Technology Dummies

Andy Cummings, Vice President and Publisher, Dummies Technology/General User

Composition Services

Gerry Fahey, Vice President of Production Services

Debbie Stailey, Director of Composition Services

Contents at a Glance

Table of Contents

Introduction

Welcome to *Renting Out Your Property For Dummies.* Many of life's lessons are discovered by on-the-job trial and error, but property management shouldn't be one of them – the mistakes are too costly and the legal ramifications too severe. In this book, you can find proven strategies to make rental property ownership and management not only profitable but pleasant as well.

About This Book

Although these pages are overflowing with useful advice and information, we present it in a light, easy-to-access format. This book explains how to wear many hats in this business: advertiser/promoter (in seeking tenants), host (in showing the property), handyman (in keeping up with and arranging repairs), bookkeeper (in maintaining records), and even counsellor (in dealing with tenants and their problems). Just as important, this book can help you maintain your sense of humour – as well as your sanity – as you deal with these challenges and more.

Conventions Used in This Book

To help you navigate through this book, we've set up a few conventions:

- *Italic* is used for emphasis and to highlight new words or terms that are defined
- **Boldfaced** text is used to indicate the action part of numbered steps.
- `Monofont` is used for Web addresses

What You're Not to Read

We've written this book so that you can find information easily and easily understand what you find. And although we'd like to believe that you want to pore over every last word between the two yellow covers, we actually make it easy for you to identify skippable material. This is the stuff that, although interesting and related to the topic at hand, isn't essential for you to know:

- **Text in sidebars.** The sidebars are the shaded boxes that appear here and there. They share personal stories and observations, but aren't necessary reading.
- **Anything with a Technical Stuff icon attached.** This information is interesting but not critical to your understanding of renting.
- **The stuff on the copyright page.** No kidding. There's nothing here of interest unless you are inexplicably enamoured by legal language and reprint information.

Foolish Assumptions

In this book, we make some general assumptions about who you are:

- You may be an unintentional property owner – someone who, through a series of circumstances, suddenly and unexpectedly came upon an opportunity to own property. Maybe you inherited a house from a relative that you don't want to let sit idle (the house, not the relative, that is), or maybe you transferred to a job in another city and haven't been able to sell your home.
- You may have intentionally entered the world of property ownership because you see the buy-to-let market as a cornerstone to your long-term personal financial planning and you've noticed that many of the most successful people are landlords.
- You hope to generate sufficient income from your rental property to cover the mortgage, cover all operating expenses, and provide some cash flow along with capital appreciation. You may even look at owning rental property as a way to supplement your current retirement plans.
- You want easy-to-understand information explaining what you need to know about property management, but you've got better things to do (like sleeping, participating in your favourite leisure activity, enjoying your retirement, or even relaxing on holiday) than become an expert on property law. In other words, you're someone who wants to make money while you retain control over your life.

How This Book Is Organised

Renting Out Your Property For Dummies is organised into seven parts. The chapters within each part cover specific topic areas in more detail. So you can easily and quickly scan a topic that interests you, or you can troubleshoot the source of your latest major headache!

Part I: So You Want to Be a Landlord?

Managing rental property is not everyone's cup of tea. The chapters in this part assist you in evaluating your skills and personality to see whether you have what it takes to be a landlord. This part can also help you figure out whether you should call in the property management cavalry. If a management company is the answer to your prayers, you can discover how to select one, what you can expect, and how much the service can cost. You can also find advice on finding the most suitable properties for your purposes and tips on what to avoid. Finally, the day you exchange contracts has arrived and the ink is dry, so you find out what your immediate priorities are as you take over your new rental property.

Part II: Renting Your Property

The most important aspect of rental housing is keeping your properties occupied with paying tenants who don't destroy them and terrorise the neighbours. In this part, you figure out how to prepare the property for rent, set the rents and deposits, develop a comprehensive yet cost-effective advertising campaign, and show your rental property to prospective tenants. Because all tenants look great on paper, we fill you in on some tricks and techniques for establishing tenant selection criteria.

Part III: The Brass Tacks of Managing Rentals

This part takes you from moving in your new tenants to moving them out – and everything in between. You get some strategies for collecting and increasing rent, retaining tenants, and dealing with those few tenants who give you a headache whenever your paths cross. Minimising vacancies and retaining tenants is the key to success as a landlord. But when your tenant complains incessantly, decides to repaint in garish colours, or stops paying the rent, the real challenge of being a landlord begins. In this part, you discover techniques for dealing with these issues – and more.

Part IV: Techniques and Tools for Managing

One of the most important keys to your success as a landlord is assembling the right professionals to help you – and that includes contractors and handymen. Maintenance can be one of the largest controllable expenses you face. In this part, we discuss how to ensure that the property is maintained to a suitable standard. And because safety is such a major issue for landlords, this part also reviews the issues of crime, fire protection, gas safety, environmental hazards, and the safety and security of your properties. Finally, we also look at insurance so that you can cover your back in case things go wrong.

Part V: Money, Money, Money!

Raising the finance to buy your rental property is one of the most important considerations you face when making a go of the rental business. In this part, we guide you through the ins and outs of buy-to-let mortgages. Even more likely than a lawsuit is taxes. So in this part, you can find out how to avoid property taxes – completely legitimately. We also offer advice on using a company to hold your property. And finally, because you probably want to know just how much cash flow your rental empire is generating, we provide you with some basics on rental accounting and record keeping.

Part VI: Only for the Daring

Many landlords automatically refuse to open their doors to tenants receiving Housing Benefit, those with pets, or smokers. But done correctly, letting to tenants who are considered undesirable by the majority of landlords can give you a niche. In Part VI, you find information on the advantages and disadvantages of letting to tenants on Housing Benefit. Niche rental markets – like those catering to students and tenants with pets – are also worthy of your consideration, and we let you know how you can use them to your advantage.

Part VII: The Part of Tens

Here, in a concise and lively set of condensed chapters, are the tips to make the difference between success and foreclosure. In these chapters, we address the benefits of owning rental properties, tips to rent your empty property quickly, and techniques to increase your cash flow.

Icons Used in This Book

Scattered throughout the book are icons to guide you along your way and highlight some of the suggestions, solutions, and cautions of property management.

Keep your sights on the target for important advice and critical insights into the best practices in property management.

Remember these important points of information and you'll stand a better chance of being a great landlord.

This icon highlights the landmines that both novice and experienced landlords need to avoid.

This icon covers the boring stuff that only anoraks would ever know. You can skip paragraphs marked by this icon without missing the point – or you can read it and impress your friends with what you know.

This icon highlights the real-life anecdotes from many years of experience and mistakes, made by ourselves and friends who are landlords. While we should all learn from our own mistakes, it's even better to learn from other people's – and we share some of them with you here.

Where to Go from Here

This book is organised so that you can go wherever you want to find complete information. Want to know how to evict a problem tenant, for example? Head to Chapter 12. If you're interested in how to improve security at your rental property, go to Chapter 15 for that. You can use the table of contents to find broad categories of information or the index to look up more specific things.

If you're not sure where you want to go, you may want to start with Part I. It gives you all the basic information you need to get started in the rental property business and points to places where you can find more detailed information.

Part I

So You Want to Be a Landlord?

"As landlord I can't see any problem over some brothers of yours stopping a night or two occasionally, Mr Francis."

In this part . . .

Managing rental property isn't for the faint of heart, but it can be very rewarding for the right person. The chapters in this part guide you through the process of figuring out whether you have what it takes to manage rental property or whether you're better off leaving it to an agent – someone you hire to do the dirty work for you. We also fill you in on what you need to know if you're taking over ownership of a rental property, including how to deal with the current tenants and inform them of your policies and procedures. This is the part for you if you're just starting to think about purchasing a rental property, but you're not quite sure what it entails.

Chapter 1

Do You Have What It Takes to Manage a Buy-to-let Property?

In This Chapter

- Being aware of the advantages of owning rental property
- Identifying the differences between owning property and managing it
- Assessing your own management skills

Congratulations! Either you already own rental property or you've made the decision to buy. Property is great whether you're looking for a steady supplement to your retirement income or a secure financial future. Most buy-to-let landlords want to become financially independent, and property is a proven investment strategy for achieving that goal.

But after you sign your name on the dotted line and officially enter the world of owning rental property, you face some tough decisions. One of the very first concerns is who will handle the day-to-day management of your rental property. You have properties to lease, rents to collect, tenant complaints to respond to, and a whole host of property management issues to deal with. So you need to determine whether you have what it takes to manage your own buy-to-let property or whether you should employ a letting agent. In this chapter, we give you the low-down on some of the advantages of owning rental property. Then we'll help you assess whether you have what it takes to manage your own property.

Recognising the Advantages of Owning Rental Property

A great advantage to building wealth through property is the ability to use other people's money – both for the initial purchase of the rental property and for the ongoing expenses.

The wide availability and low rates of interest on buy-to-let mortgages makes buying a second property a viable and realistic option for virtually everyone. Most people raise a deposit and then borrow the rest of the cash from a mortgage lender.

The deposit required for a buy-to-let mortgage tends to be higher than that needed for a 'regular' mortgage. Expect to pay at least 15 per cent of the purchase price, depending on the lender.

The ability to control significant property assets with only a small cash investment is one of the best reasons to invest in bricks and mortar. For example, you may have purchased a £100,000 buy-to-let property with a £20,000 cash deposit and a mortgage for the remaining £80,000. If the property's value doubles in the next decade and you sell it for £200,000, you will have turned your £20,000 cash investment into a £100,000 profit. This is an example of *capital appreciation,* where you are able to earn a return not only on your cash investment but also on the entire value of the property.

Rental property also offers you the opportunity to pay off your mortgage using your tenant's money. If you've been prudent in purchasing a well-located rental property in a stable area, you'll have enough income to pay the interest on your mortgage, as well as all the expenses, maintenance, and insurance. Each month your property should be appreciating in value while your tenant is essentially paying all your expenses, including the interest on your mortgage.

Your lender and tenant aren't the only ones who can help you with the purchase of your rental investment property. Even the government is willing to offer its money to help your cash flow and encourage more people to become landlords. In calculating your income tax obligations each year, the government allows buy-to-let landlords to offset their income against interest payments on their mortgage and certain expenses. For example, you can claim 10 per cent of the annual rent for wear and tear on fixtures and fittings in furnished properties.

Over time, rental income generally outstrips operating expenses. And after your tenants have finished paying your mortgage for you, you'll suddenly find that you have a *positive* cash flow – in other words, you're making a profit.

Being Honest with Yourself about Your Skills and Experience

One of the first steps in determining whether to completely self-manage your rental property or delegate some or all of the duties to other people is to analyse your own skills and experience. Many very successful property owners find that they're better suited to deal-making, so they leave the day-to-day management for someone else. This decision is a personal one, but you can make it more easily by thinking about some of the specifics of managing property.

Property management requires basic skills, including marketing management, accounting, and people skills. You don't need a university degree or a lot of experience to get started, and you're sure to pick up all kinds of ideas of ways to do things better along the way.

Examine your own personality. Are you a people person? Serving as a landlord is a labour of love; you must love people, you must love working with your hands, you must love solving problems. Most of all, you must be able to do all this without getting much in the way of appreciation.

If you're impatient or easily manipulated, you aren't suited to being a property manager. Conveying a professional demeanour to your tenants is important. You want them to see you as someone who will take responsibility for the condition of the property. You must also insist that tenants live up to their part of the deal, pay their rent regularly, and refrain from causing unreasonable damage to your property.

People who need people: Putting your interpersonal skills to the test

Whether you're confident you have what it takes to be a good manager of rental property or you're still not sure, take stock of yourself and your abilities by answering these questions. Interview yourself as though you were a job applicant. Ask the tough questions. And more important, answer honestly.

- Are you a people person who enjoys working with others?
- Are you able to keep your emotions in check and out of your business decisions?
- Are you a patient and reasonably tolerant person?

- Do you have the temperament to handle problems, respond to complaints, and service requests in a positive and rational manner?
- Are you well organised in your daily routine?
- Do you have strong time-management skills?
- Are you meticulous with your paperwork?
- Do you have basic accounting skills?
- Do you have maintenance and repair abilities?
- Are you willing to work and take phone calls on evenings and weekends?
- Do you have sales skills?
- Are you a good negotiator?
- Are you willing to commit the time and effort required to determine the right rent for your property?
- Are you familiar with or willing to find out about the laws affecting property management?
- Are you willing to consistently and fairly enforce all property rules and rental policies?
- Are you interested in finding out more about property management?
- Are you willing to make the commitment to being your own property manager?

Ideally, you answered yes to each of these questions. This assessment is not scientific of course, but it does raise some important issues, particularly the level of commitment that you need to succeed as a rental property manager.

You need to be fair, firm, and friendly to all potential tenants and those who do actually become your tenants. Treat everyone impartially and remain patient and calm under stress. Be determined and unemotional in enforcing rent collection and your policies and rules. And maintain a positive attitude through it all. Not as simple as it looks, is it?

Even if you didn't answer with an enthusiastic 'yes' to all the questions in this section, you may still make a good rental property manager if you're prepared to be flexible. Learn from your property management experiences. The really good property managers graduated from the school of hard knocks. The following sections give an overview of the key skills you need to manage your property effectively.

If your assessment revealed that your skills may be better served doing something other than managing your own property, turn to Chapter 2 for some alternatives. Owning rental property can still be a great investment, even if you don't manage it yourself.

Making sure you have good management skills

Good management leads to good financial results. Having tenants who pay on time, stay for several years, and treat the property and their neighbours with respect is the key to profitable property management. But, like most things, it's easier said than done. One of the greatest deterrents to financial independence through investing in rental property is the fear of management and dealing with tenants.

If you choose the wrong tenant or fail to address certain maintenance issues, your buy-to-let investment may turn into a costly nightmare. By doing your homework in advance, you can reduce those beginners' mistakes. Experience is a great teacher – if you can afford the lessons.

If you already own your *own* home, then you already have some basic knowledge about the ins and outs of owning and maintaining property. The question then becomes how to translate that knowledge into managing *rental* property.

Delegating management activities

As a landlord, you may choose to handle many responsibilities while delegating some of them to others. Look at your own set of skills to determine which items you should delegate. A contractor may be able to handle the maintenance of your rental property and grounds more efficiently and effectively than you can.

The skills you need to successfully manage your own rental properties are different from the skills you need to handle your own property maintenance. Most buy-to-let landlords find that using trusted and reasonably priced contractors can be a valuable option in the long run.

Ultimately, you can delegate all the management activities to a professional managing agent. But hiring a managing agent doesn't mean you're off the hook. Depending on the arrangement you have with your letting agent, you may still oversee the big picture. Most letting agents need and seek the input of the property owner before they start so that they can develop a property management plan that meets the owner's investment goals.

Keep in mind that no one else will ever manage your rental property like you will. After all, you're more motivated than anyone else to watch out for your buy-to-let investment interests. Only *you* will work through the night painting your property for the new tenant moving in the next day. And who else would spend her annual leave looking through the local newspaper classifieds for creative ad ideas?

Start by being honest with yourself. Know your strengths and your weaknesses as a property manager. You may find that you're able to do the job but wind up with frazzled nerves when you do. If you're not truly excited and challenged by handling your own property management tasks, then you're not likely to have success in the long run.

You may find that a managing agent can run the property more competently than you can. Many buy-to-let landlords possess the necessary skills and personality to efficiently and effectively manage their rental properties, but they have other skills or interests that are more financially rewarding or enjoyable. Hiring professionals and supervising them is often the best possible option.

Recognising how well you manage your time

If you're like most buy-to-let landlords, managing your property is a part-time job. You can handle calls from the tenant, collect the rent, show the property to prospective tenants, and even perform most maintenance in the early evenings or on weekends. The challenge is finding the time required to do this. The good news is that the time required to be a landlord is in your control.

If you develop proper skills in marketing, tenant screening, and tenant selection, you can greatly reduce the amount of time you spend managing your rental property. You also have to work smart or you may find that your time is better spent in other areas than management.

You can save a lot of time by asking your tenants to pay their rent by direct debit each month, with the money transferred straight into your bank account. A cheque in the post is also acceptable but not as convenient. The days of actually collecting the rent in person from the tenant are, thankfully, in the past.

Many of your contractors and suppliers will want to be paid immediately. But you can be more efficient and save time if you have a policy of paying all your invoices at the end of each month.

Time management is really about evaluating how much time you have and then looking for ways to streamline your tasks so that you make the best use of your time.

Chapter 2

Deciding Whether to Manage Your Property Yourself or to Hire an Agent

In This Chapter

- Deciding whether to manage your own property
- Assessing the benefits of working with an agent
- Knowing what to look for in a letting agent

The TV property experts can make a buy-to-let investment sound so simple. But just as important as buying the right property for the right price, the key to success is a well-managed property. Although you may lack experience of being a landlord in the beginning, this is often the easiest time to manage your property portfolio because you have just one lot of tenants to deal with and one buy-to-let mortgage to pay. To help you decide, this chapter takes a look at the pros and cons of managing your own property (as opposed to hiring an agent to do it for you).

Even if you don't hire a letting agent to manage the property for you in the beginning, once you build up the number of properties on your books, you may eventually decide to pass the job onto someone else. So this chapter also looks at tools for evaluating letting agents, from the services they offer to the fees they charge. It also explains the importance of experience, qualifications, and credentials. Also, we reveal some of the common tricks that letting agents use to generate additional income that are not in your best interest.

Managing Your Rental Yourself

When you first start out, you'll probably do all the work yourself – painting, cleaning, doing repairs, collecting the rent, paying the bills, and showing the property to potential tenants. After looking at some of the advantages and disadvantages of doing this yourself, you can decide whether you want to go it alone or whether hiring an agent is for you. If you decide on the latter, check out the information later in this chapter about working with a professional letting agent. This is one of the most important decisions you'll make as a buy-to-let landlord, so take the time to look at all your options.

Even if you ultimately decide that *you* are the best manager for your rental property, the more you learn about how the professionals manage property, the better you will be at management yourself.

Recognising the advantages of self-management

If you have the right traits for managing property, and if you have the time and live close to your property, you should definitely do it yourself. Managing your own rental property has some definite advantages. For example, by managing your own property, you don't have to pay a monthly fee to a letting agent, which can be as much as 15 per cent of the rent for a full management service.

If you purchase a small flat as an investment property, you might not be able to generate enough money to pay for a letting agent and make a profit – at least not right away.

By keeping direct control of the management of your rental property, you also may save on maintenance costs, because *you* decide who does the repair work or mows the lawn. Doing your own maintenance is usually a good idea; if you hire someone else to do it for you the cost can eat into your profits.

Develop a list of reliable handymen and gardeners who do good work and charge low rates. Even if you hire someone to let your property for you, you're better off choosing the maintenance contractors yourself, if possible, rather than turning over the decision – and your money – to a letting agent.

Paying attention to the drawbacks

If you're just starting in the world of property management you may be thinking of it as a part-time venture – something you'll do in addition to your day job. And if you want, you can keep it that way by keeping the number of properties you own to a minimum. But you may find yourself spending far more time on managing your properties than you anticipated – either because you've bought more of them, or because you just didn't anticipate the time requirements.

If you earn your living regularly from something other than managing your rental property, managing that property may not be worth your valuable time. If you're a high-income, full-time professional, rushing off on weekdays to handle some minor crisis at your property is not only impractical, it could be downright damaging to your career. Most employers have little tolerance for a second job, particularly one that often has unpredictable and unscheduled demands.

As a jobholder, look at your annual income and work out approximately what you earn per hour. Do the same for the cash you're saving by managing your own property. Unless your management efforts produce significant cash savings compared to your job, you may be better off hiring a letting agent to manage your properties. The same guideline holds true even if you are self-employed. Your schedule may be more flexible than the fixed workday of a 9-to-5 employee. But if you're earning £50 an hour as a consultant, devoting hours of your productive work time to managing property, which may only amount to savings of £100 a month, may not make sense.

Managing your property from a distance

If you own rental property at the other end of the country, you may initially consider managing it from afar. As long as your tenants pay their rent and make only a few maintenance demands, this arrangement can work – but it's a fragile one. One major problem can turn the job of managing the rental property into a nightmare.

We know someone who had a very bad experience when he rented his own house to tenants after being transferred by his company to a job overseas. He found a nice family to rent to, and everything was fine for the first six months. Then one day he got an urgent call from his tenants, complaining that torrential rain had caused the roof to leak, making the house uninhabitable. As he was still abroad, he asked his tenants to assist him in hiring someone to repair the roof. The work was botched, and he wound up flying back and forth twice to straighten out the mess before he finally managed to get the roof fixed properly. This negative experience ended up costing thousands of pounds, easily wiping out whatever small profit he could have made.

Think twice about handling your own rental property maintenance from hundreds of miles away. You need to be in the immediate area to routinely inspect and maintain a buy-to-let property, especially when a roof leak or broken pipe demands immediate attention.

Exploring Professional Management

Many first-time buy-to-let landlords frequently drift blindly into self-management by default, because they assume they can't afford to use a letting agent. 'Why pay someone to manage my rental property when I can keep the money myself?' is a common refrain.

Other owners would really prefer to hire a professional to manage their properties, but they've heard so many horror stories that they don't know whom to trust. Many of their concerns are real – some letting agents mismanage properties and have a total lack of ethics. Luckily, there is a detectable pattern that can help you avoid hiring the wrong letting agent.

If you think that hiring a letting agent may be the right choice for you, take the time to study this option. Here are some advantages to using a management firm:

- They have the expertise and experience to manage rental property, plus knowledge about relevant legislation and safety regulations.
- They're able to remain fair, firm, and friendly with tenants.
- They have screening procedures and can typically screen tenants more objectively than you can yourself.
- They handle property management issues throughout the day and have staffing for after-hour emergencies.
- They have contacts and preferential pricing with many suppliers and contractors who can quickly and efficiently get work done.
- They handle all bookkeeping, including rent collection.
- They have well-established rent collection policies and procedures to follow when tenants' rental payments are late.
- They can be excellent sources for purchasing additional properties because they are often the first to know when their current clients want to sell.

Of course there are some disadvantages to using a letting agent as well:

- Using a management company for small rental properties that you've recently acquired may not be cost-effective.
- They often won't have the same care, consideration, and concern you have for the rental property.
- They may take longer to find tenants for your property if the letting agent has several other vacancies they're dealing with at the same time.

- Letting agents may not be as diligent in collecting late rent as you would be.
- Some letting agents may try to falsely impress you by not spending enough on repairs and maintenance needed to properly maintain the property.

Be sure to consider the pros and cons to determine whether working with a letting agent is right for you.

Knowing what to look for in a letting agent

Size isn't the determining factor in whether a professional letting agent can deliver quality service. Some letting agents specialise in large rental projects, whereas small operations may focus on managing small family homes and one-bedroom flats. Don't assume that a big letting agency will do the best job for your property or that the small company has the credentials, experience, and knowledge that you need. Try to find letting agents familiar with your kind of buy-to-let property. With a little research, you can find the right fit for your property.

Professional letting agents normally handle a wide range of duties. If you opt for full management, you'll typically get the following services:

- Preparing, advertising, and showing the property
- Introducing, vetting, and selecting the tenants
- Preparing the tenancy agreement
- Advising on inventories for furnished properties, changes in legislation, and Council Tax
- Collecting the rent and paying the balance to the landlord's account
- Providing regular accounting reports
- Regularly inspecting the property and overseeing repairs
- Enforcing the property's rules and regulations
- Dealing with complaints from the tenants

More limited management services are also available from some letting agents. Maybe you just need help with finding tenants in the first place and are willing to pay a basic fee for this. Or you may want help finding tenants and collecting the rent as well. Each letting agent has his or her own scale of charges and terms and conditions.

A good letting agent may be able to operate your rental properties better and more efficiently than you can on your own. Their superior knowledge and experience can result in lower costs, higher rents, better tenants, and a property that is well maintained. Using such companies more than pays for the costs, and you have more time to pursue additional properties or other pursuits. Of course, a poor letting agent cuts into your profits, not only with their fees, but also with improper maintenance and poor quality tenants who will run your property into the ground. A bad letting agent can leave you in worse shape than if you'd never hired one in the first place.

Telling the good from the bad and the ugly

Management companies accept the responsibility for all operations of the property, including advertising, tenant selection, rent collection, maintenance, and accounting. The right letting agent can make a big difference in the cash flow your property generates, because he finds good replacement tenants quickly and makes sure that maintenance is done in a timely manner without breaking your budget. You need a letting agent who is committed to helping you get the optimum results from your properties. As the heading suggests, cowboys do exist.

Be sure to visit the office of the letting agent and spend time interviewing the specific person who will have control of the hands-on management of your property. Make a few extra phone calls to check references and don't sign a management contract until you feel confident that the company you hire has a sound track record. Checking with the letting agency's chosen referrals is not enough. Ask for a list of all their clients and contact the ones with rental properties similar in size and type to your own. Make sure the landlords you contact have been with the letting agent long enough to have a meaningful opinion on the quality of the service.

The following sections tell you specifically what to look for.

Do they manage property exclusively?

Make sure that the firm you hire manages property exclusively. This is particularly important when selecting a letting agent for a single-family home, flat, or very small rental property. Many traditional estate agents (as opposed to letting agents) offer property management services; however, property management is often a *loss leader* (meaning that it costs more for the estate agent to manage your property than they're charging you for that service, because they're hoping to get your business later on when you're ready to sell). Many letting agents who work in estate agents do not have the same credentials, experience, and expertise that an employee of a company which focuses entirely on managing properties would have. The skills required to represent clients in *selling* property are entirely different than the skills required to *manage* property.

What are their professional affiliations?

Letting agents do not have to be affiliated to a national body, but it makes sense for you to opt for one that is. Not only does this give you peace of mind, but you'll also know that they are of a certain standard. In addition, if a dispute arises, you have the right to appeal to a third party.

Examine the letting agent's credentials. Are they a member of the Association of Residential Letting Agents (Arla), the professional and regulatory body solely concerned with residential lettings? Members are kept up-to-date with changes in legislation and are governed by Arla's Principles of Professional Conduct, providing a framework of professional and ethical standards. To gain membership, agents must, among other things, demonstrate that their client accounts are professionally managed. They must also offer a full management service to landlords on top of basic letting and rent collection. Other accreditation to look out for is membership of the government-backed National Approved Letting Scheme (NALS), membership of the Royal Institution of Chartered Surveyors (RICS), or membership of the National Association of Estate Agents (NAEA).

Are they properly insured?

Verify that the letting agency is properly insured. The company should be a member of the Client Money Protection scheme, which provides professional indemnity insurance. This safeguards both the landlord's rent and tenants' deposits should the management company run into difficulties or even go bust. The management company is your agent and will be collecting your rents and deposits, so they should also have fidelity insurance to protect you in case an employee embezzles or mishandles your money. Most property managers use a single master trust bank account for all properties on their books but controls on client accounts are very strict for Arla members so this shouldn't be a problem. Every penny must be allocated to the right client at any given moment.

What's their policy on handling emergency repairs?

In most management contracts, letting agents have the ability and right to perform emergency repairs without advance approval from the owner. This allows the letting agent to take care of problems that occur unexpectedly. Most management contracts contain clauses that allow letting agents to undertake day-to-day repairs, such as replacing a faulty boiler, without the owner's advance approval. When you're in the early stages of working with a new letting agent, make sure you closely monitor their expenses. Even though they may have the legal right to use funds up to a certain amount, they should always keep you informed as the owner.

Important questions to ask

The quality of your letting agent directly affects the success of your property investments and your peace of mind. Here are some important questions to ask as you interview letting agents:

- Can you provide a list of exactly what management services are provided, including dates I will receive reports, and a breakdown of management costs?
- Can I contact several of your current and former client references with rental properties that are similar in size and location to mine?
- Is your firm a member of the Association of Residential Letting Agents (Arla)?
- Who will actually manage the day-to-day activities at my property? What are his qualifications and does he exclusively manage properties?
- Do you provide 24-hour on-call maintenance services with e-mail capability?
- Given that maintenance is usually provided in-house or by an affiliated firm, do you only charge the actual cost of labour and materials without any surcharges, markups, administrative fees, or other such add-ons?
- Do all funds collected for applicant screening fees, tenant late charges, and other administrative charges go directly to the landlord and not the letting agent?
- Do you have fidelity insurance for all employees?
- Are all individual clients' monies accounted for at all times within your single master trust bank account?

When you hire letting agents, treat them well – but be sure they know that you're paying their wages. They should ask before spending significant amounts of your money, and they should keep you informed on a regular basis.

Paying your letting agent

Letting agents are paid in a variety of ways, and the type – and amount – of fees vary widely throughout the country. Make sure that you understand how your letting agent earns his money, but never evaluate the management company based on the management fee alone as, more often than not, you get what you pay for. Don't be afraid to negotiate the fee either, especially if you have several rental properties.

Letting agents essentially charge for services based on the amount of time that is required of different staff members to manage your property. An experienced property management company owner will know the average number of hours that the property manager, the accounting staff, and other support personnel will spend each month on managing your property. The owner will then calculate a management charge that should generate the fees necessary to provide the proper management company resources to effectively manage your rental properties.

Most management companies operate on a 'no let, no fee' basis, receiving a percentage of the collected income for managing a rental property. However, a few companies also charge a flat fee per month. Try to find a company that has a management fee that is a percentage of the collected income; this kind of fee is a strong motivator to the management company to ensure that the rents are kept at market rate and actually collected on time. Never pay a management fee that is based solely on the potential income of a property.

Management fees are typically tied to the size and the expected rental collections of the property. However, for properties that may be more difficult to manage, the letting agent may have higher management fees or additional charges for certain types of services or for a certain period of time. Management companies may also propose charging a minimum monthly management fee or a percentage fee (opting for whichever of the two is greater). For example, a property that is in very poor physical condition and requires extensive repairs and renovations will require a significant increase in the time spent by the property manager in supervising the improvements. This additional time is worthy of separate compensation to the property manager.

Traditionally, agents charge 15 per cent of the monthly rent for a full management service, 12.5 per cent for rental collection or 10 per cent for simply finding tenants. But there are no hard-and-fast rules as charges vary across the country and from agency to agency. In addition, comparing fees charged by different firms can be hard because they are calculated in different ways. Some charge a set-up fee for preparing the initial contract. Others charge for preparing the inventory. You can also be charged fees if the tenant renews the tenancy. The best way to compare prices is to ask several agents for a written quote of exactly what is covered.

Additional fees for the leasing of buy-to-let properties are often justified, because the most time-intensive portion of property management is tenant turnover. When one tenant leaves, the property must be made ready for the next; then the managing agent must show the property and screen the tenants. Charges for this can vary, but are usually either a flat fee of a few hundred pounds or a percentage of the rent.

Generally, the larger the rental property, the lower the management fee as a percentage of collected income. Fees also vary by the income potential of the rental property with the higher end commanding a lower percentage management fee than the lower end of the market.

A friend was moving to Manchester for work and wanted to retain his beautiful home in West Sussex in case he was ever transferred back to the area. He inquired into the cost of hiring a professional management firm and was shocked by the wide variation in management fees quoted. So he began asking more questions of one prospective letting agent and learned that this particular property manager was already overseeing over 170 other rental properties and would be glad to add another client to his books. My friend quickly calculated that this property manager would only be able to spend an average of one hour a month on the management of his rental home, including rent collection, accounting, fielding tenant calls, property inspections, and all the other property management duties. For this, he was quoted a management fee of 15 per cent, or over £140 per month. Be sure that you know how many other rental properties will have a claim on your property manager's time before you sign up!

Making sense of management agreements

The management agreement is a pivotal document; it spells out the obligations of the letting agent to you, their client. Be sure to study the fine print – it's tedious but necessary in order to avoid unpleasant surprises. Be wary of clauses that are clearly one-sided in favour of the letting agent. Ensure that the management agreement does not call for the property manager to collect and keep all the income from late payments or from following up a bouncing cheque. Of course, property managers justify their entitlement to this money on the basis that they incur additional time and costs. But these fees should belong to you, because you want to give the letting agent a financial incentive to fill your property with a tenant who pays rent on time and cares for the property. A management fee based on actual rents collected is a better arrangement.

Some property management agreements indicate that there is no management fee charged when the property is vacant between tenants. Although this seems like an arrangement that saves you money, especially when rental revenues are not coming in, the property manager could rush to fill the property without properly screening tenants – and a destructive tenant can be worse than no tenant in the long run.

It is worth including a 'reasonable care' provision so the property manager is motivated to be diligent in the management of the property and avoid employing tradesmen to carry out repairs at your property if there has been a problem with them in the past. Your agreement should also mention such obvious requirements as informing you of what is happening with your rental property.

Some property management companies request long-term management contracts that cannot be cancelled or can only be cancelled with good reason. Avoid signing any property management contract that cannot be cancelled by either party with or without good reason upon a 30-day written notice. A property management company that knows they are only as good as their most recent month's performance will stay motivated to treat your property with the time and attention needed to get top results.

Make sure all your concerns are addressed in the management agreement. You need to know exactly what weekly or monthly reporting they provide, when your property expenses will be paid, and who is responsible for payment of critical items like mortgages, insurance, and property taxes. Leave nothing to chance.

If the property manager won't agree to reasonable clarification of the contract language or a complete list of the services provided for the fee, he may not go out of his way to help you later. Consider it a warning sign, and find a property management company willing to accept your reasonable terms.

Many property managers use their own proprietary agreements written strictly in the best interests of the property management company. So be sure to have your solicitor review this agreement very early in the discussions with your potential property manager.

Knowing the tax consequences of using a management company

As a buy-to-let landlord, you're running a business and must file a Land and Property form with your basic self-assessment tax return each year. Landlords are only taxed on their profit after allowable expenses, including the interest payments on any buy-to-let mortgage, cost of advertising, travel expenses incurred when checking the property, essential repairs, insurance, and management fees (whether paid to yourself or a property management firm).

But although your expenses are deductible, they erode your net income from your property. If your annual expenses are greater than the rent revenues, you may find that you can use those losses to help ease the tax burden from your full-time job or other sources of income unrelated to your rental property. But a loss is a loss, and trying to keep your rental property in the black is still a good idea, even if you have to pay some taxes on the income.

The advantage of using a management company is that they should be able to make life easier for you. Before employing a letting agent, find out whether they can provide you with a statement of account that is in a format acceptable to the Inland Revenue. This should include your income and outgoings, as the letting agent should have all the receipts to back these figures up. This saves you a lot of time, effort, and hassle when it comes to filing your tax return at the end of the year.

Chapter 3

Finding the Perfect Rental Property

In This Chapter

- Figuring out exactly what type of rental property you want
- Knowing where to look for a rental property
- Assessing whether there are enough suitable tenants in the area

Location, location, location is the mantra you should bear in mind when you go to buy property – particularly when you go to buy rental property. Not only do you want to pay a reasonable price for a property that increases in value over time, but you also need to find a rich source of suitable tenants to fill it, look after it, and pay the rent on time every month. This task sounds straightforward enough, but you need to do your research very carefully before committing to the purchase of a rental property to make sure that all these aims are met.

It doesn't matter how great a one-bedroom flat is if it's situated in an area full of large family homes with big gardens. You're not likely to find the single tenant or couple you need to fill it, and – at the end of the day – filling the property is your aim if you want your rental property business to be profitable. As a landlord, you have to be dispassionate and ruthless about your purchase, because the type of property you may want to live in won't necessarily appeal to tenants. In this chapter, we help identify what to look for when choosing a rental property – and the pitfalls to avoid.

Knowing What to Look For

Before you start, you need to have a clear idea of what type of rental property you're looking for. If you want a small family house, say a two-bedroom terraced house, don't be persuaded to look at unsuitable properties such as studio flats or rambling six-bedroom mansions. By focusing on exactly what you want and avoiding countless unsuitable properties, you can save yourself time and money.

While staying focused is good, don't be too narrow-minded. If you're looking for a two-bedroom house for your rental business but then stumble across a slightly cheaper two-bedroom flat in the area, you may decide that the flat is perfect for renting to tenants. If you stick too closely to your original plan and don't evaluate alternatives as they present themselves, you could find yourself missing a good opportunity.

Ask dedicated letting agents – not estate agents – for advice on renting property. Estate agents want to earn their commission and get the sale, so they are unlikely to be completely unbiased. The letting agent should provide more useful opinions on location and a particular property.

Big or little: Size matters

Letting agents will tell you that the easiest properties to let to tenants are studio apartments and one-bedroom flats. If you opt for a huge, grand house in the hope that it will generate lots more rent, you are likely to discover that finding tenants is much harder. This fact is partly down to demographics: More people are living on their own than ever before. And with property prices out of the reach of many first-time buyers until later in life – the average age of a first-time buyer in the UK is now 34 – many 20- to 30-year-olds are being forced to rent until they have saved enough for a deposit.

If you have £300,000 to invest, consider using it to pay deposits on two or three small properties rather than put all your money towards a single, larger one. Doing so is advantageous in a couple of ways:

- **Smaller properties are usually easier to let than larger ones, making life easier for you.** In fact, demand for properties with three or more bedrooms is diminishing. You're better off choosing a property suitable for the young professional who is not yet ready to buy but still wants the freedom and independence of living on her own.
- **Rent on a studio or small flat is also going to be a lot less than on a big house.** This may not sound like a good thing, but consider this: If you run into void periods, covering the mortgage yourself is likely to be much less of a burden than it would with a large property (as the mortgage is likely to be smaller).
- **Flats are much easier to maintain.** Most flats in the UK tend to be leasehold rather than freehold so you have to pay an annual service charge to the freeholder for the maintenance of the common areas. If you buy a leasehold property, you own the flat for the duration of the lease, unlike a freehold property where you purchase it outright. Watch out for properties with a lease of 65 years or less as getting a mortgage on such properties is difficult. However, leases can be extended – and you can add the service charge onto the rent.

Setting your budget

Of course, what property you buy is largely decided by your budget. You can find more about financing the purchase of your property in Chapter 16, but the key factor to bear in mind is that you shouldn't overstretch yourself. Most landlords use leverage to borrow much more than their deposit, but most lenders demand that the rental income covers at least 120 or 130 per cent of the mortgage repayments. And ask yourself this: If the property is empty for two or three months a year, can you afford to carry on paying the mortgage yourself? If the answer is no, you should think about scaling down your ambitions.

Location, location, location

Picking a good location isn't as straightforward as it sounds. What you think is a good location might not be your tenant's idea of a good location. Your ideal place to live could be a green, leafy street with minimal traffic, close to good schools. But your prospective tenants (some of whom won't have cars) may be more interested in an area that is close to shops, pubs, and takeaway restaurants with reliable public transport links.

If your tenants don't have a large family, a large supermarket two roads away isn't as important as a 24-hour convenience store where they can pick up a pint of milk late at night.

Many prospective tenants don't have the resources to run a car so require a property close to local transport links. Most don't fancy walking half-an-hour from the nearest train station when they return home late at night. For these tenants, the train station or bus stop needs to be close to a rental property: More than 10 minutes' walk and your prospective tenants are likely to be put off.

To extend the likely pool of tenants, look at properties outside major cities but with reliable transport links into the city. For example, many towns in the South East are around an hour away from London on the train. Many people prefer to live outside a city and commute in as necessary for work. Buying rental property in such an area widens your pool of potential tenants.

When you buy a property, keep your potential tenants in mind. You should have a good idea what type of person is likely to want to live in your rental property. If not, you'll find buying the right property very difficult. For example, if your rental property is near a college, university, or hospital, a house that several students or colleagues can share for a reasonable monthly rent may be easier to let than a luxury one-bedroom flat with a hefty rent to match.

Ex-council flats

In big cities in particular, you often find lots of ex-council flats for sale at cheaper prices than swanky Victorian conversions. While you personally might not want to live on the edge of an estate in an ex-council property, tenants often aren't bothered about renting such a flat or house, as long as the inside is up to scratch. If the property is clean, and everything in good working order, you shouldn't have much trouble renting out an ex-council flat.

The benefits of buying locally

If you plan to manage your rental property yourself, without the help of an agent, buying locally makes sense. If the tenant has a problem in the middle of the night or complains of a malfunctioning boiler – problems you'd prefer to check out yourself before calling in a tradesman – your life is a lot easier if the rental property is just down the road rather than three hours away up the M1.

The other advantage of buying locally is knowing the area inside out. Many landlords feel more confident buying property in an area they know, especially when they start out. You are likely to know what is a bargain in terms of property prices – and what isn't. Finding that bargain and snapping it up quickly is also easier: You might be driving down a street on your way to work and spot a property that you think would be ideal for letting. A quick call to the estate agent handling the sale, and you're on hand to view it immediately. A scenario like this could save you the hassle of trawling through newspapers, property magazines, the Internet, and estate agents, and puts you in a position to find a good deal.

Buying too close to your own residence

Be wary of buying a rental property too close to your main residence. Buying the empty house next door to yours, for example, with a view to letting it out may seem like a good idea. But while you can keep a close eye on the rental property, tenants living on your doorstep can be a pain in the neck, particularly if they're the type to constantly badger you for this and that.

Just as you may regret having your tenants living next door, you may also find it difficult to rent the property in the first place. Tenants can be wary of living in close proximity to their landlord, fearful of being closely watched and monitored. It may be better for all concerned if you buy your rental property in another part of your town.

Buying in an area you don't know

Buying in an area that you don't know well is fraught with potential problems. The property you have your eye on may look like a bargain, but it could be in an area beset with problems, none of which are apparent to someone not familiar with the locality. The area could also be declining rather than improving in the long term, and you're not likely to know that until too late.

If you want to spread your wings and buy further afield, do your research carefully first. The Internet is a great place to start when you want to research an area. You can get an idea of the type and price of property available, local amenities, and schools and transport. Once you have a general idea of where a good place to buy may be, visit the area to get a feel for whether it actually is a good place to buy in. Visit local estate agents and speak to letting agents to get an idea of what property is available and what sort of rent you can expect.

Dilapidated properties

A rundown property needing complete renovation may be well within your budget, but there's probably a very good reason for that – the property is likely to need plenty of work. It may look like a bargain, but if the property takes months to get ready to rent, it'll cost you money, not just in renovations but also in lost income. Also, most mortgage lenders only offer buy-to-let loans on properties ready to let to tenants (see Chapter 16).

Converting an old rambling house into several flats may be tempting, but leave this well alone until you're more experienced in property management. Over time, you'll build up contacts, including a network of tradesmen and builders, who will be able to complete the work for a good price. Nicholas Walliman's *Self Build and Renovation For Dummies* (Wiley) gives more advice.

Letting out a basement in your home

If you live in a large property with a basement, you may be tempted to convert it into a self-contained flat to rent out and generate some extra income. But bear in mind that this strategy is feasible only if the property has space for a separate entrance. If you're planning a new self-contained flat and building work is required, you also need planning permission. Building regulations also have to be followed concerning all structural aspects of the property, as well as the size of the windows, ventilation, drainage, and escape routes. Information on planning and building regulations can be obtained from your local council.

While converting your basement into a self-contained flat is potentially a good idea, think it through very carefully. Check with local letting agents as to the amount of rent you can expect to generate to see whether you'll get a good return on your investment.

Where to Go to Find Your Rental Property

Wherever you decide to buy your property, prepare yourself for plenty of legwork. If you know the area well, perhaps because you live there, keep your eyes peeled when you're out and about to see whether you can spot any houses and flats for sale that would be suitable for your purposes. You can take several other routes to find the right property for you, and these are explained in the following sections.

Using an estate agent

Although letting agents are more useful to landlords than estate agents when it comes to managing your property, you will need the services of an estate agent when you are purchasing a rental property. Although everyone loves to hate them, estate agents are very useful when you're looking to buy a rental property. You can't get round it – you'll have to befriend an estate agent if you want to get ahead of the game. If you get on with your agent and prove that you're a serious buyer, your agent is more likely to ring you first when suitable properties become available.

Estate agents are paid by commission, which they get by selling a property for their client – the seller. As a result, they want the property to fetch the highest price possible. Don't forget this during your negotiations.

To prove that you're a serious buyer, make sure your funds are ready to move forward with the purchase of a property as soon as you find a suitable one. Be proactive: Keep in touch with estate agents to see what new properties come up and make an effort to see these new properties as quickly as possible.

Buying at auction

Auction is the place to go if you want to buy a property with development potential. Hundreds of auctions take place across the country every week, organised by the big estate agents. But while auctions are good sources of properties, they can be intimidating places. If you plan to buy at auction, attend one or two first, purely as an observer, to see how they operate. Having done so, you may decide that such a process is not for you – and then you can channel your energies into buying property by another route.

If you go to an auction, set a limit beforehand as to how much you are prepared to bid for a property and stick to it. Exceeding this budget may be tempting if you have set your heart on a property, particularly if you get caught up in a bidding war. It is likely that the property requires quite a bit of work, so if you blow your budget buying it in the first place, you'll be left with no funds to pay for refurbishments.

If you successfully bid for a property, the offer becomes binding and you have to exchange contracts immediately. You also have to pay a 10 per cent deposit on the day and complete the purchase within a stated period of time, usually 28 days. If you don't, you lose your deposit, could be sued for breach of contract, and be liable to pay the difference between the price you agreed to pay for the property and the price it eventually fetches. So make sure you don't bid until you have

- **Finished your homework:** Never bid for a property, even if it sounds like a bargain, without seeing it first. Look through the auction catalogue and visit any properties you're interested in. If the property needs a considerable amount of work, take a builder with you so that he can give you an estimate.
- **Arranged your financing:** Unless you have enough cash to pay for the property outright, you should have the mortgage agreed in principle with your lender before the auction. You must also ensure that you have enough cash available to pay the 10 per cent deposit on the day of the sale: Most auctioneers require that you pay this via banker's draft, so make sure the funds are available in your bank account.

Some auctioneers require that you register as a bidder at the start of the sale, so ensure you get there early on the day if this is the case.

It is possible to grab a bargain at auction, but it's also just as easy to make a terrible, costly mistake. Think carefully before you buy and don't get carried away in the heat of the moment.

Using the Internet

The Internet has really taken off in recent years as a source of properties for sale. Many of the big estate agents have realised the value of having some sort of online presence, as have sellers who want to avoid using the services of an estate agent altogether. Sites to look out for include `www.assertahome.co.uk`, `www.fish4homes.com`, and `www.findaproperty.com`.

Local and national newspapers tend to have good Web sites featuring properties for sale. These sites are likely to be updated more frequently than the paper, particularly in the case of weekly local papers. Make a habit of checking these sites on a regular basis.

Checking Out the Tenant Pool

It doesn't matter how great your rental property is, or how close it is to major transport links, if the area doesn't have sufficient tenants to ensure it is rented out virtually all of the time. Before buying a property, establish whether the property is located in a serious rental market. In areas that have lots of small 'starter' homes, for example, people may tend to buy rather than rent. If you have a property there, you'll struggle to find tenants who want to rent your property.

An area with more tenants looking for somewhere to live than available rental properties is the ideal location for your rental property. To get a feel for the rental market in the area, try gauging how busy letting agents are. If the market doesn't appear to be strong, you may want to look somewhere else.

Markets can change quickly as well – an area that is rich with potential tenants working for a big company located in the area can change dramatically should that company close down or relocate. If you already own a rental property in such an area, you may decide to sell up and buy another property elsewhere with a stronger source of tenants. As a landlord, you have to move quickly if you are going to keep ahead of the game.

Part II
Renting Your Property

"The carpet's new – my husband chose it while he was working in the CID."

In this part . . .

The chapters in this part guide you through the process of actually renting your property – everything from getting the property ready, to setting the rent, to advertising. We also give you some great tips for showing your property to prospective tenants and fill you in on the importance of good tenant-screening policies. So if you have a vacancy on your hands – or you will soon – read on.

Chapter 4

Preparing Your Rental Property for Prospective Tenants

In This Chapter

- Knowing what to upgrade and what to repair
- Renovating to get more out of your rental property
- Paying attention to the exterior of the property
- Getting everything done on time in an order that makes sense
- Working with a professional to get your property ready to rent

You may think of preparing your rental property as one of the most basic skills, but it is critical to your overall success. Because vacant rental properties don't generate rental income, you need to fill them with good, reliable tenants who pay their rent on time, and you need to do this as quickly as possible. One of the best ways to attract responsible tenants is to make sure that your vacant rental properties are clean and ready to rent when you show them.

You may think you're saving time and money by allowing a new tenant to rent a property that hasn't been properly prepared. After all, if they don't mind that the property isn't ready to rent, why should you? Unfortunately, this strategy isn't as problem-free as it seems on the surface. In fact, it's a big mistake. Why? Because the kind of tenants you attract with a rental property that hasn't been properly prepared is someone who has lower standards and may even be desperate. New tenants who accept a dirty and poorly maintained property are surely not going to make any effort to leave it in good condition when they leave.

This chapter helps you to figure out whether you need to upgrade your rental property before a new tenant moves in. It also fills you in on the proper methods of preparing the rental property so that you can get the kind of tenant you want in as little time as possible.

Coming Up with a Plan to Handle Vacancies

Because a poor first impression of your rental property's exterior is hard to reverse – regardless of how great the inside may look – the first step in getting good tenants is to develop a plan to get each vacant property in top condition. Ideally, your vacating tenant will be cooperative and allow you access to the property so that you can determine what items need to be cleaned, repaired, replaced, or even upgraded. As you walk through the property, take lots of notes on its condition and what needs attention in order to get it ready to rent again. These notes serve as the foundation for a detailed plan for getting the property ready to rent. That plan in turn helps you attract several suitable prospective tenants who want to lease the property at the rent you're asking.

Not everyone appreciates or values the same features in a rental property as you do. Although you may prefer curtains and carpets in your own home, for example, you may find that tenants prefer Venetian blinds and wooden floors. Although cleanliness has universal appeal, some features such as fitted wardrobes and microwave ovens will appeal more to some prospective tenants than others.

Considering renovations and upgrades

Almost every rental property has potential for renovation or upgrades. Often these upgrades are where you can create the real value in buy-to-let properties: When you have a rental property that is dated, you can renovate it and increase the rent.

If you have an older rental property, renovating may be more difficult due to some of the hazardous materials used in your property's original construction. Although asbestos is banned by law (breathing it in can cause cancer), it was commonly used in construction of many older properties. Removing asbestos can be quite costly because a contractor specialising in asbestos removal must perform this work to ensure that the material is disposed of safely. Your local council may have a specialist department dealing with the removal of asbestos so consult them first.

When you're considering renovations, keep these points in mind:

- **Before you start renovating, be sure to evaluate the cost of renovations or upgrades versus the rent increase that you'll be able to get because of the improvement.** You need to be sure of getting your money back from your investment. But remember that there's no way you can come up with an exact answer to what amount of increased rent a particular improvement will generate; some tenants value certain improvements more than others. A separate walk-in power-shower in the bathroom, for example, will have a different impact on each prospective tenant; some are willing to pay more for such amenities, and others won't. When you think about what to upgrade, pay particular attention to those items that would be quick, easy, and inexpensive to replace but that can really improve the overall look of your rental property.
- **Think about what features and strengths your prospective tenants will find in other rental properties.** Look for outmoded or outdated features in your own property. For example, if most rival landlords offer dishwashers but you don't have one, you may want to install a dishwasher so that you remain competitive. Your property may have a very old light fitting in the dining room that you can easily replace with a modern light fixture. Another simple upgrade is to replace your old electrical switches and sockets for a more modern look.

- **When upgrading or replacing electrical appliances, try to standardise the brand and model and buy white versions wherever possible to give a uniform, tidy impression.** It is often worth buying a well-known brand as well even though little-known brands tend to be cheaper. While buying the cheaper version may save you money up front, it can cost you much more in the long run when you're unable to find replacement parts. Many oven and cooker parts are easily replaceable, but this fact will be worthless if you bought an obscure brand that doesn't have replacement parts available either from the manufacturer or from a third party.
- **When you are considering renovations or upgrades to your rental properties, make sure that you obtain the appropriate planning permission as required.** Check with your local council's planning department to see whether any restrictions apply to renovation plans. Taking this step is important even if you're just replacing the windows or building a garden wall. Also get any permission you need in writing so that you don't have to remove your improvements at a later date – at your own expense. You definitely need permission if your property is a listed building or situated in a conservation area.

Even if your renovations are fairly straightforward and not extensive, it is worth checking with the council to avoid having to undo all your good work at a later date.

Paying attention to the exterior or common areas

You want to make sure that your prospective tenants' first impression of your rental property is a positive one. If the property exterior and garden isn't up to scratch, your potential tenant won't even bother to see the interior – where you may have just installed new appliances and expensive carpets. Start at the street and carefully evaluate your property as if you were entering a contest for the best-looking property in your area.

If you own a rental property that is leased to a Housing Association, the responsibility for the maintenance and repair of the common areas during the lease period may fall to the Association. If this is the case, contact the Association to advise them of any common area concerns that you have. The Association has a vested interest in ensuring the proper maintenance of the premises as well as maintaining a sense of desirability for owners and tenants.

To attract tenants who treat your property properly and stay for a long time, pay special attention to these things as you spruce up the exterior of your property:

- **Be sure that your garden and exterior areas are sparkling clean and well maintained.** Renovating the grounds by making sure that no rubbish, junk, or weeds are present is often a very inexpensive task. A nice green lawn, pretty flowerbeds, and neat hedge enhances any rental property.
- **Make sure that the structure of your building is presentable and inviting.** Although major architectural changes are often cost-prohibitive, you can do a lot with a little paint, landscaping, and a good clean. The good news is that such attention to detail generally doesn't cost much compared to the positive benefits you gain. Some specific exterior improvements to consider are hanging baskets, brass house numbers, or freshly painted fence or window frames.

- **First impressions are critical, and one of the key areas seen by all potential tenants is the front path and doorway of a house.** Make sure these are clean, well kept, and well lit. The front door should be cleaned or freshly painted or stained. Buying a new welcome mat also sends the right vibes out to potential tenants.

There are no shortcuts when it comes to showing a rental property

Early in their property management career, landlords tend to learn a valuable lesson about the importance of cleanliness and first impressions. We know a landlord who had just arrived at one of his vacant rental properties for a management inspection and was speaking to the letting agent at the same time as a potential tenant was viewing the property. The prospective tenant was a local university student who was looking for a flat with her mother. The letting agent went ahead and showed the property while the landlord tagged along. The grounds of the block of flats were very well maintained, and the letting agent was doing a great job getting to know the prospective tenant's needs.

Everything was going great, and it seemed almost certain that the prospective tenant would become the landlord's newest tenant. But when they got to the rental property itself, things immediately went downhill. The hallway was full of cobwebs and dirt; the interior of the property had been cleaned but had not been tidied up for at least a week, and a large tree branch was hanging precariously over the rail of the balcony. Immediately there was a change in the young lady and her mother's attitude. Up to that point, they had been very positive and had been talking about how soon she could be approved and move in. Suddenly, they stopped asking questions, barely answered any, and became very noncommittal.

The lesson the landlord learned? That the cleanliness of the rental property is paramount, and that you should never show a property without having inspected it yourself just prior to the viewing.

Making sure the interior of the property is up-to-scratch

The most suitable, reliable tenants will always have choices, no matter how good or bad the rental market is. You are in competition for these excellent tenants, and you need to make sure that your rental property stands out from the rest. The positive first impression of the exterior of your rental property will soon disappear if the interior is not just as sharp, well aired, and well maintained.

Don't show your rental property until it is completely ready for the tenants to move in. Prospective tenants understandably have little imagination, and if you show them a dirty rental property, that's the way they will always think of it. Although you may lose a couple of potential showing days by taking the time to get the property ready to rent, you benefit in the long run with a more conscientious tenant.

When preparing a rental property for a new tenant, make sure that you don't overlook or forget a single item. We recommend using an inspection checklist to guide you through the process and as a final inspection tool. Here's a list of things to check:

- **When you have legal possession, check to make sure that the prior tenant didn't leave anything behind.** Remove all of the prior tenant's personal possessions and rubbish.
- **Check all plumbing (toilets, taps, and pipes) for proper operation.** Make sure that there are no leaks, that the stopcock is on, and that the drainage is adequate.
- **Check all appliances for proper operation.** Run the dishwasher through a full cycle. Be sure that all the shelves are in the oven.
- **Check all hardware.** Be sure the locks have been changed and are operational. Pay attention to all latches and catches, doorknobs, and any sliding doors.
- **Check all windows.** They should be clean, unbroken, secure, and operate properly. All window locks should work as well.
- **Check all walls, ceilings, and skirting boards.** The paint and/or wall coverings should be clean, without holes, cuts, scratches, nails, or bad seams.
- **Check all floor coverings.** They should be clean and in good condition. The flooring should be properly installed, with no bad seams.
- **Check bathrooms.** Thoroughly clean the toilet, bath, shower, sink, mirrors, and cabinets. Check the toilet roll holder and towel rail to be sure they're clean. Put a new toilet roll in each bathroom.
- **Check all wardrobes, cupboards, and storage areas.** Hooks, shelves, lights, floors, and walls should be clean.
- **Check all work surfaces, cabinets, and doors.** They should be clean and fully operational, presenting no hazards.
- **Check smoke detectors, all lighting and electrical sockets, and circuit-breakers for proper operation.** Fix or replace any that don't work.
- **Check all patios, balconies, and hallways.** They should be clean and any railings should be secure.
- **Check the heating to make sure it's working properly.** Be sure the thermostat, boiler, and radiators are in working order.
- **Check the property's external appearance, including the garden, drive, and paths.** Keep them as neat and tidy as possible.
- **Perform a final check of the entire property for appearance and cleanliness.** Be sure to recheck the property every few days while it is empty.

To furnish or not to furnish, that is the question

If your property is unfurnished, you may want to think about furnishing it. Unfurnished properties can look rather bleak when bare; with the right furnishings, however, you can make your rental property look cosy and inviting to prospective tenants. Done properly, furnishing your property can generate extra rent and may well make your rental property more desirable to tenants in the first place. In letting agents' experience, furnished properties are quicker to let than unfurnished, so ask yourself whether you will recoup the money you lay out for the furniture by having the property vacant for shorter periods of time.

Most prospective tenants have little imagination when shown an empty property. They can't envision what it would look like with furniture or how nice it could be. The whole idea of the show home in a new development of flats is to show potential buyers just what they could do with their properties. If you furnish your rental property, you are doing the work for the prospective tenants, demonstrating how great the place is.

Pay attention to your windows. The right curtains or blinds can really make your rental property look great. Not only will your prospective tenant want attractive and functional window coverings, you will also want to control the appearance of your rental property from the street. Appropriate window coverings vary; some tenants prefer curtains, whereas others may appreciate blinds or shutters. You want window coverings that appeal to your prospective tenants and are easy to maintain. We recommend blinds or curtains, because they are easy to maintain and clean.

If you decide to furnish your property, keep these tips in mind:

- Don't think of your rental property as home for all the old, worn-out furniture you don't want or need any more. If you don't have any use for worn-out items, chances are your tenants won't either. The furniture doesn't have to be new, but it does have to be smart and clean.
- Buy hard-wearing, reasonable quality sofas and beds, tables, and chairs. Don't forget table and bedside lamps, chests of drawers, and bedside cabinets. Remember also that there should be ample wardrobe space in the bedroom.
- Keep patterns and colours fairly neutral and plain. Sofas should have washable covers, and the upholstery fabric shouldn't be a light colour. Light fabrics are very hard to keep clean and will probably need replacing after a short period of time.

- Bear in mind certain safety regulations when furnishing your rental property. It is an offence to let a property that contains furniture that doesn't comply with the 1988 Fire and Safety Regulations. If found guilty of breaking these regulations, you can be fined up to £5,000 or, worse still, imprisoned for up to six months. Sofas manufactured before 1988 are considered a fire hazard and should not be used. Check for the relevant safety label and, if in any doubt about the age of your sofa, throw it out and buy a new one. It's not worth taking the risk.

Whether you furnish your rental property or not, every property should have a fully-fitted kitchen with fridge, freezer, cooker, and perhaps washing machine. A dishwasher is another useful addition that appeals to many prospective tenants. Cupboards should ideally be matching and of a neutral colour, preferably white.

Preparing Your Rental Property the Right Way

One of the best ways to maximise your rental income is to develop a system to improve your efficiency by making sure your property is ready to let again in the minimum amount of time. But you may be so overwhelmed by the amount of work you need to get done in the amount of time you have that you don't stop to consider which order you should do it in. Here's the order we recommend to make the most of your time and be as efficient as possible:

1. **Do the general cleaning.**
2. **Perform the required maintenance, including making repairs and necessary improvements.**
3. **Paint anything that needs it.**
4. **Do a final cleaning, to clean the mess you made painting and repairing things and to catch anything you missed before.**
5. **Clean the carpets or floor coverings.**

The following sections explain in more detail what each of these steps involves. Keeping handy a copy of Jeff Howell's *DIY & Home Maintenance All-in-One For Dummies* (Wiley) is also a good idea.

Keeping up appearances

As soon the old tenants move out, clean the vacant rental property. This initial cleaning should include the following:

- **Remove all rubbish left behind by the former tenant.** Remember to check drawers, cabinets, and wardrobes.
- **Wipe down all surfaces.**
- **Sweep or vacuum the floors.**
- **Wash the windows and doors.**
- **Clean out the storage areas or garage as well.**

If you were unable to gain access before the tenant vacated, this is when you should walk through the property and come up with your plan for getting it ready to rent again. See the earlier section 'Coming Up with a Plan to Handle Vacancies' for details.

Keeping everything ticking over

The majority of the items requiring maintenance in your vacant property will be minor items such as cupboard doors that have come off their tracks, door knobs and towel rails that are loose, and burned-out light bulbs. But be sure to carefully evaluate the current condition of all systems and equipment, including plumbing, electrical appliances, heating, and ventilation:

- **Carefully inspect all plumbing fixtures.** Look for leaky taps, blocked extractor fans, or leaky toilets. Test the stopcock under each sink and look for signs of leaks.
- **Inspect and test the electrical components of the rental property.** Make sure that fuses are all operating properly. Replace burned-out light bulbs and check light switches. If possible, verify that the cable television and telephone lines are working, too.
- **Inspect each of the appliances and make sure that they are operating properly.** Cookers and ovens contain modular parts and you can replace the grill pans and control knobs very easily because replacement parts for most major-brand appliances are readily available. Run the dishwasher through a cycle and look carefully for any signs of leaks around underneath near the pump housing.

- **Conserve energy by turning off the water heater and setting the refrigerator to a low setting.** Tenants are becoming increasingly aware of the importance of conservation and energy-efficiency when selecting their homes. If you install energy-saving features such as insulated windows and doors, loft insulation, weatherproofing, pilot-less ignition gas cookers and water heaters, water-saving fixtures, and other energy-efficient appliances, you'll have a competitive advantage in the rental marketplace.
- **Take steps to minimise the likelihood of pests.** Seal all cracks around the windows, foundations, drains, and pipes that might afford entry into the rental property. Almost every rental property will have the need for pest control at some point in time. An occasional mouse or ants in search of water or food are commonplace, and there are consumer products available to handle these limited situations. However, use professional exterminators to treat more significant problems, and talk to your exterminator about establishing a regular schedule of follow-up treatments to be sure your rental property is free of pests.
- **Perform regular checks as necessary on other areas.** If your rental property has a fireplace, for example, be sure to clean out the ashes and debris as well as have the chimney flue inspected periodically based on the amount of usage. If your property has a pool or spa, have a professional company evaluate the condition and provide a written report documenting its condition, including the equipment and water quality. This evaluation establishes a baseline and often can head off any tenant complaints later on.

Brush strokes

The next step in getting your vacant rental property ready is painting. Painted walls are much easier to maintain than those covered with wallpaper. And the key to success in painting is preparation and having the proper tools.

To prepare your walls, follow these guidelines:

- Make sure that all nails, screws, picture hooks, and other similar items are removed and that any holes in the wall have been filled in with filler.
- Remove all doorknobs and electrical socket covers before you start.
- Make sure the walls have been cleaned of any dirt. Treat grease, water stains, and other blemishes with special products designed for this purpose.
- You may also need to do some scraping and sanding to ensure that the new coat of paint will adhere properly.

One coat of a high-quality white or off-white matt emulsion is usually sufficient, unless the colour of the walls is currently of a much darker colour. If so, you may need another couple of coats. Use silk emulsion in kitchens and bathrooms for easy cleanup and resistance to moisture. Unless you have recently painted the rental property in its entirety and only need to touch up one or two walls, you should paint throughout, including the walls, doors and doorframes, skirting boards, windows and frames, and cupboards and wardrobes, where appropriate.

Don't forget to paint the ceiling! Sparkling white walls will only make it look dirty and in real need of a lick of paint.

When you finish painting, be sure to replace any light switches and sockets that are damaged or covered with paint. Remove any paint that has strayed or splattered onto the floor, windows, work surfaces, cabinets, appliances, and woodwork, and be sure to clean out sinks or baths if you used them to clean paintbrushes or hands.

Keep it clean, vicar

Cleanliness sells. And the only people you want as tenants are ones who will only accept dirt in their home as a temporary condition.

Pay particular attention to the kitchens and bathrooms. A dirty or grimy kitchen and bathroom can be a real turnoff to a potential tenant. Be sure that you clean and re-grout the tiles, and scrub the shower, bath, toilet, and sinks. Another final touch is to install a new toilet seat, if required.

For many landlords, the thought of cleaning up after someone else is too much to bear. Luckily, many local cleaning services do a great job for a very reasonable price. Remember, you don't have to do everything yourself.

If a rental property doesn't smell clean, it won't matter how diligently you've cleaned it. Use a pine or lemon disinfectant and cleanser to neutralise any bad odours from the previous tenants. Buy an air freshener specifically designed for the fridge and pour bleach down the drains to remove any bad odours. Some great air-freshener products are available, but you need to be careful because certain fragrances may be offensive to your prospective tenant. We recommend placing a cinnamon stick in a shallow pan of water and placing it in the oven on low heat. In a short time, the rental property will be filled with a smell that will remind your prospective tenants of homemade apple pie.

The floor's no walkover

Cleaning the carpet or floor is the last step you take in preparing your rental property for new tenants. You can clean wooden and tiled floors during the final cleaning stage; however, if carpets are particularly dirty, you may have to get in an outside contractor to do the job with professional steam-cleaning equipment. If carpets aren't too dirty, you can clean them yourself with the hand-held equipment that is available for rent.

If the carpets are too old, severely worn, or badly stained and damaged, replace them. Be sure to select colours and styles of carpet that are designed for use in rental properties. We recommend selecting a standard carpet for all your rental properties, in a neutral colour. Avoid loud prints or colours that might be to your taste but not necessarily to everyone else's. If you own a lot of rental properties and have proper storage space available, purchasing your standard carpet by the roll can offer significant savings. You can use the extra carpeting to patch or even replace a full room if needed; however, be aware that each roll of even the same carpet style and colour can be different, because the manufacturer's dye may vary slightly each time the carpet is produced.

Many rental property owners make the mistake of purchasing a more expensive carpet than is necessary and try to save money on the underlay. But the underlay can make all the difference in the world. Consider using a higher-grade of underlay with a medium-grade carpet for competitively priced, excellent results.

Unless they're damaged, thoroughly clean your wooden, tiled, or lino floors before deciding to make replacements. Lino is very competitively priced, and the range of materials available is impressive. The most common problem with a roll of lino is that any damage requires complete replacement. Some landlords prefer individual floor tiles that can be replaced as needed; however, these tiles quickly trap dirt at the seams and can look unsightly. The best choice in floor covering material will be determined by your tenant profile and the expectations of your prospective tenant and your competition in the area. Be sure to select neutral colours and basic patterns.

Inspecting Safety Items

Although tenants need to take an active role in, and have the ultimate responsibility for, their own safety you need to check all safety items every time you let the property to a new tenant. The most basic items found in virtually every rental property include door locks, window locks, and smoke detectors. Be sure that these items are in place and working before the new tenant takes occupancy.

Every door should have adequate locking mechanisms. Many insurance companies have specific requirements concerning the type and specifications of door locks. All windows that open and are accessible from the ground should have proper window locks.

London's burning . . . pour on water

Providing each tenant with a small fire extinguisher and fire blankets for the kitchen is a good idea. Although there is always the possibility that the tenant will not use the fire extinguisher properly, using a fire extinguisher quickly can keep a fire from spreading. Of course, the tenant should first ensure that someone is immediately dialling 999 before attempting to put out the fire single-handed.

Smoke detectors are inexpensive and extremely important to the safety of the tenants. Any building constructed after June 1992 is required by law to have smoke detectors on each floor. But it is good practice, and important for the safety of your tenants, that your property has working battery-operated smoke detectors dotted around. Make sure that your records clearly indicate that you tested the smoke detectors and that they were operating properly before your new tenant moved in. Then the tenant needs to take an active role in regularly testing the smoke detector and must not disconnect or disable the smoke detector in any way. The best way to do this is to have your tenant sign a Smoke Detector Agreement (see Chapter 9) whereby the tenant agrees to check the smoke detector on a regular basis, usually at least once a month.

Bad things happen in threes

Here are three more points for you to ponder when you're considering safety in and around your property:

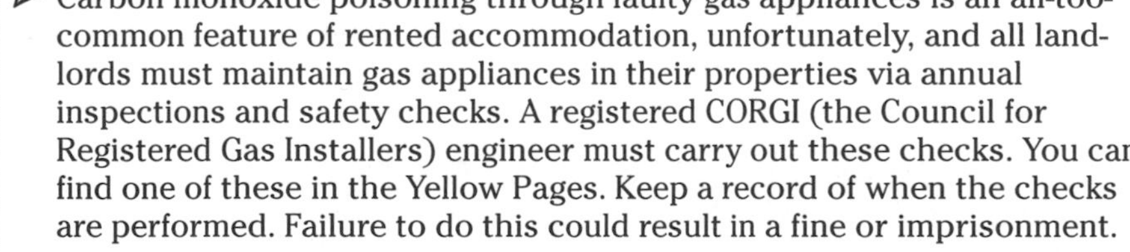

- Carbon monoxide poisoning through faulty gas appliances is an all-too-common feature of rented accommodation, unfortunately, and all landlords must maintain gas appliances in their properties via annual inspections and safety checks. A registered CORGI (the Council for Registered Gas Installers) engineer must carry out these checks. You can find one of these in the Yellow Pages. Keep a record of when the checks are performed. Failure to do this could result in a fine or imprisonment.

- If you have a flat roof, your tenants may be tempted to use portions of it for their personal use, such as for sunbathing (if the weather is nice), hanging out washing, watching fireworks, or hosting parties. This is never a good idea, because roofs are only designed to shelter the rental property from the natural elements, not to hold people. In addition to potential premature damage to your roof, you could be liable if someone gets injured.

- Be sure that the house number or address is clearly marked on the exterior of your property so that it is easy to locate it from the street. This simple measure can be a huge help to fire or ambulance crews in an emergency.

Using Outside Contractors

Determining how to handle the work required to get the property up to scratch so that it's ready to rent to tenants again is one of the toughest decisions that landlords have to make. Most landlords of small properties are typically on their own to either handle the work personally or find contractors to do the necessary work to prepare their vacant properties as quickly as possible.

Even if you're inclined to do all the work on the property yourself, certain maintenance jobs are best handled by outside contractors. Use outside contractors for those trades that require specialised licensing or training. For example, it would be unwise for you to act as an exterminator or a contractor dealing with an environmental hazard. Specific regulations are in place, and unique knowledge is required in these areas.

Your skill level and time constraints may help determine whether you do some chores yourself or hire a professional. For example, cleaning, painting, and light maintenance may be items that you feel qualified to handle, can complete promptly, and will not cause you to forgo significant income in other areas. The ultimate answer is to let others do what they do best while you focus on what *you* do best.

Every day your rental property sits empty costs you rental income you can never recover. If painting your own rental property takes you six days, working in the evenings and weekends, for example, you may actually lose money doing it. How? Well, if the rental market is strong and the daily rental rate is £50 per day, you're actually spending £300 (£50 a day for six days) for a job that you may have been able to hire a professional painter to do in one day for £200.

Chapter 5

Rent, Deposits, and Tenancy Agreements: The Big Three of Property Management

In This Chapter

- Determining the appropriate rent for your rental property
- Using deposits wisely
- Deciding on what to include in your tenancy agreement

Before advertising and showing your rental property, you need to set the rent, determine the appropriate deposit, and have a tenancy agreement ready to go. All of these decisions are important ones. Setting an appropriate rent is important because your net income from your rental property is determined by the amount of rent you charge. Determining an appropriate deposit is important because you need to make sure that the deposit adequately protects you from tenant damage or default. And a tenancy agreement is important because it outlines the terms and conditions of the agreement you have with your tenant.

In this chapter, we give you some tips on setting the asking rent and determining the appropriate deposit. We also guide you through the tenancy agreement so you know what to look out for.

Even if you buy a property with tenants already in place, you need to determine market rents so that you can calculate the appropriate rent when the time comes to renew the tenancy agreement or consider increasing rents to market level.

In addition to setting the rent, you need to make sure that the deposit on hand adequately protects you from tenant damage or default. Deposits serve as the lifeline or protection you need before you turn over your significant property asset to a tenant. The deposit needs to be large enough to motivate the tenant to return the rental property in good condition, plus serve as an accessible resource to cover the tenant's unpaid rent or reimburse the costs to repair any damage. But if your deposit is set too high, many suitable prospective tenants may not be able to afford it, and you'll have fewer rental applicants.

You will also need to draw up a tenancy agreement so that it's ready to go as soon as you find a tenant for your rental property. Most tenancy agreements are for six months in duration although you may want to draw up a shorter or longer one.

Setting the Rent

For most landlords, setting the rent is one of the most important yet difficult tasks. Although you may be tempted to pull numbers out of the air, resist that urge. If you set your rent too high, you'll have a vacant rental property. And if you set your rent too low, you'll have plenty of prospective tenants but not enough money to cover your costs and generate a return on your investment. Your profits will suffer, or, worse, you won't have enough money to even cover your expenses. Finding the optimum price takes time and effort.

If you currently own a rental property, you probably already know how much rental income is necessary to cover your mortgage and other basic running costs. And if you're looking to buy a rental property, you want to determine your minimum income needs *before* the deal is final. Having this information is essential because buy-to-let mortgage lenders can require that your rental income covers at least 130 per cent of the mortgage repayments: any less, and they won't lend you the money to buy the rental property in the first place.

You can use two common methods for determining how much rent you should charge for your rental property – return on investment and market analysis.

Examining the return on your investment

The first step in determining your rent based on the return on your investment is to calculate the costs of owning and operating your rental property. You need to estimate the costs for your mortgage, managing agent fees (where applicable), insurance, maintenance, and how much of a profit you want to make on your invested funds.

If, for example, your annual expenses per rental property are £6,000 for your mortgage and another £2,500 for other annual operating expenses (which include things like managing fees, insurance, and so on) and you want a 10 per cent (or £2,500) annual return on your original cash deposit of £25,000 in this rental property, you need to generate a total rent of £11,000 per year. That's £917 per month. (Of course, this simple calculation doesn't account for the increase in the capital value of the property, but it gives some indication of the costs involved.)

Knowing how much money you need to break even is important for evaluating the potential return on your property investment. But the reality is that the amount you need or want to collect in rent is subject to market conditions and your abilities as a landlord. Although you may have calculated that you need £917 a month for your rental property to achieve your estimated breakeven point (including your 10 per cent profit), if the rental market has determined that comparable properties are available for £850, you may not be able to make the profit you want. With most property investments, the initial returns may not match your original projections; however, in the long run, rents often increase at a greater rate than your expenses, and your return on your investment is likely to improve.

Many new landlords make a major mistake by overestimating the potential income from their rental property. They develop unrealistic operating budgets or projections, using above-market rents and anticipating virtually no void periods or bad debt. When reality strikes, they're faced with negative cash flow, and ultimately they may even lose their rental property. Don't fall into this trap yourself.

Setting the rent is particularly critical if you own just one or two small properties because the rent loss from an extended vacancy or one bad tenant can seriously jeopardise your entire investment. A landlord who owns 20 rental properties and has one tenant who absconds without paying the rent he owes can use a little of the surplus from each of the profitable properties to cover that month's rent on the vacant property. But if you only have two rental properties, you don't have that luxury. If you are a small-time landlord, follow these suggestions:

- **Be conservative in setting your rents.** To avoid surprises, use a conservative budget for your rental property that anticipates rental income at 95 per cent of the market rent for a comparable rental property plus provides for a void period of one to two full months each year.
- **Be very cautious in tenant screening.** To find out how to screen for the tenant you want, head to Chapter 8.
- **Be aggressive in maintaining your rental properties.** To attract good, long-term tenants who pay on time, keep your rental properties in excellent condition.

Conducting a market analysis of the rent in your area

Although you can determine the amount of rent to charge by calculating a desired return on your investment and setting the rent accordingly, as explained in the preceding section, typically the best way to set your rent is to conduct a market survey of comparable rental properties in your area.

Evaluating how much rent is being charged for similar rental properties in comparable locations is a great way to gather information before setting your own rent. Make minor adjustments in your rent because of variations in the location, age, size, and features of the properties you're comparing. If, for example, one of your competitors has an available house to rent that is nearly identical to yours, your rent should be slightly higher if you also have off-road parking. Of course, be honest and make downward adjustments for aspects of your rental property that aren't as competitive or as desirable as well.

The rental value of a particular property is subjective and can vary dramatically from one person to another. When estimating the proper market rent for your rental property, be careful not to make adjustments based strictly on your own personal preferences. You may prefer a first-floor flat and believe that such flats should be priced higher than comparable ground-floor flats. But although many prospective tenants may, like you, prefer living on the first floor, just as many prospective tenants would similarly value the ground-floor flat because they may not want to climb stairs or use a lift.

In order to determine the going rent in your area, do your homework and locate comparable rental properties. *Comparable properties* are those properties that your tenants are most likely to have also considered when looking for a rental property. They may be located in the next road to your property or across town. For example, many of your prospective tenants may work at the local hospital, two miles away from your rental property. But these prospective tenants are just as likely to choose a property that is within two miles of the hospital in another direction. So your comparable properties could be four miles away. Don't assume that your comparable properties are only in your street.

After you determine which rental properties are comparable, finding out the current market rent is easy. Begin by checking the To Let signs in your area and ring to ask how much the rent is and other details. Your local or regional newspaper generally has ads listing the properties for rent in the area, along with some details and a phone number to call for more information. Although looking at ads gives you some good general information, you need to go and see the properties in person to truly determine whether the rental properties are comparable to yours.

There are two schools of thought when performing a rent survey to determine the proper asking rent for your rental properties:

- **You can be honest and tell the landlord that you're also a landlord and you're doing market analysis.** While you may find that some landlords might co-operate and share the information you need, the majority are likely to be more cagey about sharing such information with a rival.
- **You can pose as a prospective tenant and ask all the typical questions that a tenant might ask.** The landlord or managing agent will give you only the information that a prospective tenant would need about the rental property. Although this strategy may seem a bit sneaky, you're more likely to get the information you require if you pose as a prospective tenant.

If you're competing against a large management company in your area, the company isn't likely to provide you with any information about its current occupancy rates. Its actual occupancy rate is important, however, because this information can provide a good indication of overall demand for rental properties. Over the years, we have discovered some creative ways to determine the actual vacancy levels, such as talking with the postman who delivers to the block of flats run by the management company. The postman won't have exact numbers, but he can tell you whether the block is completely full or whether there are a good number of vacancies. You can also drive past the property at night and see how many parking spaces are being used.

Rental rates can vary greatly from town to town and even from street to street because many factors affect rents. Determining the proper asking rent is not scientific; views, landscaping, and traffic noise are just a few examples of the issues tenants take into account. So be realistic in setting your asking rent. Starting a little too high is better than starting too low, because you can always reduce your asking rent slightly if you encounter too much resistance. But you can't very easily raise your asking rent if you get a large response to your ads.

Setting your rents properly is an independent decision based on current market conditions. Unfortunately, the realities of the rental market may put limits on the rent you can reasonably charge for your rental property, regardless of your costs of owning and maintaining that property.

Coming Up with a Fair Deposit

You should collect a deposit from your tenant when she moves into your property, and you can hold it until the tenant leaves. The general purpose of the deposit is to ensure that the tenant pays rent when it's due and keeps the rental property in good condition. If you collect the first month's rent upon move-in, this amount is *not* considered part of the deposit.

Most landlords ask for the equivalent of one month's rent as a deposit, although some ask for two months. The law doesn't regulate the length of time it takes the landlord to return the deposit and any deductions, although there are plans to change this (see Chapter 13 for more on this).

Deposits are more than just money that you hold for protection against unpaid rent or damage caused by your tenant. Although the actual cash amount may be relatively small compared to the overall value of your rental property, the deposit is a psychological tool that is often your best insurance policy for getting your rental property back in decent condition.

Don't lower or waive the deposit. If the required funds to move in are too high for your tenant to manage, collect a reasonable portion of the deposit prior to move-in and allow the tenant to pay the balance of the deposit in instalments. If you don't collect the deposit in full, you lose your bargaining tool. Your tenant could well abscond further down the line without paying the rent he owes you if he doesn't have the incentive of the return of his deposit. Or he might think nothing of making cigarette burns on the sofa or wine stains on the carpet if he knows he won't be penalised for it by losing some of his deposit.

Keeping deposits separate from your other funds

Deposits are a liability, because they are funds that legally belong to the tenant. You hold these funds in trust as protection in the event that the tenant defaults in the payment of rent or damages the property.

Because the funds don't belong to you, you may want to hold the deposits in a separate bank account rather than mix it in with the other funds from your rental properties or personal resources. Keeping the deposits separate from the rest of your funds ensures that whenever a tenant moves out and is potentially entitled to the return of some or all of that money, the deposit is available. Besides, it's a nice gesture to pay the tenant the interest earned on the deposit when you return it at the end of the tenancy (see the later section 'Paying interest on deposits' for information on this option). However, you're not legally required to do this.

Setting a reasonable deposit

Most landlords opt for the equivalent of one month's rent as a deposit. One problem with this approach is that tenants may misconstrue that the deposit is to be used as the last month's rent (because it's equal to a monthly rent payment).

The deposit is absolutely not for this purpose. If any damage has occurred to the property or professional cleaning is required, such as having the carpets steam-cleaned, you don't have any recourse but to subtract these costs from the deposit. If the deposit is used as the last month's rent, you're out of luck entirely.

We recommend that you collect slightly more than a month's rent as a deposit. To avoid tenants using the deposit as the last month's rent, we suggest that you ask for five or six weeks' rent as a deposit and explain your policy to minimise any confusion.

Avoiding non-refundable deposits

Some landlords charge non-refundable fees, for cleaning or keeping a pet. But we recommend avoiding such non-refundable fees and just incorporate these charges into your rent. This way, you avoid potentially time-consuming disputes with your tenants.

If you have a specific concern, such as a tenant's pet, increase the amount of your refundable deposit to protect yourself from any damage.

Having the deposit fully refundable is an incentive to the tenant to return the premises in good condition. A non-refundable deposit can actually deter the tenants from making any effort to return the premises in good condition, because they figure that they're forfeiting the deposit anyway.

Paying interest on deposits

No law requires that landlords pay interest on the tenant's deposit. However, you may want to offer to pay the interest generated by the deposit to the tenant at the end of the tenancy agreement – this policy is likely to act in your favour and make your rental property more attractive to prospective tenants.

If you're going to pay interest, put the deposit in the savings account paying the highest rate of interest that you can find. The best savings rates are available via Internet-based accounts rather than high-street banks, so shop around online for a reasonable rate. The tenant is unlikely to receive back a lot of interest, but it's a nice gesture which is likely to be appreciated.

No law prevents you from voluntarily paying interest on deposits, and some owners offer to pay interest as a competitive advantage or as an inducement to collect a larger deposit. If you are able to get a much larger deposit, we recommend paying interest on that deposit. The additional peace of mind is worth the relatively small amount you will lose by not receiving the interest yourself.

Increasing deposits

If you have a long-term tenant and your rents have increased significantly over time, you may want to consider increasing your deposit. Doing so is legal as long as you comply with the normal requirements for any change in the terms of the agreement.

If you have a six-month tenancy agreement, for example, you must wait until that agreement expires before you request an increase in the deposit. If you have a shorter tenancy agreement, then you can increase the deposit the same way that you raise the rent, typically by giving the tenant a written 30-day notice in advance.

Using a Tenancy Agreement

The tenancy agreement is the primary document that specifies the terms and conditions of the agreement binding the landlord and the tenant. It is a contract between the owner of the rental property and the tenant for the possession and use of the rental property in exchange for the payment of rent.

Most landlords use the Assured Shorthold Tenancy agreement. When this tenancy agreement was introduced in 1988 and later amended under the 1996 Housing Act, it revolutionised the residential letting market. For the first time, it granted the landlord a series of guarantees that made it easier for the landlord to let property at a market rent and to recover possession of the rental property if needed. The tenant has no security of tenure after the end of the term agreed between landlord and tenant; the landlord is certain to obtain possession of the property and doesn't have to give a reason as to why he wants possession. You will still have to follow the correct procedure, however, and give two months' notice in writing.

An Assured Shorthold Tenancy tends to start with an initial fixed period. No upper limit is specified, but six months to a year is normal. If you opt for six months, for example, you can't repossess the property during this length of time unless the tenant breaks the terms of the agreement. After the fixed term, you can renew the agreement for another fixed period or allow it to continue indefinitely on a periodic basis, such as month to month.

If you're renewing for a fixed period, you need to draw up a fresh tenancy agreement. If you're continuing indefinitely on a periodic basis, you don't need to take action to continue the letting, but you do have to make the tenant aware that you're continuing on the same terms.

You don't have to employ a solicitor to draw up a complicated tenancy agreement because the Assured Shorthold Tenancy is a fairly standard form. All letting agencies have them, but if you're going it alone and managing your own rental property, you can use the tenancy agreement printed later in this chapter (see Form 5-1). An Assured Shorthold Tenancy is legally binding between landlord and tenant; however, it can be difficult to enforce if one of the parties decides not to abide by it.

Before you can offer an Assured Shorthold Tenancy agreement on your rental property, certain conditions must be met:

- The tenant (or each of the joint tenants) must be an individual, not a company.
- The tenant must occupy the dwelling as his only or principle home.
- The annual rent must not be greater than £25,000.
- The landlord must not live at the rental property. However, if the landlord has converted the basement in his house into a self-contained flat with separate entrance and lets this to tenants, an Assured Shorthold Tenancy can be created as normal.

The tenancy agreement must also include certain definitions as to what you mean by the terms *landlord* and *tenant* and on what grounds the tenancy can be terminated. You should also clearly state the notice period to be served by either party – one month by the tenant; two months by the landlord – and the agreement should state that the tenancy must run for at least six months.

You and your tenant have to sign the tenancy agreement in the presence of witnesses. It then becomes legally binding.

With an Assured Shorthold Tenancy, you cannot increase the rent or change other terms of the tenancy until the current agreement expires. Also, you cannot terminate or end the tenancy before the agreement expires, unless the tenant does not pay his rent or violates another term of the tenancy agreement. (The majority of tenants move only because of a job transfer or another significant reason, or because the landlord does not properly maintain the property.)

Although the tenancy agreement legally binds both you and the tenant, it's not difficult for a tenant to walk away from a tenancy agreement. The tenant is responsible for paying the rent for the whole of the initial period even if he leaves early. If you find a replacement tenant during that time, you should let your former tenant off the hook and only charge him for the rent up until the new tenant moves in and begins paying rent. However, you are not obliged to do this.

Although oral rental agreements are binding, make sure all your tenancy agreements are in writing, because so many issues surrounding those agreements involve monetary considerations. Memories fade, and disputes can arise that could well be resolved in the favour of the tenant should legal action be required. Oral agreements also create the potential for charges of discriminatory treatment. Always put all terms and conditions in writing, even if you know the tenant personally or you only intend to let the property for a short period of time. Oral agreements are only as good as the paper they are not written on because they can't be substantiated and they're not always enforceable.

Rent Assessment Committee

Under an Assured Shorthold Tenancy agreement, if the tenant feels the rent you're charging is too high – and if it's higher than rents on comparable properties in the area – the tenant can apply to a Rent Assessment Committee for the rent to be reduced. (Keep in mind, however, that few tenants actually apply to the Rent Assessment Committee because they feel they are being charged too much rent.)

The tenant can take this action only within the first six months of a tenancy. And the committee can make a decision only if enough similar properties in the area are let on Assured Shorthold Tenancies. The committee compares the rents charged on similar rental properties in your area with what you charge and decides what the rent for your property should be. You don't have to panic, though, because this amount will never be lower than the market rent.

You are only at risk of being forced to accept a lower rent if you charge significantly higher than the going rate for a similar property in your area.

A standard tenancy agreement

Form 5-1 shows a standard tenancy agreement. For peace of mind, it is worth asking your solicitor to review these documents and all other forms in this book before using them, particularly as you may well want to add your own terms and conditions.

TENANCY AGREEMENT

THIS AGREEMENT is made on the date specified between the Landlord and the Tenant. It is intended that the tenancy created by this Agreement is and shall be an assured shorthold tenancy within the meaning of the Housing Act 1988 as amended by the Housing Act 1996.

DATE: ______________________

LANDLORD: ______________________

LANDLORD'S ADDRESS: ______________________

____

LANDLORD'S AGENT (if applicable): ______________________

TENANT(S): ______________________

____

____

PROPERTY: ______________________

____

CONTENTS: The Landlord's fixtures, fittings and furniture listed in the attached Inventory, and signed by the Landlord and Tenant.

TERM: For the term of _________ months
Starting from: _____________

RENT: £__________ (______________________ pounds) per calendar month, in advance. Tenant is to make the first payment on the signing of this Agreement, and subsequent payments on the same day of the month as the start date.

DEPOSIT: A deposit of £ __________ (__________________________ pounds) to be paid to the Landlord on the signing of this Agreement.

1. The Landlord agrees:

1.1 To let the Property and its Contents to the Tenant for the Term at the Rent payable as above. As long as the Tenant complies with the Tenant's obligations (see below), the Landlord agrees not to interfere with the Tenant's use and enjoyment of the Property.

1.2 To pay the balance of the Deposit to the Tenant as soon as possible after the conclusion of the tenancy, minus any reasonable costs incurred for the breach of any obligation. Where applicable, the Landlord may retain the Deposit until the Local Authority confirms that no Housing Benefit paid to the Landlord is repayable.

1

Form 5-1: Tenancy Agreement (Page 1 of 6).

1.3 To keep the structure and exterior of the Property in good repair.

1.4 To keep the installations of the Property in good repair and proper working order for water, gas, electricity, sanitation and heating.

1.5 To ensure that the Property has an up-to-date gas safety certificate under the Gas Safety (Installations and Use) Regulations Act 1998. All gas appliances, flues and other fittings to be checked annually to ensure they are safe and working properly.

1.6 To comply with the obligations under the Fire and Safety Regulations 1988. All of the Landlord's furniture and furnishings, including sofas, beds, cushions and pillows, must meet these fire safety standards.

2. The Tenant agrees:

2.1 To pay the Rent on the days and in the manner stated in the Agreement without any deduction, and by direct debit to the Landlord's bank account.

2.2 To pay the Deposit as security for the performance of the Tenant's obligations and to pay and compensate the Landlord for the reasonable costs of breach of these obligations. It is agreed that this sum shall not be transferable by the Tenant in any way, and at any time against payment of the Rent and that no interest shall be payable on the Deposit.

2.3 That if the Landlord has recourse to the Deposit during the tenancy, the Landlord may immediately demand from the Tenant whatever amount is required to restore the amount of the Deposit to the original sum.

2.4 To arrange immediately with the relevant supply company for all accounts for water, gas, electricity and telephone (where applicable), and television licence, at the Property to be addressed to the Tenant in their own name and pay all standing charges for these.

2.5 To pay the council tax, water, gas, electric, telephone bills and television licence for the Property. The Tenant shall also pay for the total cost of any re-connection fees relating to the supply of water, gas, electricity and telephone, if disconnected. The Tenant also agrees to notify the Landlord before changing supplier for any of the utility services.

2.6 Not to damage the Property and Contents or make any alterations or additions. Before embarking on any redecoration the written consent of the Landlord or Landlord's Agent must be obtained first.

2.7 Not to leave the Property vacant for more than 28 consecutive days without notifying the Landlord in writing beforehand, and to properly secure all locks and bolts to the doors, windows and other openings when leaving the Property unattended.

2.8 To keep the interior of the Property and its Contents clean and tidy and in good decorative condition up to the standard existing when the Tenant moves in (reasonable wear and tear excepted). To remove rubbish from the property on a daily basis, to clean the windows regularly both inside and out, and to keep all rooms well ventilated.

2.9 To immediately pay the Landlord or Landlord's Agent the value of replacement of any furniture or effects lost, damaged or destroyed, and not to remove or permit to be removed any furniture or effects belonging to the Landlord from the Property.

2

Form 5-1: Tenancy Agreement (Page 2 of 6).

2.10 To pay for any cleaning that may be required to reinstate the Property to the same order that it was provided at the beginning of the Tenancy, including the washing or cleaning of all carpets and curtains which have been soiled during the Tenancy.

2.11 To ensure the drains, drainage system and gutters are free from obstruction.

2.12 To replace all broken glass in doors and windows damaged during the Tenancy.

2.13 To promptly notify the Landlord of any defect, damage or disrepair in the Property, especially if it compromises health and safety or may give rise to a claim under the Landlord's insurance policy.

2.14 To permit the Landlord or any person authorised by the Landlord or Landlord's Agent to enter the Property on giving 24 hours' notice (except in case of emergency) to inspect its condition and Contents; repair or replace the Contents; replace locks; carry out gas and electrical safety checks or repairs, or show prospective tenants or buyers round the Property.

2.15 To use the Property as a private residence for occupation by the named Tenant(s) and, if the Landlord has given his consent, by the named Tenant's children under the age of 18.

2.16 Not to assign, sublet, or part with, possession of the Property, or let any other person live at the Property.

2.17 To use the Property as a single private dwelling and not to use it or any part of it for any other purpose nor to allow anyone else to do so.

2.18 Not to receive paying guests or carry on or permit to be carried on any business, trade or profession on or from the Property.

2.19 Not to do anything that gives the insurers of the Property and its Contents any reason to refuse payment or increase the premiums.

2.20 Not to keep any animals, birds, or other living creature at the Property without the Landlord's written consent. Such consent, if granted, to be revocable at any time by the Landlord.

2.21 Not to keep any dangerous or inflammable materials at the Property or in any outbuildings.

2.22 To keep gardens (if any) including all driveways, paths, lawns, hedges and flower beds neat and tidy and properly tended at all times. The Tenant is not to cut down or remove any trees or shrubs without the Landlord's prior consent.

2.23 Not to alter or change or install any locks on any doors or windows in or about the Property or have any additional keys made for any locks without the prior written consent of the Landlord.

2.24 Not to use the Property for any illegal or immoral purposes.

2.25 Within seven days of receipt thereof to send to the Landlord all correspondence addressed to the Landlord and any notice order or proposal relating to the Property (or any building of which the Property forms part), given, made or issued under or by virtue of any statute, regulation, order, direction or by-law by any authority.

3

Form 5-1: Tenancy Agreement (Page 3 of 6).

2.26 To pay and compensate the Landlord fully for any reasonable costs, expense, loss or damage incurred or suffered by the Landlord as a consequence of any breach of the agreements on the part of the Tenant in this Agreement and to indemnify the Landlord from, and against, all actions, claims and liabilities in that respect.

2.27 Not to deface or damage the Property by fixing anything whatsoever to the interior or exterior using glue, Sellotape, pins, nails, hooks or screws, without the Landlord's written consent.

2.28 To take all reasonable precautions to prevent damage to the Property by frost.

2.29 To comply (where the Property is a leasehold dwelling) with the rules regulating the use of the Property and the conduct of its occupiers.

2.30 In order to comply with Gas Safety Regulations, it is necessary:

2.30.1 that the ventilators provided for this purpose in the Property should not be blocked.

2.30.2 that a build up of soot on any gas appliances should immediately be reported to the Landlord or the Landlord's Agent.

2.31 To ensure the chimneys (where applicable) are swept when necessary.

2.32 Not to use any portable gas or electric heaters in the Property without the Landlord's prior written consent.

2.33 To be responsible for testing all smoke detectors fitted in the Property once a month and replace the batteries as necessary.

2.34 Within the last two months of the Tenancy to allow the Landlord or any person authorised by the Landlord or Landlord's Agent to enter and view the Property with prospective tenants at reasonable hours.

2.35 That where the Property is left unoccupied, without prior notice in writing to the Landlord or Landlord's Agent, for more than 28 days and the Rent for this period is unpaid, the Tenant is deemed to have surrendered the Tenancy. This means that the Landlord may take over the Property and take steps to find another tenant.

2.36 To return the keys to the Property to the Landlord or Landlord's Agent at the end of the tenancy. The Tenant also agrees to pay for any reasonable charges incurred by the Landlord or the Landlord's Agent in securing the Property against re-entry where keys are not returned.

2.37 That Housing Benefit, where applicable, is paid direct to the Landlord.

2.38 Not to be a nuisance to the neighbours. The Tenant will not make any noise that is audible outside the Property from 11pm to 8am daily, or be guilty of harassment or abuse on grounds of sex, sexual orientation, disability or race.

3, The Landlord can terminate the Tenancy on the last day of the Term, or after the Term, by service of the Landlord's notice of intention to seek possession.

3.1 The Tenant can terminate the Tenancy by vacating the Property on the last day of the Term, or after that by giving the Landlord one month's notice in writing.

4

Form 5-1: Tenancy Agreement (Page 4 of 6).

4. If the Tenant does not pay the rent due to the Landlord under this agreement within 14 days of the due date, the Tenant will be issued with a reminder from the Landlord, in writing, for which there is a charge of £20. Interest will also be charged at the rate of 5 percent per annum, calculated on a daily basis from the due date until the rent is paid.

5. By obtaining a court order, the Landlord may re-enter the Property and immediately thereupon the Tenancy shall absolutely determine without prejudice to other rights and remedies of the Landlord if the Tenant has not complied with any obligation in this Agreement or should the Rent be in arrears by more than 14 days.

6. The parties agree:

6.1 Notice is hereby given that possession might be recovered under Ground 1, Section 2 of the Housing Act 1988 if applicable. That is, that the Landlord used to live in the Property as his or her main home; or intends to occupy the Property as his or her only or main home.

6.2 Before the Landlord can end this tenancy, he shall serve any notice(s) on the Tenant in accordance with the provisions of the Housing Acts. Such notice(s) shall be sufficiently served if served in accordance with section 196 of the Law of Property Act 1925. Under this, a notice shall be sufficiently served if sent by registered or recorded delivery post (if the letter is not returned undelivered) to the Tenant at the Property or the last known address of the Tenant or left addressed to the Tenant at the Property.

7. The Tenant irrevocably authorises the Local Authority, Benefit Office, Post Office and the relevant utility companies (including electricity, gas, water and telephone) to discuss and disclose to the Landlord or Agent all financial and other information relating to the Property or any housing benefit claim. This authority shall extend to disclosure of the Tenant's whereabouts if the Tenant has left the Property with rent or other money owing.

8. This Agreement, which includes all the attachments referred to below, constitutes the entire Agreement between Landlord and Tenant and cannot be modified except in writing and signed by all parties.

9. Addenda. By initialling as provided, Tenant acknowledges receipt of the following optional addenda, as indicated, copies of which are attached hereto and are incorporated as part of this Agreement:

_____ A, Policies and Rules
_____ B. Inventory
_____ C, Animal Agreement
_____ D. Other ______________________

SIGNED by the LANDLORD: **In the presence of:**

5

Form 5-1: Tenancy Agreement (Page 5 of 6).

SIGNED by the LANDLORD:
(or the Landlord's Agent)

____

In the presence of:

Name ____________________________

Address __________________________

____

Witness Signature ___________________

SIGNED by the TENANT(S):

____

____

____

In the presence of:

Name ____________________________

Address __________________________

____

Witness Signature ___________________

6

Form 5-1: Tenancy Agreement (Page 6 of 6).

Standard tenancy agreements are great because they save you the expense of getting your solicitor to draft an agreement for you. But they don't allow you to add your own clauses. However, you can modify the terms of your tenancy agreement fairly easily with the Addendum to Tenancy Agreement, shown in Form 5-2. For example, maybe you want to include a clause stating that smoking or pets are absolutely forbidden in your rental property. You can easily incorporate this clause into the tenancy agreement by using the Addendum.

Be careful about adding additional clauses or language to your tenancy agreement unless you seek the advice of a solicitor.

Addendum to Tenancy Agreement

This Addendum to the Tenancy Agreement entered into on ____________________ (date), between ____________________ (Tenant) and ____________________(Landlord) for the property located at: ____________________

This Addendum shall be and is incorporated into the Tenancy Agreement dated ____________________ between Tenant and Landlord.

Tenant and Landlord agree to the following changes and/or additions to the Tenancy Agreement:____________________

This Addendum is to be effective as of ____________________ (date).

Signed: ____________________ ____________________

LANDLORD/MANAGING AGENT TENANT(S)

Date: ____________________ Date: ____________________

Form 5-2: Addendum to Tenancy Agreement.

The number one reason for tenants to insist on a tenancy agreement is that the rent is fixed for a minimum period of time. The landlord cannot unilaterally vary the terms of a tenancy after it has been granted. So you cannot increase the amount of rent without the consent of the tenant, unless the terms of the tenancy allow you to do so. Therefore, be sure to include a term in the tenancy agreement allowing you to increase the rent.

Chapter 6

Generating Interest in Your Rental Property

In This Chapter

- Planning your marketing strategy
- Figuring out what role advertising plays
- Making sure you don't break any anti-discrimination laws
- Finding the methods of advertising that will work best for you

More than almost any other single factor, good quality tenants make your experience as a landlord enjoyable and profitable. But finding a good tenant can be a long and arduous process if you don't know how to do it well. So in this chapter, you can see the process from beginning to end – from creating a marketing plan (which helps you narrow your focus and set goals) to writing good copy for your ads. This is the place to start if you've just found out one of your properties will be vacant in a month, and it's the place to turn to if your property has already been empty for twice that long. It's never too late to start advertising effectively, and this chapter gives you all the tools you need to do exactly that.

Developing a Marketing Plan

The key to success in owning and managing rental properties is to keep your rental properties full with long-term paying tenants who treat your rental property and their neighbours with respect. But first you need to determine the best way to attract and retain these highly desirable tenants. A marketing plan can help you do just that.

A *marketing plan* can be anything from a formal written outline of your marketing strategies to some general marketing ideas you keep in mind as you try to find tenants for your property. If you only own one or two properties, or even if you own 20 or 30 rental properties in several towns, you may not think that you need a marketing plan. Developing a marketing plan may seem like an unnecessary use of your time and energy. But the basic concepts of a marketing plan are important for *all* owners of rental property, regardless of the number of flats or houses they may own.

A good marketing plan consists of strategies for attracting prospective tenants as well as retaining your current tenants. The importance of retaining your current tenants is so vital to your long-term success as a rental landlord property owner that there's an entire chapter devoted to it. Turn to Chapter 11 for more information.

If you don't attract and retain tenants, you can rest assured that your competition will. And you are in competition with other owners and property managers for the best tenants, even if you only have a few rental properties. In most rental markets, prospective tenants have many options, and the most responsible tenants are very selective, because the rental property they select will be their home.

The likelihood of finding responsible tenants is often a numbers game. The more prospective tenants you are able to attract, the greater your opportunity to carefully evaluate their qualifications and the higher the probability that you will be able to select the most qualified applicant.

Determining your target market

One of the first steps in developing a basic marketing plan is to determine the *target market* for your rental property. The target market consists of prospective tenants who are the most likely to find that your property meets their needs. The target market can be relatively broad or it can be fairly narrow, depending on the location, size, and features of your property. If you have several properties, you may find that each one has a different target market or you may find that the target markets overlap.

To determine your target market, first carefully evaluate your property by looking at the location, size, and the specific features that make it unique.

- **Location:** What are some of the benefits of your property's location? Is your property located near transport links, factories or offices, a hospital or doctor's surgery, shops, or other important facilities, such as a sports centre? Paying attention to your property's location may provide you with a target market that includes employees of certain companies or people who have a need to live in close proximity to certain facilities, such as a mainline train station.

- **Size:** Larger properties tend to be more attractive to families or several tenants who wish to share accommodation (such as students), whereas studio flats are more suitable to a single tenant or a couple on a budget.
- **Amenities:** A property that allows pets and has a large garden typically appeals to pet owners and/or tenants with children. If your property has storage space or a garage, this is often an additional attraction to prospective tenants.

When you consider your property's features, you will probably discover that it meets the needs and requirements of certain tenants more than others. You can use this knowledge to target specific audiences, but your rental efforts must never discourage, limit, or exclude *any* prospective tenants from having an equal opportunity to rent from you.

Knowing what your tenants stand to gain from your property

When you have established who your most likely tenants are, you need to shift your focus to incorporating and implementing the concept of a target market into the marketing plans for your rental property. This is when we usually think of the WIFM approach. *WIFM* stands for 'What's In It For Me?' (yes, we know that it technically 'WIIFM', but that just doesn't look right!), and it represents the thought process of virtually all consumers (including your potential tenants) when evaluating a purchase decision. The WIFM concept can be used in all business and reminds us that, in general, people are most interested in the benefits that they personally will receive in any given relationship or business transaction.

When it comes to marketing and advertising your rental property, the important concept of WIFM can help you see the rental decision process through the eyes of your prospective tenants and makes your goal of finding long-term, stable tenants more attainable. Unfortunately, owners and managers of rental properties are human and, just like most people, although they are very good at seeing the world from their own perspective, they often fail to critically evaluate the advantages and disadvantages of the product that they are selling – their rental property. As a landlord or manager, you have a competitive advantage if you understand the opportunities and challenges presented by your particular property. You can also have a competitive advantage if you find ways to enhance the deficits or narrow your marketing focus to those specific types of tenants who will be attracted to your property.

Looking at your property through your prospective tenants' eyes

One landlord we know owns several 2-bedroom flats in a large development near Bristol University. When he first bought them, he was wary of renting to large numbers of undergraduates, so his plan was to attract post-graduates who could share a 2-bedroom flat. Although many prospective tenants looked at the flats, few decided to rent one out. Clearly, the landlord was trying to define and force the rental market and prospective tenants to adapt to his perception of their needs.

When it became obvious that his rental efforts were not having much success, our landlord friend began to carefully review the comments of prospective tenants and actually listen to their needs. What he found was that there were plenty of post-graduate students in need of accommodation, but that they preferred to live alone. The WIFM from the perspective of the post-graduates was the desire for a quiet place to work or study without the distraction of flat mates. With this new perspective on the needs of the prospective tenants, he quickly realised that he could market these very same 2-bedroom flats to this new target market.

Armed with this knowledge, he revised his marketing efforts and changed his advertising in the university newspaper to read, '1 bedroom plus study.' This change led to an increased interest in the property and more tenants. Just by changing the way the flats were advertised, he found that he was able to reach his original target market of post-graduates who wanted to live off campus.

Remember: Look at your rental property from the perspective of the most likely tenants. Then promote and accentuate the features of your property that will be of greatest interest to that market.

Understanding the Importance of Good Advertising

Tenants rarely come looking for you. Your local newspaper may have a column for 'Properties Wanted to Rent' or one of your current tenants may contact you enquiring on behalf of a friend who is looking for a rental property. But this is the exception, not the rule. The majority of your tenants will come from the efforts you make to find suitable tenants for your property.

Advertising is how you let people know that you have a vacant property available to rent. When it's done well, the money you spend on advertising is money extremely well spent, but when it's done poorly, advertising can be another black hole for your precious resources. Advertising is more of an art than a science at times, because what works for one particular property may not work for another.

Advertising rental properties is no different in many ways than all other types of advertising. The key to success in rental property advertising is determining how you can reach that very small, select group of suitable tenants who will be interested in your rental property when it's available to rent. In your ads, you want to show that your property offers what your target market is looking for.

The best way to determine the most desirable features of your rental property for your target market is to use the WIFM approach and ask your current tenants what they like about where they live. You may also figure out from talking with the *rental traffic* (all the people who look at your property, whether or not they agree to rent) what they found of interest in your rental property. The key is to remember that your rental property has different features that appeal to different prospective tenants, but over a period of time you will be able to determine certain common factors that most prospective tenants desire. Incorporate these selling points into your marketing and advertising efforts.

Review the information from your marketing plan about the most marketable features and attributes of your property and present it to prospective tenants in your advertising.

Rifle versus blunderbuss: Picking an advertising approach

Creating interest in your rental property used to be as simple as putting up a sign or placing an ad in the local newspaper. Although these tried-and-tested methods of notifying potential tenants that you have a property to rent are still very successful, many other excellent options are available for you to consider. The target market for your property has a lot to do with which method of advertising works best for your particular rental property. Here are your options:

- **The rifle approach:** Advertising that is very specific and targets a narrow group of prospective tenants is often described as a *rifle approach.*
- **The blunderbuss approach:** Advertising that blankets the market with information to tenants and non-tenants, suitable and unsuitable alike, is commonly called a *blunderbuss approach.*

Many methods of advertising your rental property fall into the blunderbuss category and very few fall into the rifle category. Big regional newspapers (blunderbuss approach) often have impressive circulations. However, they can't tell you how many of those readers actually read the rental property ads or are actually looking for a flat on the specific day your ad will run. Advertising is, for the most part, a numbers game. Reach enough readers and you are bound to find a few that will be looking for a rental property like yours on a given day. Two good rifle approaches to advertising are word-of-mouth referrals and postcards on student notice-boards under 'Accommodation'. But if you rely solely on these approaches to find tenants, you may end up with an empty property for much longer than you'd like.

One size rarely fits all. When it comes to advertising a rental property, you need to employ a combination of both the blunderbuss and the rifle approach to be successful. Clearly, both methods have advantages. Referrals and student notice-boards often give you good exposure to prospective tenants in your local area, whereas newspaper and Internet ads let people moving to your area know about your rental property as well. Check out Table 6-1 for a comparison of the pros and cons of various approaches to advertising.

Table 6-1 Pros and Cons of Different Advertising Approaches

Approach	*Pros*	*Cons*
Flyers	Allows more details	Limited distribution
Internet	Ease of use	Uncertain effectiveness
Local employers	Suitable tenants	Narrow market
Newspaper	Widely used by prospective tenants, broad reach	Potentially expensive
Notice-boards in supermarkets and sports centres	Inexpensive	Narrow market
Property signs	Very effective, inexpensive	Narrow market
Specialist rental publications	Widely used by prospective tenants	Expensive for small properties
Word of mouth	High credibility, inexpensive	Narrow market

Kerb appeal: Getting your property to rent itself

The best advertisement for your property is its exterior appearance. The *kerb appeal* is the impression created when the building is first seen from the street. Properties that have well-kept grounds with green grass, trimmed hedges, beautiful flowers, and fresh paint are much more appealing to prospective tenants than a property that looks as though it has seen better days.

Kerb appeal can be positive or negative. Positive kerb appeal can be generated by having a rubbish-free garden, well manicured landscaping, well-maintained walls and fences, a clearly identifiable address, and clean windows. All extras (such as the driveway) should also be clean and well maintained.

Properties with negative kerb appeal can be rented, but finding a tenant often takes much longer. You may have fewer suitable tenants to choose from or you may have to lower the rent. Because time is money in the rental housing business, the lost revenue caused by poor or negative kerb appeal is often much greater than the cost to repair or replace the deficient items. Besides, a well-maintained and sharp-looking property often attracts the type of tenant who will treat your property with care and respect and pay a higher rent.

Kerb appeal is also important to retaining your current tenants. One of the most common complaints of tenants and a major reason for tenants to move is the failure of the owner or property manager to properly maintain the rental property. If the tenants are frustrated with the property's appearance or if they get the runaround when they need things repaired, the tenants have little reason to remain unless the rent is significantly below market value. Poor kerb appeal is the direct result of poor management. There is no excuse for poor kerb appeal, and there are no benefits to anyone involved, because the lost revenue is never regained, and the property value ultimately declines.

Even the best advertising campaign in the world cannot overcome a poor physical appearance. Making sure your property looks good on the outside as well as the inside significantly improves your chances of finding just the right tenants.

Before you spend money on advertising, take another look at your property with a critical eye or ask someone you know to do this for you. You probably have a relative or friend who has a sharp eye for finding those little details that aren't quite right. So put those people to work helping you identify and then correct those niggling aspects that detract from your rental property.

Looking at Your Advertising Options

When it comes to advertising, you need to think like a tenant. Many landlords have been a tenant at some point in time. You may have personal experience yourself as a tenant looking for the right place to live. You may have found the experience very frustrating, or maybe you developed a successful system for finding quality properties at a fair price in your area. Your experience as a tenant can be helpful as you place your current ads as a landlord.

Many landlords may remember that, when they began looking for their own buy-to-let property years ago, they either drove around the area or looked for advertising that was specific to a particular geographic location. That strategy still holds true, because tenants typically look for a property in a specific location and try to find ads on supermarket notice-boards; in gyms, health clubs and colleges; or in the local newspaper that cover just their area of interest.

Most tenants dislike moving. Although moving is enough of a disruption in your daily routine, adapting to a completely different neighbourhood is even worse. Thus, the majority of tenants move to another address within the same geographic area, unless they are forced to move for work, for their children to attend another school, or for another significant factor that requires relocation to another part of the country.

The following sections outline the different ways you have to reach your prospective tenants; everything from word-of-mouth to the Internet. Use more than one form of advertising and you'll find a new tenant more quickly.

Word-of-mouth

Often the best source of new tenants is a referral from one of the neighbours near your rental property, one of your other tenants, or possibly even the tenant who has just vacated your property. Many times, referrals also come from work colleagues or friends. Word-of-mouth is often your most effective and least expensive method of finding new tenants, especially if people like your property or like where it's located. In the long run, your best source for new tenant leads is other satisfied tenants.

Many of your tenants or other people who own or rent in the area may have a family member or friend who is looking to move into the area as well. Creating a sense of community in which your tenants have friends in the immediate area can persuade tenants to stay longer. This means less hassle and better cash flow for you.

You need to put all applicants referred by word-of-mouth through the same tenant application and thorough background check as any other applicant. Always screen every referral carefully, but be particularly careful if the referring tenant has a poor payment history or has created other problems in the past. Just as a referral from an excellent tenant often leads to another excellent tenant, a referral from a problem tenant often leads to another problem tenant.

Suitable tenants are the name of the game

Unsuitable applicants can be a major waste of time. You only want suitable potential tenants to apply. There are always going to be some prospective tenants who do not pass your financial checks or who have a poor rental history. But if you receive applications from several unsuitable prospective tenants from a certain source of advertising, re-evaluate either the method of advertising or the message in your ad.

Answering phone calls and showing your rental property are two of the most time-consuming areas of property management. These areas are also two of the most critical for determining your success in the long run. The last thing you need is for unsuitable prospective tenants to call and ask numerous questions or even arrange to view the property, only to find out that they do not meet your requirements to rent your property. In Chapter 7, you can find out about techniques for using the initial telephone call to determine whether the potential applicant is suitable.

Property signs

A property sign is the first step in renting most properties because it is one of the most economical ways to promote a vacant flat or house. The use of a simple 'For Rent' or 'To Let' sign can be very effective and generate great results for only a minimal cost. In certain areas with only limited availability of rental properties, a sign on the property is all that you need to generate several queries from suitable potential tenants.

Unless your property's kerb appeal is poor or signs are not allowed in your flat's lease, you should immediately put up a property sign when you find out that you're going to have an upcoming vacancy.

An advantage of the property sign is that applicants already know the area and have seen the exterior of the building. The attractiveness and aesthetic qualities or kerb appeal of a rental property are essential. The rental property must look good from the street, or prospective tenants won't even bother to stop and see the interior of the property.

When putting up a sign, keep these things in mind:

- **Use signs that are in perfect condition, with large, crisp easy to read lettering.** The condition of the sign reflects the image of your rental property – whether good or bad. A well-maintained sign provides a good first impression. A faded, worn out, or tacky sign is worse than no sign at all.

- **Make sure that the sign is clearly visible from the street and that the lettering is large enough to read.** The two-sided sign should ideally be placed perpendicular to the street so that it is easier for passing vehicles to view the sign.
- **The sign does not need to include too many details about the property, but the phone number and the date of availability should be very clear.** You can also add the number of bedrooms and bathrooms, as well as any special features. Don't get carried away or put so much information on the sign that it cannot easily be read from the street.

- **Drive by your property from both directions at the usual speed of traffic and make sure that the sign can be seen and understood easily.** The main objective is to get the driver's attention with the words 'For Rent' or a similar basic message. The driver should pull over and stop to write down the details and the phone number.
- **When the exterior of the property does not do justice to the actual rental property itself, you're better off *not* including the amount of rent on your property sign.** The value of some rental properties cannot be appreciated until the prospective tenant has seen the interior of the property. Because you will typically not be there to actually show the property at the time the prospective tenant sees the sign, the prospective tenant may think that the rent is either too high or too low and immediately decide not to call.

Generally, we don't recommend indicating the amount of rent on the property sign. You've got a better chance of convincing a potential tenant who didn't want to pay quite as much money that your property is worth the extra if you get a chance to speak to them on the phone. If the prospective tenant doesn't even bother calling because the stated rent is more than they wanted to pay so your property seems out of reach, you could be missing out on someone who would have made a good tenant. The other problem with advertising the rent is that you lose any competitive advantage you have as other landlords in the area will find out how much you are charging your tenants.

Property signs don't work as well if your rental property is not on a busy street or your property sign is not clearly visible from a main road. Property signs on dead-end streets or cul-de-sacs are still worthwhile, but don't expect the kind of response you would get if your property were on a main road.

A disadvantage of signs is that they announce to the world that you have a vacant property, which, in some cases, can lead to vandalism or squatting. To avoid this happening, many landlords use a rental sign while the property is still occupied by the outgoing tenant and then remove the sign once the property has been vacated. Depending on your tenants and their level of co-operation, you may also want to indicate on the sign that the current tenant should not be disturbed.

To minimise the chances of vandalism when the property is vacant, you can indicate on the property sign that the property is occupied and include a statement such as, 'Please do not disturb the occupant'. Although not a guarantee, this simple statement may deter the amateur criminal elements who don't want to take the chance of running into any residents.

Newspapers

The most commonly used medium for advertising rental properties is the newspaper classified ads. These ads can be very effective if you follow some basic rules of advertising:

- Attract the reader's attention.
- Keep the reader's interest.
- Generate a desire to learn more about your property.
- Convince the reader to contact you for more information.

Important considerations when using newspaper advertising include selecting which newspaper to advertise in, the size of your newspaper ad, what to include in the newspaper ad, and how often or on which days the newspaper ad should run. We cover each of these issues in the following sections.

Which newspaper should you advertise in?

Most towns have at least one local newspaper to advertise your rental property in. Those living in a city have more choice with one major regional morning or evening newspaper covering the whole area to choose from, plus several weekly or fortnightly local newspapers as well. Such papers are usually reasonably priced and can reach prospective tenants already living in the area. Some local papers even offer free ads.

Another source of ads for properties to rent is the dedicated property sections of national newspapers. The burgeoning interest in buy-to-let means several pages are often dedicated to rental ads. Of course, such ads cost much more than those that run in local papers, so you need to weigh up whether you'll reach more suitable tenants by advertising in the nationals.

If your rental property is located near a big company, be sure to run an ad in the in-house newspaper. Advertising in magazines such as *The Lady* or *The Spectator* will also reach more upmarket tenants. See the later section 'Local employers' for details on tapping into in-house publications.

Should you advertise in the local weekly throwaway, the regional major daily, or the property section of a national? Unfortunately, there is no right answer to this question. You need to try each newspaper and see which one works best for a particular rental property.

Often the local newspapers offer cheap or even free ads. You may think you can't go wrong with a free ad. But when your phone begins ringing every few minutes and none of the callers are suitable, you pay for that ad again and again with your most precious resource – your time. Dealing with unsuitable prospective tenants can be very time-consuming and frustrating.

Although many newspaper sales representatives proudly speak of their total circulation or readership, the only number that matters to you is the number of suitable prospective tenants that see your ad for your property. For example, the *Daily Telegraph's* circulation is just under 1 million readers. Although the potential of that many people reading your ad may sound enticing and the cost per reader is miniscule, the actual number of suitable prospective tenants nationwide for your 3-bedroom rental property in Scunthorpe will be measured in dozens.

Evaluate the cost-efficiency of regional papers such as London's *Evening Standard* by comparing the cost of the ad with the best estimate of the actual number of readers of your specific ad. If the cost per suitable prospective tenant is reasonable, then you may be wise to use this resource.

Keep your advertising costs under control, but don't overlook the fact that each day that your property sits empty is another day of lost income that you will never see. Just as airlines lose money for every empty seat on a plane, you can end up being penny-wise and pound foolish with your advertising, particularly if your best advertising source is *The Sunday Times'* property section and you need to wait until the following week to place another ad. In that week, you may have lost a couple of hundred pounds (or many times the cost of the ad).

The key to effective advertising is not the overall number of calls that you receive but the number of suitable prospective tenants per pound you spend on advertising. Typically, advertising that costs £10 to £30 per suitable prospective tenant is an effective ad in most major regional newspapers. So if your ad in the *Evening Standard* costs £55, you should expect to receive inquiries from two to three suitable potential tenants every time the ad runs. Of course, you'll receive additional inquiries from people who aren't suitable, but you can also measure the effectiveness of your ad by noting how *few* unsuitable prospective tenants call in response to your ad.

How big should your newspaper ad be?

Newspapers typically offer two different types of rental ads: display and classified. Display ads can be (but aren't always) more effective and eye-catching. However, they are significantly more expensive and beyond the needs and budgets of most small-time landlords. Typically, only the owners or property managers of large blocks of flats in your area use display ads on a regular basis. And most of these advertisers also use classified ads to augment or supplement the display ads, particularly on the days when their display ad is not running.

Newspapers are in the business of selling space, and large classified ads cost more than smaller ads. The good news is that the larger ads are not always more effective. A large classified ad that fails to attract readers' attention and keep their interest is a complete waste of money.

Owners or property management companies with several properties in a certain geographic area often use display ads because they can combine more than one rental property into one large display ad, making the ad more cost-effective. If you are a small-time landlord, unless you have several properties with vacancies in the same general geographic area, use the classified 'Property to Let' advertising section of your newspaper.

The trick is to develop a classified rental ad that does its job of promoting your property but doesn't place a higher priority on low cost while sacrificing the ability to attract and keep the attention of the prospective tenant. Your potential tenant needs to be able to easily read your rental ad. One of the best ways to make your ad readable is through the use of white space in the ad. *White space* is the blank space that makes your ad stand out from the others, many of which are so crammed with information that readers instinctively skip them.

You'll be lucky if a prospective tenant spends more than just a few seconds looking at your rental ad. If you cannot attract and keep the attention of prospective tenants in those brief seconds, they'll move on to the next ad. So when it comes to writing your ad, you want to provide as much information as possible, while also keeping the ad readable. But the overall size of the ad also needs to be kept to a minimum, or you risk a major shock to your advertising budget.

Most tenants actually prefer to rent from small-time landlords rather than big agencies, which is why classified ads can be very effective. Classified ads need to be directed to a specific target market and should stress the particular advantages of a property from the tenant's point of view, as explained in the following section.

What should you include in your newspaper ad?

An effective newspaper ad (like the ones shown in Figure 6-1) provides the basic facts, plus a *hook,* which is a call-to-action that helps your rental ad stand out from the rest:

The basics

Every ad should include the following basic information:

- **General geographic location of the property:** The most important aspect of promoting your rental property is to identify the location. Most newspapers sort their rental ads by location, and if your ad isn't listed properly, then all the prospective tenants who want to live in your area will miss your ad. Some newspapers automatically put your ad in a certain geographical area based on the property's address. In many cities, the property's postcode makes an immediate impression on potential tenants. This impression can be very positive or very negative, depending upon the reputation of the particular area. So if the address would give a negative impression, leave it out. (The sidebar 'Considering whether to include the address in your ad' outlines the advantages and disadvantages of including the property address in your ad.)
- **Number of bedrooms and bathrooms:** After the location, this is the second most important aspect of the rental property that the tenant is interested in. If four friends want to share a house, for example, a two-bedroom flat is unlikely to be big enough. A three-bedroom house might be okay, as long as they are prepared to use the lounge as a fourth bedroom. But one bathroom for four tenants may not be enough so they will be looking for a rental property with more than one bathroom.
- **Major features or amenities:** This should include anything that makes the property stand out and would be considered desirable by tenants. If you have a swimming pool, for example, you are onto a winner and should obviously mention it in your ad. Likewise, if the property boasts original fireplaces or there is a garage or off-road parking, it is worth mentioning these as they could persuade a prospective tenant to opt for your property over another.
- **Monthly rent:** Include the amount of rent you charge per month. This info lets prospective tenants know what you're expecting upfront. Most prospective tenants are scanning through the newspaper rental ads just trying to eliminate the ads that are not worthy of their time to call. Generally, any ad that does not give the prospective tenant enough information to determine their level of interest will be immediately dismissed.
- **Telephone number where you can be reached:** See Chapter 7 for details on using the phone to your advantage.

- **The date when the property becomes available:** This lets the tenant know whether the property is right for them: if you want to let it immediately but they have only just given a month's notice on their current rental property, you would clearly prefer someone who could move in straightaway.
- **Who pays the bills – landlord or tenant?** This is a major factor when the tenant is working out whether he can afford the rent on the property. If the rent is a bit higher than he was hoping to pay but the landlord pays the utility bills, he may well find that it is affordable after all.
- **Whether the property is furnished:** Some tenants have their own furniture, others don't. And if a tenant doesn't have her own furniture, there is a strong likelihood that she won't want to fork out hundreds of pounds buying furniture until she buys her own property. If you state in the ad whether your property is furnished, you won't waste time fielding calls from tenants looking for an unfurnished property.

The hook

The hook can be monetary or it can be an improvement to the rental property – anything that makes your ad grab the prospective tenant's attention. For example, offering the tenant the opportunity to select new tiles for the kitchen floor or hallway is an excellent hook.

First Class Schools

Impressive and beautifully presented 1920s house close to excellent primary and secondary schools in Guildford. Entrance hall, 2 receptions, kitchen/breakfast room, utility room, 4 bedrooms, 2 bathrooms, triple garage, gardens of approx 1 acre, pets welcome. Unfurnished. £3,600 pcm. Available immediately. Call 01234 567 890.

Farnham: Close to Everything

Large 1 & 2 bedroom townhouse apartments, on bus route. Within walking distance of schools, shops and main railway station. No pets. Furnished or unfurnished. From £600 pcm, bills included. Call 01987 654 321.

Figure 6-1: Good newspaper ads like these can help you find the right tenant quickly.

If you are in a soft rental market with many of your competitors offering good deals, such as lower rent, you may need to match or even outdo them. This is when using the upgrades to your rental property as an incentive comes in handy. Besides providing new floor tiles, common upgrades landlords can offer include a new kitchen or walk-in power-shower. You can also offer new appliances, double glazing, or a burglar alarm. For rental properties in which the tenants are responsible for garden maintenance, a new lawnmower might be handy for both the new tenant and for the landlord concerned about absent-minded tenants who may forget to mow the lawn.

Although prospective tenants who are looking for the absolute lowest rent won't be interested in rental property upgrades, the tenant who is aware of the competitiveness of the rental market and wants to be treated fairly will often appreciate the upgrades more than the cash in their pockets. Plus, you are making improvements to your own rental property, and these upgrades make your property more desirable now and for future tenants as well.

Other stuff

In addition to the basic information and the hook, be sure to include in your ad every detail that your prospective tenant wants to know. Remember the concept of WIFM (what's in it for me; see the earlier section 'Knowing what your tenants stand to gain from your property' for details) and be sure to include the features of your rental property from the point of view of the prospective tenant.

Although leaving out some information saves you money in the cost of the classified ad, don't forget that incomplete information either leads to suitable prospective tenants skipping over your ad or may lead many unsuitable prospective tenants calling to ask you every question under the sun.

Abbreviations: Should you or shouldn't you?

Be careful with abbreviations in newspaper ads. Although abbreviating some words can stretch your advertising budget without cutting into your message, the use of abbreviations often discourages tenants from reading your ad. An ad that's hard to understand won't generate the phone calls you want. And if your ad doesn't generate phone calls, you've wasted your time and money.

We recommend using only basic abbreviations – and then only if most landlords advertising in your area commonly use them. Although you can ask your newspaper classified advertising representative, we strongly recommend that you determine which abbreviations are commonly used by reading through other rental ads in the section yourself. When in doubt, don't use abbreviations. Table 6-2 lists some common abbreviations used in newspaper ads.

Considering whether to include the address in your ad

Although there are differences of opinion regarding including a property's address in a newspaper ad, we generally recommend including the name of the road or street where the rental property is situated. This informs prospective tenants of the exact location of your property and enables them to independently determine whether the property is one they're interested in renting.

Table 6-2 Common Newspaper Ad Abbreviations

Abbreviation	*Translation*
bath/WC	bathroom/toilet
bed	bedroom
dbl	double
furn	furnished
GCH	gas central heating
gdn	garden
hse	house
incl	included
lge	large
mth	month
nr	near
pkg	parking
pw	per week
refurb	refurbished
unfurn	unfurnished

Some newspapers even provide a key of the common abbreviations and print this index in the 'Property to Let' section. This key can be very helpful to prospective tenants. But remember that you want to attract and keep the attention of the prospective tenant. And one of the best ways to do this is to make your ad one that is the easiest to read and provides the most information. Prospective tenants who are looking to solve puzzles are typically more interested in the newspaper crossword than trying to decipher the abbreviations commonly found in many 'Property to Let' classified ads.

How often or on which days should your newspaper ad run?

Many local and national newspapers have dedicated property sections that run on certain days of the week. Find out which days these appear and ensure that your ad is submitted in time to meet the deadline; otherwise, you'll have to wait another seven days to have it published. Following are some tips that may make your ad more cost effective:

- Check with your local newspaper to see whether they offer any discounted rates for running consecutive days or weeks.
- If you have many rental properties, look into advertising contracts where you agree to run a minimum number of ad lines over a given period of time at often greatly reduced rates compared to the single insertion ad rate.
- Some newspapers even offer special ads that offer guaranteed results. For example, if you haven't found a tenant for your property after the ad has run for a certain period of time, the newspaper will give you up to an additional week for free.
- Check with your newspaper sales representative for special sections that are run featuring editorials on rented housing and news features. These special sections are written with the tenants in mind and can increase the likelihood of your ad being seen by prospective tenants.

When your ad first appears, be sure to check the newspaper personally to see that it is listed in the proper section of the classifieds and is worded exactly the way you wrote it. The newspaper ad representatives are very skilled at taking down complicated ads with abbreviations, but mistakes can and do occur. Nothing is worse than not receiving any phone calls because your ad was placed in the wrong section or because the phone number was listed incorrectly. If you find a mistake, be sure to notify the paper at once, and, if the paper made the mistake, they should run the corrected ad at no charge.

Checking your ad for accuracy may be relatively simple if you regularly buy the newspaper. However, if you don't, be sure to have your newspaper ad sales representative send you a copy of your ad.

Be sure to change your ad regularly. Tenants often look for several weeks when they are just beginning to search for a new rental property. If they see the same ad for more than a week, they could assume that your rental property is undesirable.

Flyers

Distributing and posting flyers informs the neighbours that you have a property available to rent, which can be helpful to them because they may know someone who would like to live close by. You can also pin flyers onto noticeboards in local hospitals, colleges and universities, supermarkets, and personnel departments of large companies.

The cost to reproduce flyers is nominal. If you have access to a computer you can produce a very simple flyer yourself for just the cost of the electricity and paper. Alternatively, plenty of printing shops will do the job for you, which can result in a more professional end product.

If you decide to use a printing shop, remember that prices vary considerably, so shop around and get a couple of quotes. The Internet is a good source of competitive quotes. For example, we found a print company offering 500 flyers for £121, using one colour. Prices increase the more colours you use, so two colours will cost £151 for 500 flyers, or £191 for three colours. All come with a good quality matt finish. The extra money is well worth it – anything that can make your flyer stand out from the others is worth considering. Although keeping your costs low is always important for landlords, remember that you may be losing £20 to £50 each day your property is vacant – and that is money you will never get back again! So if you have a property that looks great with a three-colour flyer, spend the extra money and generate those important rental leads today!

An advantage of flyers is that they allow you a lot more space in which to describe your rental property. You can go into detail and list many of the features that you couldn't afford to list in a newspaper ad.

You can also use flyers to direct people to more information (including maps and additional photographs) on a Web site. See the later section 'Internet' for more information on using the Internet to advertise your rental property.

High-tech flyers

With the wide availability of word-processing programs, making great-looking rental flyers that contain all of the pertinent information, plus even a photo and a map, is very easy. Although the widely used word-processing programs have everything you would need to make basic flyers, we highly recommend that you invest in a basic desktop publishing software package. Several great desktop publishing programs are available, but two of the easiest to use are Quark XPress and Adobe PageMaker. These programs have templates that simplify the process and can provide you with the graphics and additional features to make your flyer really look sharp.

Another invaluable tool for all rental property owners is a digital camera. A digital camera helps you prepare advertising that works! There is nothing like a photo to separate your rental property flyer from the others that may be circulating at any given time. Check out Figure 6-2 for a great example of a flyer that effectively uses photographs to draw attention to the property.

Converted Barn For Rent

Situated in the charming village of Windlesham, Surrey, this two-bedroom converted barn has plenty of character. Boasting many original features, the unfurnished property comprises a large drawing room and open-plan kitchen. The master bedroom comes with en suite bathroom, and there is a second bathroom and shower room. There is parking for two cars and a private orchard. Windlesham itself has a lot to offer, with a variety of shops and good restaurants a short drive away and easy access to the M4, M25 and M3. The nearest mainline station is Sunningdale, which is two miles away from the property, with an approximate journey time of one hour to London Waterloo. Available immediately for £2,500 per calendar month.

Call 01344 873081.

Figure 6-2: Flyers are a great way to attract attention to your property, giving you the space to highlight the extra details you may not have room for in a small newspaper ad.

Some people think that a handwritten flyer actually has greater appeal and implies that the owner is a non-professional who has a rental property at a below-market rental rate. Although this may be true, we believe that the benefits of having a sharp, easy-to-read, typeset flyer with a high-quality photo and detailed map provides superior results.

Although your goal is to rent your property quickly, the reality is that you are likely to be marketing your rental property over a couple of weeks. This is particularly true if you are able to start your marketing during the current tenant's notice period. One of the problems with flyers is that knowing which ones are current and which ones are out of date is difficult. We recommend that you put a date on your flyers and keep them fresh. You should also consider having a series of flyers with a different look. Include the monthly rent on your flyers so prospective tenants can immediately determine if your rental property is in their price range.

Flyer distribution

The key to success when it comes to flyers is distribution. Either distribute the flyers personally or consider hiring a reliable individual to distribute flyers door-to-door in the area where your rental property is located. You can also have the flyers distributed to locations that current and prospective tenants are likely to visit.

Flyers can be targeted to a specific geographic area and can be very effective in reaching good prospective tenants. Because they are most often distributed in the area near the rental property, the flyers are effective; tenants looking to relocate already live in the local area and want to stay close by or know someone who would also be interested in living in the area. Flyers, like all forms of advertising, are only as good as their distribution, so be sure to distribute the flyers to the places where potential tenants are most likely to see them.

Although some people suggest that tenants look for a new property in the last two weeks of the month, we find that, in most rental markets, there are always tenants on the look out throughout the entire month. Begin distributing your flyers as soon as you can. Each week, distribute the latest version with the current information and dates so that they are fresh.

Rental publications

A number of publications carry classified and display 'Property to Rent' ads. *Loot,* the daily free ads paper, has a number of South East editions, covering London, Bedfordshire, Buckinghamshire and Hertfordshire, Kent, Croydon and Surrey, and Essex. There are also a number of North West editions covering Manchester, Cheshire, Lancashire and North Staffordshire, Liverpool, Chester, Wirral, and North Wales. *Loot* also has a major presence on the Internet, as outlined in the next section.

Hot Property is an alternative weekly rental publication offering advertising for London and the South East. It also has an accompanying Internet site where prospective tenants can search for suitable properties to rent. Landlords can choose between text-only ads or add a picture to illustrate their property. The rental publications are a good source of potential tenants and often allow your ad to run for a number of consecutive issues, without you having to give instructions to run the ad again.

If you're thinking about using a rental publication, take the time to determine which one has the best distribution in your area for your target market.

Internet

As more and more people have access to the Internet, it is becoming more useful as a source of prospective tenants even for owners of small rental properties. However, if you are a small-time landlord, you probably shouldn't rely solely on the Internet to find prospective tenants. More conventional advertising methods, discussed throughout this chapter, should be used alongside the Internet. The problem with relying solely on the Internet is that prospective tenants are unlikely to find your specific ad on the Internet, because the Internet is so vast and contains so much information that it can be difficult to search for rental ads in specific locations.

One of the reasons for the difficulty in sifting through the numerous ads is the minimal barriers of entry and low cost of placing information about your rental property on the Internet. Although the likelihood of someone actually finding your specific rental property on the Internet may be minimal, unless you utilise the services of a major rental property marketing firm, rental publication or regional newspaper, the Internet still has tremendous potential to assist the small-time rental property owner.

Although online advertising is primarily for major property managers with lots of properties on their books, there is one way that the Internet can be invaluable to owners and managers of small-to-medium rental properties or even a single-family rental home. If you have developed flyers or brochures, you can easily post these marketing pieces online. You can then put the Web page address (or URL) in your newspaper ad and allow prospective tenants to gain additional information at their convenience. When a prospective tenant calls, you also have the option of referring them to the Web page, if they have access to the Internet, for more information.

The online rental information you can offer is virtually unlimited. With a digital camera, you can place photos of the rental property online. If you have a wide-angle digital camera, you can even put interior photos online, which is very helpful if the property is currently occupied and you cannot or do not want to bother the current tenant by showing the place. You can also show floor plans and provide detailed directions. If you are really computer-savvy, or know someone who is, you can add a narrative soundtrack or some music. (Keep in mind that music can be annoying to Web site viewers, however. The last thing you want to do is frighten potential tenants off with a medley of your favourite punk songs.)

Of course, be careful that the graphics do not slow down the loading of the Web page so significantly that it takes too long to load the page. Just like the short attention span of your prospective tenant when scanning through the newspaper ads, you want to make sure that your Web site loads very quickly with all of the basic information. Use a simple text file format that loads quickly. If you get the attention and interest of the prospective tenant, you can offer links to the graphics of floor plans and property photos.

Local notice-boards

As with posting flyers, notice-boards can also be very effective in small villages or towns. Often the local newsagents, pharmacies, hospitals, or corner shops have notice-boards or window space that is available at no cost or for a small charge. You may find that you are limited to a postcard, but you can tailor it to the people who will be most interested in and attracted to your rental property.

If your rental property has unique features like a garage or large garden, you may have some additional promotional opportunities. Carefully evaluate your rental property and determine the unique aspects of the property and the specific target market that will be most interested in these specific elements. For example, a rental property with a large garden appeals to tenants with pets, so a listing on a notice-board at a local pet shop may reach that specific target market. Likewise, a rental property with a garage appeals to customers of a hardware store.

As with any ad in which the property address is clearly stated, a disadvantage of local notice-boards is that you may be promoting the fact that your rental property may be vacant to squatters or burglars. One way to minimise this problem is to use this method only when the property is still occupied and clearly state that it will be available at a future date. You should also consider indicating that the current tenant should not be disturbed.

Local employers

Another great source for prospective tenants are the local employers in your area. Employees of these companies will, most likely, have stable employment and will be looking for long-term rental properties.

Many firms offer employees assistance or have ads in in-house magazines to help workers find reasonably priced housing. Most rental properties located in cities or towns are located near at least one major employer. As a sharp rental property owner, you may already have determined that the employees of certain major firms are part of your target rental market.

Likewise, the major firms in your area have a vested interest in their employees being able to find good quality and affordable rental housing in close proximity to their location. Progressive employers are always looking for inexpensive ways to assist their employees and improve morale. You can even offer all employees of companies an incentive to rent your property, such as offering a discount on the rent.

Letting agencies

One of the recent trends in the property market are firms that assist tenants in finding suitable rental properties. These services are available in virtually every major city. Some offer their services for no charge to the tenant and are paid by the property manager when the tenant signs a rental agreement. Other firms charge tenants for their service and are only paid when they find a rental property that meets the tenant's needs.

Although most owners of small-to-medium size rental properties don't need the services of a letting agency, there are some definite advantages to consider. Letting agencies often have close working relationships with major companies and relocation services and have excellent tenants looking for rental properties at the top-end of the market. These tenants relocating into an area typically don't have the time to search for a rental property and want the letting agency to handle matters for them. Also they are not usually candidates for purchasing a home because they'll only be staying for a specific period of time or because they want to rent in the area before deciding if, and where, they are going to purchase a property. There is often a trade-off with these tenants: They are usually very suitable with good references, but they are not as likely to rent long-term. But the reality is that not all tenants will stay for a long period of time anyway, and if you know that the tenant will only be with you for a set period (such as a 1-year lease), you can adjust the rental rate to reflect this rental term.

Agent referrals

Besides selling properties, many estate agents are also in the business of referring tenants to property managers. Many of the calls that estate agents receive are from individuals moving from other areas who contact an estate agent to enquire about the future purchase of a home. Although they may have long-term plans to purchase, they often rent while they become familiar with the area.

Estate agents don't mind referring tenants to an owner or property manager, because they know that today's tenant may likely be a homebuyer further down the road. Estate agents are also very interested in referral fees from owners or property managers. Although the referral fee may be a small amount of money compared to the potential commission the estate agent would earn on a sales transaction, agents are willing to be patient and accept a small reward in the short run knowing the big money will be earned down the road.

Advertising Without Discriminating

Whether you are the owner of a one-bedroom flat or several small-to-medium size family homes for rent, when you advertise you are subject to the law. All landlords are required to comply with anti-discrimination laws and human rights legislation. For instance, you will need to know what the legal situation is regarding the Sex Discrimination Act, the Race Relations Act, and the Disability Discrimination Act to ensure you don't violate any of them, even inadvertently. For example, the Race Relations Act makes it illegal for a landlord to discriminate between tenants because of their race – and this applies to advertising for new tenants too. Likewise, you cannot discriminate against people on the basis of religion, sexuality, or disability.

Any discrimination when advertising a property to rent is illegal and can result in very severe penalties.

While it's understandable that you want to rent your property to the tenants of your choice, as a landlord you must not discriminate or show any preference, limitation, or discrimination based upon race, colour, ethnic origin, religion, sex, or physical disability. You are only allowed to discriminate on critical factors such as whether your prospective tenant has the ability to pay her rent or has references that back up her good character.

Compliance with the law is critical for all owners of rental property, and you can read about this topic in more detail in Chapter 8. This begins with advertising to all suitable prospective tenants, continues throughout the screening and tenant selection process, and remains a key issue throughout the entire tenancy. If you plan to be in the letting business, you need to make sure that all of your advertising, tenant screening, and selection and management policies reflect the intent as well as the letter of the law. Also, be aware that these laws are constantly being redefined and expanded. Ignorance is not an acceptable excuse if you are challenged for your policies.

Chapter 7

Handling Prospective Tenants and Showing the Property

In This Chapter

- Using technology to your advantage
- Showing your rental property
- Letting your rental property
- Taking a look at environmental issues in rental housing

In virtually all instances, the tenant/landlord relationship actually begins with an initial phone call. If you successfully develop a skill in ascertaining the suitability of prospective tenants, and become a master of selling your property to them, you will find owning and managing rental property to be a profitable and even pleasant experience.

Armed with the information in this chapter – and some practice – you will become adept at quickly screening callers and convincing suitable prospective tenants that you have the rental property they want. In this chapter, we explain the importance of preparing for calls from prospective tenants, using the telephone as an effective marketing tool, and handling potential tenants all the way from the first phone call to the completion of the rental application.

Making the Most of Technology

The goal of advertising your rental property is to reach the pool of suitable prospective tenants who are currently looking for a new rental property and inform them that you have a rental property that they may be interested in. When your advertising and promotion generates interest in your rental property, your phone will ring. But if your prospective tenants can't reach you,

Don't neglect your dog & bone

Some property management books recommend never placing your phone number in your rental ads. Instead, they suggest that you market your rental property strictly by advertising and by holding open houses where interested tenants can all view the property at the same time. The concept of an open house is very good, but not until you have narrowed down the prospective tenants to those who are genuinely suitable.

In our experience, omitting your phone number from your ads eliminates a large number of suitable prospective tenants who don't have the time or interest in racing all over town to attend open houses at rental properties that may not even meet their needs. We live in a world of information, and the most desirable prospective tenants are often people who value their time very highly.

You may think that you are able to conserve some of your *own* time by not taking phone calls, but you'll have a different opinion after your first three-hour open house where only a couple of unsuitable prospective tenants show up! Or, even worse, you may not get any prospective tenants at all. Now *that* is a counterproductive afternoon!

Use the telephone as your primary business tool. Take advantage of all the advances in communications technology to improve your success rate in locating and selling the benefits of your rental property to the most suitable prospective tenants.

they'll immediately lose any potential interest in you and your rental property. So you need to make sure that prospective tenants – and current tenants, for that matter – can easily reach you at all times.

Advances in telecommunications technology have made the management of rental housing much more efficient today than it was even just a few years ago. With so many options, however, you need to know how to use this technology effectively and efficiently. The following sections cover the basics of using technology to your advantage. Later in the chapter, you can find more specific information on using the telephone in particular – because the telephone is still your main link to your prospective tenants.

Using your telephone's special features to your advantage

The telephone is your primary way of staying in touch with your prospective tenants. But using the telephone isn't just about putting your phone number in your classified ad or on the 'To Let' sign outside your rental property. Telephones come with all kinds of special features that can help you manage your property more effectively. We cover these features in the following sections.

Mobile phones

The best way of finding prospective tenants is to put your mobile phone number in your property ad. This enables potential tenants to get in touch with you at any time – preferably as soon as the ad appears in the paper. This accessibility could make the difference between finding the most suitable prospective tenants out there or losing them because they couldn't get hold of you.

The other advantage of mobile phones is that you can switch them off whenever you want. So, if speaking to prospective tenants isn't convenient for you, for whatever reason, you can simply switch the phone off and let your voicemail pick up any messages.

Call forwarding

If you're advertising a property for rent and the only contact number you provide is your home number, for example, but you work outside of the home all day, you won't be available to take the incoming calls until the evening or weekends. If this is the case, you may want to consider using a phone number where you *can* be reached during the day or where you can at least be immediately notified of incoming calls.

But if you don't want to list your work phone number in your advertisements, you can still use your home phone number, a separate rental property phone line at home, or even a pager by using the *call forwarding* feature available through most phone companies. With call forwarding, you simply set up your phone to forward all calls to another phone number – such as your work number, a mobile phone number, or any other number where you can be reached. And you can turn the call forwarding off when you return home.

Which mobile's right for me?

Choosing the right mobile phone can be quite a challenge because so many models and price plans are on the market. A friend may have recommended Vodafone to you while another swears by Orange. You may also be taken with a picture messaging phone. But for the purposes of running your letting business you only require a bog-standard mobile and one of the most basic ones will do the job. As for the price plan, check out what the main suppliers are offering and decide how much you're going to use it and what times of the day you are likely to make those calls. All this affects how much you pay. If you only use the phone for incoming calls, for example, you may decide to opt for a Pay As You Go package, which doesn't charge a fee for a monthly line rental.

Caller ID

Another great phone feature you can use to increase your time management efficiency and lower your costs is caller identification (ID). When you pay for caller ID through your telephone company, you have either a special display unit or a special phone that displays the phone number of the party placing the incoming call. Caller ID is a great way to get the return phone number of your prospective tenants in case they neglect to leave their contact information for you.

Why do you need to have the telephone number of a prospective tenant? First, having a prospective tenant's number allows you to call him back and follow up with more information or get an update on his rental status. You can also use his number to reconfirm an appointment to see the rental property. And later, during the applicant screening process, you can use the phone number as a crosscheck when he submits his rental application, to be sure he's giving you the correct information.

Voicemail

As a rental property manager, you should have a voicemail system or an answering machine that can handle calls 24 hours a day. The outgoing voicemail or answering machine message should provide callers with your mobile number or pager in case of emergencies (this is important for current tenants, and it lets prospective tenants know that you'll be there for them if they need you).

You can also record detailed information about the rental property for your prospective tenants; this helps tenants pre-screen themselves (they won't waste their time – and yours – if the property you describe is out of their price range, for example). So in addition to your name, include on your voicemail system or answering machine recording the following information about your rental:

- Location, including directions
- Number of bedrooms
- Rent and deposit requirements
- Additional information, such as whether pets are accepted
- Property features and benefits

Most tenants spend quite a bit of time looking through various rental housing advertising publications. They typically make many phone calls before actually beginning the process of looking at a rental property. So you want to make the information-gathering process as smooth and efficient for the prospective tenants as possible because you're in competition for the most suitable tenants.

Working holiday

Recently, a friend and his wife, who happen to own several flats that they rent to tenants, were in Scotland on holiday. They had already seen the traditional sights and had a little extra time to spare, so his wife went shopping in Edinburgh. As shopping isn't our friend's favourite activity, he found a public library and checked his e-mail on his free e-mail account. You can get a similar service through a number of service providers (such as Yahoo! and Hotmail). These services enable you to access your e-mail from anywhere in the world, as long as you have access to the Internet.

While he was in Scotland, he could access all his e-mails, enabling him to read and respond to the most urgent messages. He could also use his mobile to call home and check his voicemail. His wife may not have been too impressed, but we have to say that technology at work is a wonderful thing.

The prospective tenants are interested in knowing certain basic information up front; this allows them to narrow their choices. Many potential tenants may not even be aware of this but subconsciously they're often looking for any excuse to eliminate your rental property from their list. You need to develop an information system for your rental property that makes the tenant feel relaxed, comfortable, and interested in actually seeing your rental property.

Knowing which additional technological devices you need

In addition to a mobile phone and landline, landlords don't need much else in terms of equipment. However, you might find that a personal digital assistant (PDA) comes in useful. When you're planning appointments with contractors or prospective tenants, you can immediately record your schedule on your PDA – a small, handheld computer (such as a PalmPilot). With many PDAs, you can download and synchronise your mobile database with your main PC back at your home and/or office.

Preparing for Phone Calls

Whether you were ever a Boy Scout or not, you have probably heard the Boy Scout motto, 'Be prepared'. This motto applies to the management of rental properties in many ways, but one of the most important is being prepared when the telephone rings. If you handle the rental enquiry call properly, you not only make your life much easier, you also get the tenants you want.

In the following sections, we discuss the importance of preparation and the steps necessary to make sure that you are ready when the phone rings. Handling a telephone rental enquiry involves eight basic elements:

- Having the basic tools ready and available
- Answering the telephone professionally
- Providing and obtaining basic information from the caller
- Using open-ended questions and building the conversation
- Selling the prospective tenant on your rental property
- Ensuring the prospective tenant is suitable
- Anticipating and being prepared for objections
- Encouraging the suitable prospective tenant to visit the property

The rental enquiry phone call is just the beginning of the rental process, but it is a critical step. Virtually all of your interested prospective tenants first contact you by phone. But the only purpose of the phone call is to get to the next step, the showing of the rental property. Master the art of the rental enquiry phone call, and most of the time you'll be able to set appointments with only suitable prospective tenants. And that is the name of the game in property management!

Having the basic tools ready

Advertising costs you a lot of time and money, so you don't want to begin to look around for a pen and paper and your notes about the rental property as the phone starts ringing. Prospective tenants can tell the difference between the prepared landlord and the one who doesn't seem to have a clue. They also form an impression of how you are likely to handle any problems they may encounter with the rental property in the future. Most sharp tenants (and those are the ones you want) are looking for a professional, business-like landlord, so that's what you need to be.

The benefits of a professional phone technique are one of the main reasons that we recommend having a separate business location for the management of your rental properties. This does not have to be a separate office in a commercial setting; it could be simply the corner of your bedroom or an office at home. Consider having a separate phone line put in as well. A separate phone line allows you to quickly distinguish between personal phone calls and rental business phone calls, and to treat each kind of call accordingly.

You can find many great resources on the proper use of the telephone in business, and the very first advice these resources typically offer is how to answer the phone and what to say. But when it comes to the management and letting of rental properties, we believe that success with the telephone begins with being prepared to use the phone even *before* your first rental enquiry call comes in. In the following sections, we cover some basic tools to have on hand before your first call comes in.

Telephone card

A *telephone card,* like the one shown in Form 7-1, is a useful tool to assist you in gathering from your prospective tenants information such as their name and telephone number, how they heard about your rental property, and their particular needs in terms of move-in date, size, and other requirements. This information can help determine whether your rental property meets the needs and wants of a prospective tenant.

You can also use the telephone prospect card if you show your rental property to a prospective tenant or need to follow up on suitable potential tenants. Finally, you can use it to track which of your ads are most successful, which means you can ensure you continue using only the advertising media that pay off.

One of the primary reasons to track your rental calls is so that you can clearly see the results generated by your advertising. The number of phone calls generated is not the most important factor in determining which advertising medium is the best for your rental property. The key factor is the number of suitable prospective tenants. In an ideal situation, getting just a few calls from ideal potential tenants is much better than getting a number of rental enquiries from unsuitable tenants (which is just a waste of your valuable time).

Property knowledge sheets

One of the best ways to have the answers to the questions that may be raised by your prospective tenant is to prepare a *property knowledge sheet* for each rental property. A property knowledge sheet contains all the basic information about your rental property, such as the size and type of the property, and the property number if you own more than one flat in a block. Also, you should include on the property knowledge sheet the age, type of construction, and other important details about the rental property.

A thorough property knowledge sheet also contains important information about the local area. Just like a tourist information centre, you want to be able to answer questions about the locality. Prospective tenants are very interested in knowing about employment opportunities, public transport, local schools, childcare, places of worship, shopping, and medical facilities. You can really make a positive impression on your prospective tenant if you can tell them where the nearest dry cleaner or Thai restaurant is located.

Telephone Card

Name ______________________ Date of initial call ____ Time ______
Current address ____
Daytime phone __________
Rental property discussed ______________________ Mobile number ________
Email ____________

How did you learn about our property? ______________________
When are you hoping to move in? ______ How many bedrooms do you need? ____
How many people will be living in the property____Do you require a parking space? ________
How much rent were you expecting to pay? ______
What do you do for a living? _____________ Where do you work? ________
What is wrong, if anything with your current rental property? ______________________
Why do you want to move? ____
Do you have any pets? ____
When can you view the property? ______________________________________
What other properties have you seen/plan to see? ______________________________
Notes
____
____
____

Follow-up

Property shown ____________ Date shown ___________ Quoted rent/deposit __
What did prospective tenant like most about the property? ________________________
Objections, if any? ____
Most important features and amenities to tenant ______________________________
Rental application completed? __ Holding deposit? ____ Date to follow-up ____

Form 7-1: Telephone Card.

You want to have all this vital information from your property knowledge sheet at your fingertips so that you can be ready to answer your prospective tenant's questions. The more you know about your property, the better able you'll be to find some important reasons for your prospective tenant to select your property over the competition's.

Check out Form 7-2 for an example of a property knowledge sheet.

The time you spend answering all of the prospective tenant's questions can provide you with useful information. Be sure to take good notes about the source of your rental traffic and any important comments made by prospective tenants. Then you can improve your results by incorporating this feedback into your future advertising for that same rental property.

For example, prospective tenants may indicate that they had trouble finding the property. This is a common problem and one that successful landlords know is a serious challenge to success. If your prospective tenants cannot find the property, there is very little chance that they will rent.

You are in competition with a lot of other landlords, and the most desirable tenants don't need to make extraordinary efforts to find a good quality rental property.

Comparison charts

You may find that you have a vacancy in a *soft rental market*, when more properties are available for rent than there are tenants to rent them. Using a comparison chart can be very helpful in this kind of market, especially if your rental property has distinct advantages over other rental properties in the area. Comparison charts are really just a marketing strategy that owners and managers of large rental properties commonly use, but the concepts are very helpful for the owners of small-to-medium size rental properties or even those with a small studio or 1-bedroom flat to rent.

A comparison chart can provide very useful information to prospective tenants who may not be aware that they are comparing apples to oranges when looking at various rental properties. Comparison charts are particularly useful to landlords who may have a competitive advantage that isn't readily apparent to the uninformed prospective tenant.

For example, your rent may be slightly higher than the rent charged by your competitors, but you may pay the gas and electricity bills whereas tenants renting other landlords' flats or houses have to pay for their own utilities. Another potential advantage of your property may be that it has reserved parking, but the competition requires their tenants to scramble for their parking spaces on the street. Or maybe your 1-bedroom flat is much bigger than a rival landlord's. Many older properties are more aesthetically pleasing, with mature landscaping and beautiful shady trees. These are all factors that may not be readily apparent to the prospective tenant, and they can give you a competitive advantage. A rental comparison chart levels the playing field and allows you to inform your prospective tenants of the actual costs of your property (and the housing provided by your competition).

Property Knowledge Sheet

Property Information
Address Street________________________ City ____________ Postcode______
Property type (circle) Studio 1Bedroom 2 Bedroom 3 Bedroom 4 Bedroom
Rent ____
Deposit____
Age of property ____________ Type of construction _______________________
Furnished?__________________________ Parking _______________________
Recreational facilities_______________________________Pets__________
Utilities (who pays?)______________________ Central heating?___________
Applicances_____________________________ Floor coverings__________
Special features/comments____
____
____

Local information
Schools: Primary ____________________ Senior _______________________
Sixth form _______________________ Tech college ______________________
University ______________________ Childcare ________________________
Places of worship ____
Police station ______________ Fire station ____________________________
Hospital ____
Doctor's surgery ____
Pharmacy ________________ Vet _________________________________
Library ______________________ Post Office _________________________
Supermarket/local shops ____
Parks/sports centre ____
Local transport ____
Restaurants/ cinema ____
Comments ____
____

Rental market information
Competitors/ Rent charged ____
____
Other competitive advantages ____
____
Other disadvantages ____
____

Form 7-2: Property Knowledge Sheet.

Check out Figure 7-1 for an example of a comparison chart highlighting four properties. By providing an honest comparison chart, you're saving your prospective tenants a lot of legwork, and you're highlighting the advantages of your apartment over others.

Comparison Chart

Property	Rent	Landlord Paid Water and Heating	Tenant Paid Water and Heating (with estimated costs)	Reserved Parking	24-hour Porter	Lush landscaping
Riverview Apartments	£550	No	Yes (£50 a month)	No	No	No
Meadow Brook Apartments	£615	No	Yes (£45 a month)	No	No	Yes
Maple Grove Apartments	£580	Yes	No	Yes	Yes	Yes
Prospect Place	£660	Yes	No	Yes	No	No

Figure 7-1: A comparison chart is a great way to advertise your property's advantages over the competition.

Answering the phone

As your key marketing tool, when your phone rings, you need to stop what you are doing. Take a deep breath and even close your eyes briefly so that you can be focused on this call. Be sure to answer the telephone no later than the third ring; prospective tenants generally have a list of calls that they plan to make, so they are rarely patient. If you don't answer in the first few rings, they'll begin dialling the next phone number on their list and probably won't take the time to call you again.

If you have an exciting and chaotic home life, then you need to take steps to make sure that you can distinguish your rental enquiry from general household calls. See the earlier section, 'Using your telephone's special features to your advantage' for information on the options you have.

First impressions can occur in just a few seconds. If you run your rental management business from your home and your prospective tenant calls and hears children screaming in the background or the dog barking, you will be making a very unprofessional impression. Controlling the atmosphere is essential in order to maintain a professional image.

When you have your initial contact with the prospective tenants, you want to come across as polite, knowledgeable, organised, and confident. So when you answer the phone, have a smile on your face and speak clearly; this is one phone technique that really does make a difference. Your positive attitude and enthusiasm can make a very important first impression. You want your prospective tenant to respect your skills as a professional landlord and to see that you treat the rental of your property as a business, not a part-time hobby. Even if you are not in the best of moods, at the moment the phone rings, don't sound rushed or hurried. You don't want your prospective tenants to feel that they're imposing upon you. If you sound disorganised and hesitant on the phone, the prospective tenants are likely to feel that you are incompetent and not the type of landlord whom they can trust and count on if they have a problem or need something repaired.

You may think that, if you are not prepared, you should let your answering machine take a message. We don't recommend this approach because most callers aren't willing to leave a message, and you'll lose an opportunity to personally speak with the prospective tenant. Believe us, they won't call back! Remember that the majority of calls made by prospective tenants to small-time landlords require leaving a phone message, and you can really stand out by answering your calls personally.

As with any business, you may find that a rental enquiry call comes in when you are right in the middle of another task that can't wait. If you find yourself in this situation, we suggest that you still answer the call right away and give your caller the choice to be placed on hold or to have you call them right back.

Asking the caller to call you back in a few minutes is a very risky strategy, and one that we don't recommend for the simple reason that the odds of your prospective tenant calling back are remote. Of course, if your only alternative is to leave the caller on hold indefinitely, this may be an option you can consider.

Because positive first impressions are always very important, remember that your goal in your initial contact is to project a friendly, helpful, and professional image.

Providing and obtaining the basic information

Typically, the caller's first comments will indicate that she is enquiring about your rental property and whether it is still available. Then she'll typically ask about the size of the flat or house and how much the rent is. Always answer the questions presented by the caller directly.

One common and effective way to develop rapport with your prospective tenant is to address the person by name. People generally like to be called by name, and they'll appreciate your addressing them accordingly. If the caller has not already volunteered this information, you may want to mention your first name again and ask for her name. If she gives you her name, be sure to ask her permission to call her by her first name. Often the prospective tenant provides only her last name, and you should show respect by using an appropriate title when you call her by her surname. You also want to ask the prospective tenant for her return phone number. (If you have caller ID, you should verify that you have the best telephone number to reach her.)

Then prompt the caller for the information that you both need. For example, you need to know when she is looking to move in, how many people (and the number, type, and size of pets, if applicable) will be residing in the property, and how much rent she is prepared to pay. Here are some examples of questions that will assist you in determining the needs of the prospective tenant (an easy way to remember the basic questions that you need to ask are to remember the six *w*s – who, what, where, when, why, and how – yes, that's technically five *w*s and one *h*, but you get the point):

- When will you need to move in?
- How many bedrooms do you need?
- How many people will be living in the property?
- What size property are you looking for?
- How much rent were you hoping to pay?
- How long do you intend to live at the property?
- Do you require parking?
- Where are you living now?
- What is wrong, if anything, with your current rental property?
- Why are you looking to move now?
- Where do you work?
- What do you do for a living?
- What type of pets do you have?
- When can you come and view the property?
- How can I reach you by telephone?

Take notes so that you can summarise the prospective tenant's needs and wants during the initial phone conversation. You can use these notes to provide the prospective tenant with immediate feedback so that she knows that you are really interested in her call and are really trying to determine whether your property meets her needs. Then remember to bring these notes on each caller to rental showings so that you know what aspects of your property are of greatest interest to each prospective tenant. (People will really appreciate the fact that you care enough to write down what they are looking for rather than just try to sell them what you have to offer.)

This basic initial give-and-take of questions and answers helps you quickly determine whether there is any point in continuing the rental enquiry conversation. The prospective tenant is looking for the opportunity to eliminate your property if you do not have what she needs at the time that she needs it. Likewise, if it appears that your property may be a good fit, you still need to explore whether the prospective tenant is suitable and meets your screening requirements.

Rental enquiry calls are different from most of the calls we normally make in business. In a rental enquiry call, we often find that both parties are trying to eliminate the other as a potential tenant or landlord and both parties are trying to get as much information without giving out any information of their own. But this is not the best approach. Remember that you are making a telephone presentation of your property. You need to have a give-and-take approach whereby you share the basic information that the prospective tenant needs while you make an initial assessment of their suitability.

Convincing the prospective tenant to rent your property

A key element to success in convincing prospective tenants to actually rent your property is your ability to build rapport with them on the phone. As you answer the initial questions presented by the potential tenant, you should take the opportunity to highlight some of the desirable or unique aspects of your property. For example, if the prospective tenant asks about the number and size of the bedrooms, you can reply, 'The house has four bedrooms, each with a built-in wardrobe. The master bedroom is very large at 15 feet by 12 feet. Will this accommodate your needs?' Or maybe you can say, 'The garden is completely fenced and is very large. Do you have any pets?'

Your goal is to turn the features of your property into benefits for the prospective tenants. You do this by painting a picture of the property in the mind of your potential tenant. For example, if your property has a swimming pool, you can talk about how nice it is to come home at the end of a long day and enjoy a refreshing swim or a cocktail by the pool.

The goal of the telephone call is to get the suitable tenant to see your property. You can't – and shouldn't – sign a rental agreement on the phone!

As the landlord, you definitely want to tell your story about what a great property you have. Then when you've grabbed the caller's interest and determined that your property meets her needs, you want to begin to evaluate the prospective tenant's suitability in light of your requirements and needs. If you fail to hook the prospective tenant, you'll never get to the next step. Of course, you want to be sure to prescreen the prospective tenant during this initial phone call so that you invest your valuable time only with suitable potential tenants.

Checking the prospective tenant's suitability over the phone

After your prospective tenants have found answers to their initial questions, and you have passed the test in being able to provide their basic needs, you need to begin asking your own questions. You need to confirm when they are looking to move, the size of the property they require, and whether they can afford the rent. Both you and the potential tenant need this basic information, and together you go through this ceremonial dance with the goal being to advance to the next stage – the showing of the rental property.

Rather than presenting a boring monologue or reading from a piece of paper, a rental enquiry call should be more like a tennis match, with each side taking a turn presenting their questions and gathering the answers they need to make a decision. Ultimately, both parties need to agree that the property may meet the needs of the prospective tenant and the prospective tenant may meet your screening criteria. This is the first step toward achieving your main objective of the property – getting a commitment from the potential tenant to make an appointment to see your property in person.

The answers to your basic questions (see 'Providing and obtaining the basic information' earlier on in this chapter) determine whether you need to go on to the next step. For example, if currently you have only a studio flat available, there is likely to be no need to show this particular property if the prospective tenant says she is looking for a property for four people to share.

You also want to make sure that you are not dealing with a *professional tenant,* someone who frequently jumps from rented accommodation to rented accommodation. Even in your very first phone call, certain red flags may indicate that you are dealing with someone who will be nothing but trouble. Signs of potential trouble include:

- A prospective tenant who asks very few questions about the property and the area but is very interested in getting a discount on the rent or an arrangement in which you allow him to pay his deposit over three months.
- A tenant who seems interested in moving in too quickly. Although you may think that finding someone who wants to move in right away is great and will minimise the length of time that your property is empty, this may be an indication that the person has something to hide or is just looking for his next landlord victim. Maybe his landlord has just served him with eviction papers for non-payment of rent and he needs to find somewhere else to live as quickly as possible.

Be sure to check each applicant's references before taking him on as a tenant. You would also do well to be very careful and wary of subtle hints, even as early as the very first phone call.

Using open-ended questions and a pleasant and friendly manner, you need to get the basic information from the tenant to determine if he meets your rental requirements. It is also important to determine whether you are speaking with the actual decision-maker, or whether this caller is only making the initial contact and gathering information for someone else. Although you always prefer to deal with the primary decision-maker from the initial contact, you need to be skilled in assessing all applicants without alienating your immediate contact, because the immediate contact may have considerable influence on the decision as well.

You will know that you have suitable prospective tenants when you have determined that:

- You have a property of the appropriate type and size available when the prospective tenants need it.
- The prospective tenants meet your minimum requirements in terms of income, credit history, and employment history.
- The prospective tenants have enough cash to pay the entire first month's rent and the full deposit.
- At least one of the prospective tenants is 18 or over so that they can sign the rental contract.

- The proposed number of occupants is appropriate for the particular property.
- The prospective tenants have an acceptable rental history and are vacating their current living accommodations legally.
- The prospective tenants are willing to live within your guidelines, such as no pets or no smoking allowed in the property.

Of course, you need to verify this information before making a commitment to rent your property. However, you can begin this pre-qualifying process over the phone instead of having to wait until you meet the prospective tenants when they tour the property or complete a rental application. You have already begun the important process of screening your prospective tenants with the very first phone call.

Naturally, not every rental property matches every prospective tenant. Your goal is not to convince *all* the callers that they must see your property in person. Showing a property to an uninterested or unsuitable applicant is one of the most frustrating experiences of being a landlord. Showing property to only suitable and interested prospective tenants is one of the most important factors in successful time-management for landlords.

Handling phone objections

If you've done your homework, you're well prepared and you know the answers to questions about the property and the surrounding area. But you'll still have to deal with objections raised by some of your prospective tenants during the initial phone rental enquiry. Again, your goal is not to convince an unsuitable prospective tenant, who is not a good match for your property, to waste everyone's valuable time by coming to view the property when it obviously won't work. Instead, your goal is to anticipate some of the more common objections and have information that allows you and the prospective tenant to determine whether there is enough mutual interest to go to the next step – the showing of the property.

We know a landlord who once owned a rental property in Putney, South-West London – a handy location for anyone working in the City – but it also happened to be right under the flight path of Heathrow Airport. The property's ideal location near restaurants and bars made it very desirable, but the proximity to the airport was quite obvious, and it was well-known that many rental properties in the area had significant problems with aircraft noise. Virtually all of the potential tenants who visited the property raised this concern, but even those who rang up brought up the subject of noise, because they were familiar with the area. However, when the property was built, the architects had designed it with special triple-glazed soundproofed windows and extra insulation so exterior noise was not a problem. Knowing the perception of rental properties in the area, the landlord began to notify potential tenants of the soundproofing design features of the property during the initial telephone conversation.

Being prepared for rental enquiries for your property includes anticipating reasonable objections and providing an honest answer to the prospective tenant.

Converting phone calls to rental showings

If your initial phone conversation goes well, the prospective tenants will want to tour your property. You have already invested a lot of time and energy into the rental enquiry calls. This is the moment of truth when you find out whether the prospective tenants really are interested in your property. Maybe they are just gathering information for a future move, or maybe they're checking out similar properties to determine if the rent increase they just received from their current landlord is justified.

You have answered a lot of their questions, taken careful notes highlighting their needs and wants, and you have built up a rapport with each prospective tenant. You wouldn't have invested this much time in a prospective tenant unless you felt that your property met his needs and that he was very likely to pass your tenant screening criteria. So now is not the time to become passive and tell him to call you back if he's interested. And it's not the time to sheepishly suggest that he 'Stop by the house this weekend, if you're in the area'.

You need to be assertive and direct. Ask him to come to your rental property so that you can personally show him round. If the tenant shows any signs of hesitating, you need to directly ask him if there is a problem. The tenant may then admit that he has just been declared bankrupt or he plans to use your property and adjoining land for a pig farm. Asking questions is one of your best tools – be sure to use it.

The prospective tenant may indicate that he's interested in the property based on your conversation, but he would like to drive by the property before actually making an appointment for a viewing. This is fine and can be another useful tool in maximising your efficiency as a landlord. Two things can happen if the prospective tenant wants to do his own drive-by before scheduling a viewing with you:

- He calls back and asks for an appointment and you can rest assured that he will show up.
- He drives by the property and finds it's not suitable for him.

Creating a sense of urgency

When you ask your prospective tenant to view your rental property, you may get a noncommittal response or an excuse that she can't make it no matter how many different appointment times you offer over the next week. Of course, the most popular excuse you will hear is that that she has just begun calling and your rental ad is the first one she followed up. This may be true, so you need to be polite and patient. But if you are truly her first call, then it is likely she called you first for a reason – your advertising made your property sound like her best option. So patience can be a virtue as long as you are not *too* patient.

Be honest, but don't hesitate to let the prospective tenant know that you already have, or will soon be receiving, many more rental enquiry calls. Let her know that it is your intent to sign a rental agreement with the most suitable tenant, but you process the rental applications in the order in which they are received so if there are two or more suitable applicants you may lean toward the first one who submitted an application. This creates a sense of urgency for the caller.

If you anticipate receiving interest in your property from several people, set up one or two open houses so that you can show the property to more than one person on the same day in just a couple of hours rather than making multiple trips. In good rental markets, the open house method often creates a competitive, or even an auction-like environment, in which the tenants don't want to lose out to another applicant. There's nothing like a little competition to instil the call to action for potential tenants.

In both cases, this is a positive step. In the former case, the prospective tenant is not convinced by the area and kerb appeal of your property alone; in the latter, the prospective tenant won't waste your time arranging a personal tour.

Many rental management advisers suggest you improve your efficiency by allowing prospective tenants to tour your property on their own. They suggest allowing the interested party to call by and pick up a key. They usually suggest that you ask for a £25 cash deposit or that you hold the prospective tenant's driver's licence (as long as they aren't driving to your property!) as an incentive to return the key. We don't recommend this strategy for a couple of good reasons:

- You might not live or work near your rental property so it might not be convenient for the prospective tenant to drop by on his way for a viewing.
- You could find that your prospective tenant has stripped the appliances or severely damaged the property while he's been there. Even a worse result could be that he decided he liked your property so much that he just moved right in!

In our experience, many prospective tenants make an appointment to view only to drive by the property a few minutes before the actual appointment and then skip the appointment if they don't like what they see. Another common scenario is one in which the prospective tenant has already decided that your property is not going to be his next home no matter how great the interior and how competitive the rent. But they feel guilty and don't want to let you down, so they show up for the appointment and go through the motions of looking at everything for nearly an hour. Imagine how many hours are wasted because the prospective tenant could have taken the opportunity to check out the area and the kerb appeal of the property before arranging a viewing.

Planning Ahead for Open Houses and Individual Viewings

One of the most time-consuming aspects of owning and managing rental property is the time spent filling vacancies. And the biggest time trap for most owners who do not have a system already in place is showing the property to prospective tenants. If you were to schedule a separate appointment with every interested potential tenant, you would be making trips constantly back and forth to the property. Unless you live or work very close to your rental property, you can quickly find that you're spending hours showing the property to one person after another. That's why having a strategy for showing your property – whether you plan to have an open house or set up individual appointments – is the best way to go.

Holding an open house

Because your time is valuable and you'll have many suitable prospective tenants interested in seeing your rental property, you may want to consider holding an open house. An open house gives you an opportunity to efficiently show the property to several interested tenants within a couple of hours. A successful landlord won't make a dozen trips to show her property to a dozen different potential tenants.

Select a time for your open house that is convenient for you and most working people (preferably during daylight hours). For example, an open house on Saturday from 11:00 am to 2:00 pm usually gives prospective tenants a good opportunity to see the property at a convenient time for them, while saving you from having to make multiple trips. In the summer months, a weekday afternoon from 4:00 pm to 7:00 pm may also be a good option. Combining a weekday afternoon open house with one on the weekend can also be very effective. That way, virtually all interested parties can fit the rental viewing into their busy schedules.

One of the other benefits to holding an open house is that many tenants feel more comfortable touring a property when there are other potential tenants around. Many prospective tenants may be concerned about meeting someone they don't know in an empty property. And you, too, should be very concerned about your own personal safety for the same reasons. Holding an open house can eliminate or at least reduce any safety concerns you – and the prospective tenants – may have.

Open houses are also beneficial because having several potential tenants viewing the property can create a sense of urgency and competition, which often generates more than one application to rent your property.

An open house, where you invite all the suitable prospective tenants with whom you have spoken in response to an advertisement, is a good way to efficiently let your property and even create a sense of urgency and competition among the potential tenants.

Scheduling individual appointments

If you are in a depressed rental market or find that you need to fill a vacancy during the holidays, you may not be able to generate enough interest from prospective tenants to schedule an open house for more than one of them. In this case, you need to be prepared to show your property in the evenings and on weekends, because that is often when your prospective tenants are available. Of course, you can still try to consolidate your appointments to a certain timeframe, but don't push this too far. Asking the potential tenants to conform to your schedule may put them off.

If you have to schedule individual appointments to show your property, be sure you have the phone numbers for your potential tenants. Call each person to verify the viewing before making a special trip to the property. By calling, you are also reassuring the tenant that you will be there and are not going to be delayed.

Crime is a concern in all parts of the country. Making an appointment to show a stranger your property can be an opportunity for someone criminally inclined. Be alert and take reasonable steps to protect yourself. If you ever have an uneasy feeling about a prospective tenant, just decline to show the property rather than risk personal injury. If you can, bring someone with you to the showing, and limit your rental showings to daylight hours. You can also tell your potential tenant that you will meet him outside, right in front of the property or at another public location and require some form of identification with a picture before showing the property. You then can use your mobile to call a family member or friend and tell that person the name and driver's licence number of your potential tenant. You can also ask someone to call you on your mobile to check that everything is okay throughout the showing. Of course, if you ever feel uncomfortable, be polite yet firm, end the rental tour, and leave immediately.

Providing directions to the property

When you have a commitment from the tenant to come to the property for an open house or rental showing, you need to make sure that you can provide clear and easy-to-follow directions from anywhere in your area. Giving directions may not be quite as simple and effortless as you may initially think. So you need to carefully consider the best route for your potential tenant. Take into consideration the traffic conditions he'll face at the time of the open house or appointment. Think about which route presents the area in the best light. You want the route to be direct, but don't hesitate to take the tenant via the best route for him to observe the great shopping, schools, or other benefits of the area near your property.

If you're not good with directions, seek the input from someone who has a knack for giving them. Be sure to avoid someone who knows the area too well. Someone too familiar with the area may know how to drive the route by memory, but he may be completely unable to provide any street names or the details that a first-time visitor needs. Remember that the directions need to spell out each road and turning and should be very precise.

Showing Your Rental Property

When your potential tenants arrive, be sure to greet them and introduce yourself. Ask for their names and shake their hands. Refer to your notes on the telephone card from your initial phone conversation to let them know that you remember speaking with them. This will give the prospective tenants a good feeling that you are not just going through the standard rental spiel.

Listen to any questions or concerns that may have come up since you spoke on the phone or while travelling to your property. Ask them whether they found your directions accurate and easy-to-use. Also ask them if they have any other needs that they are looking for in a property that haven't already been discussed.

Don't just let the prospective tenants wander around the property by themselves. (Of course, this is particularly true if you are showing an occupied property.) Listen carefully to your prospective tenant and anyone they brought with them as you informally guide them through the property. Pay close attention to the features that your tenants have indicated are of particular interest or comments made during the viewing.

For more information on preparing your property for viewings, see Chapter 4.

Showing a vacant property

If you're showing a vacant property, begin the tour of the flat or house and act as a tour guide. Don't be too controlling; instead, let the prospective tenants view the property in the manner that suits them. Some go right to a certain room, which gives you a clue about the importance they place on that aspect of your property. Of course, if they hesitate, or are reluctant to tour on their own, you can casually guide them round the property yourself.

Encourage your potential tenant to see the entire property, including any garage or storage areas and the exterior grounds or garden, if there are any. You want to be sure that they have the opportunity to observe the condition of all aspects of the property and ask any questions.

There are as many different ways to show a property as there are landlords. Keep in mind the information provided by the prospective tenant and customise the tour by beginning with the feature or room that you feel has the most interest to that person. This is not the time to head straight to *your* favourite feature. When in doubt, start with the kitchen, then move on to the living areas and the bedrooms.

As you begin to show the interior of your property, avoid making obvious statements such as 'This is the living room' or 'Here's the bathroom!' Instead, listen and observe the body language and facial expressions of your interested viewers as they walk through the property. You don't need to oversell if they seem pleased, but you should feel free to point out the benefits of your property (for example, 'It sounds like this neutral coloured carpet will go great with your living room furniture' or, 'The view from the kitchen of the sunsets is so relaxing').

During an open house you might quickly find yourself dealing with several people at once all of whom seem to have better timing than a synchronised swimming team. Do your best to courteously greet and speak with each potential tenant individually. At least cover the basic information and get them started on the property tour before beginning to work with the next interested party. Be sure to communicate clearly that you will answer all of their questions, and be sure to treat all potential tenants openly and fairly to avoid any allegations of favouritism or discrimination.

Showing an occupied property

If your current tenants are at the end of their lease or have given notice of their intention to leave, you, as the landlord (or your managing agent) are usually allowed access to the property, by arrangement, in order to show it to a prospective tenant, during the last 28 days of the tenancy. (To avoid problems or confusion, the tenancy agreement might include a clause expressly allowing such access. See Chapter 5 for details.)

Showing a vacant property is generally much easier, but guiding your prospective tenant through an occupied flat or house does have some distinct advantages. Your current tenants can actually be a real asset if they are friendly and co-operative and take care of the property. The prospective tenants may want to ask the current tenant questions about their experience of living at your property.

If you're showing an occupied property, try your best to co-operate with the current tenants and schedule mutually convenient times to show the property. Be sure to respect their privacy and avoid excessive intrusions into their lives.

Still, showing an occupied rental property can have some disadvantages: Although the current tenant may legally be required to allow you and your prospective tenants to enter the property for a viewing, they don't have to make any efforts to ensure that the property is clean and neat. They also are not required to help you in your efforts to impress the potential tenant. Keep this fact in mind when deciding whether you want to show your property while it is still occupied.

If your current tenant is being evicted, is not leaving on good terms, or has an antagonistic attitude for any reason, don't show the property until she has vacated it. Be sure to complete your rent-ready preparation work and any upgrades to the property. This strategy is also more suitable if your current tenants have not taken good care of the property or if their lifestyle or furnishings could prove to be objectionable to some potential tenants.

If you can, get copies of recent utility bills from your current tenant, in case your prospective tenants have any questions about utility costs. Utility costs for electricity, gas, and water are becoming significant items in the budgets of many tenants. You don't want your tenant to be unable to financially handle the typical monthly utility costs, because that may affect their ability to pay your rent. You may also be able to use low utility costs as a marketing tool.

Checking if the prospective tenant is suitable during the property viewing

While you're touring the property, you can verify the information that the prospective tenant provided during your initial phone conversation. Refer to your notes and verify his desired move-in date, the number of occupants, the rent, his employment and other important information. Also make sure the tenant is aware of your rental policies and any limitations on pets or other important issues.

You don't want to be abrupt or refuse to let the prospective tenant and the other rental applicants begin looking at the property until they answer numerous questions, but verifying the basic information upfront can save a lot of time if there was a misunderstanding or if the prospective tenant's needs have changed.

If you don't take the time to review the information a prospective tenant provided to you on the phone as well as your rental terms and expectations, you may find that some of them have glossed over certain problems or indicated your rental policies were fine when really they're not. Of course, their strategy is to wait until you think you have successfully rented the property and you are just about to sign on the proverbial dotted line when they spring the truth on you. Maybe their sick aunt has suddenly asked them to care for her Rottweiler or their pay-cheque was delayed and they can only pay your deposit in installments. These are surprises that you don't need and if they are sprung on you at the last minute, you have the tough decision of whether you should go ahead with renting your property to the tenant or risk having your property empty for some time while you start the screening process all over again with another tenant. You have to weigh up whether you can live with the tenant's last minute revelation – or not.

Resolving objections

Almost every prospective tenant will express some concerns or reservations about some physical aspects of the property, the rent or other terms, or about the area. This is to be expected, because it is unlikely that any property exactly meets the needs of a prospective tenant.

You'll encounter different types of objections. Some prospective tenants use objections as an effort to test you and see whether you'll lower the rent or make some improvements to the property. The other forms of objections are sincere issues that are generally more tangible and specific in nature.

If you have been listening carefully to the prospective tenant and taking notes, then you can anticipate some objections and handle them even before they're raised. In many instances, objections can actually present the opportunity to reassure the applicant that your property meets her needs.

If the prospective tenant raises a question and you don't know the answer, make a note of the question and promise to get back to her as soon as possible. You can overcome most objections by openly discussing them and giving honest feedback. Giving a response and attempting to answer positively is important.

Convincing the prospective tenant

After you have confirmed the suitability of the prospective tenant, you need to convince her that you have the best property available. Remember that people

- Want more than just a place to live
- Want to feel they can communicate with you if a problem arises
- Appreciate it when someone shows an interest in their lives

And by showing an interest, you are clearly setting yourself apart from other landlords. We believe that tenants will even accept a property that is not exactly what they're looking for if they have a positive feeling about the landlord.

We have never seen a property that can rent itself. So *you* need to make the difference. No matter how close your property meets the stated needs and wants of your potential tenants, they'll often hesitate and doubt their own judgment. You don't need to be pushy, but you should be prepared to actively convince them that your property is right for them.

Inviting the prospective tenant to rent your property

When you've convinced your prospective tenants that your property is the right one for them, it's time to close the deal. This is one area where many landlords and managers suddenly get cold feet. They can do a great job handling the initial telephone rental enquiry, the preparation and showing of the property, and even objections, but when it comes to shaking hands on the deal – they become shy and freeze.

Your goal is to receive a commitment from the prospective tenant to rent by getting him to complete your rental application and pay his first month's rent, and a month's rent as a deposit on the spot. Of course, you still need to thoroughly screen the prospective tenant and confirm that he meets your rental criteria before signing a rental agreement.

If, despite your best efforts, the prospective tenant is still undecided, you should make sure that he gives you a holding deposit. Remind him that you may make a deal with the very next applicant and he'll be out of luck. Of course, if you have a lot of demand for your properties, you should develop a priority waiting list, covered later in this chapter.

Persuading the prospective tenant to complete a rental application

You need to offer every interested tenant the opportunity to complete a written rental application (like the one shown in Form 7-3). There are two important reasons for this policy:

- **You want to have all of the information so that you can begin the screening process and select the best tenant for your property using objective criteria and your rental requirements.** The rental application is the key document you use to verify information and conduct your entire tenant screening procedures. We discuss tenant screening in more detail in Chapter 8.
- **You want to avoid the situation where prospective tenants accuse you of discriminating against them by not permitting them to fill out the rental application.** It is important not to prejudge an applicant. The prospective tenant may have already volunteered enough information about his financial situation and tenant history to make you believe having him complete an application would be a waste of time and effort. But even in these situations, always be sure to offer your rental application form to every prospective tenant old enough to legally rent the property.

Have several rental applications and pens available at the property. Although you want to make sure that you offer a rental application form to every prospective tenant, you don't just want to hand them out and let them leave without making a commitment.

Here are some important guidelines to remember when accepting rental applications:

- **Every prospective tenant who is currently 18 years of age or older should complete a written application.** This applies whether the applicants are married, related in some other way, or unrelated housemates.
- **Before accepting the rental application, carefully review the entire form to make sure that each prospective tenant has clearly and legibly provided all requested information.** Pay particular attention to all names and addresses, employment information, national insurance numbers, driver's licence numbers, and emergency contacts. Any blanks should be marked with a 'N/A' if not applicable so that you can tell that they were not inadvertently overlooked.
- **Each prospective tenant must sign the rental application authorising you to verify the provided information and to run a credit check.**
- **Ask each prospective tenant to show you his current photo-ID driver's licence or other similar photo identification so that you can confirm that the applicants are providing you with their correct names and current addresses.**

RENTAL APPLICATION

SURNAME________________ FIRST NAME ________________________
CO-APPLICANT SURNAME _____________ FIRST NAME _____________
TELEPHONE _______________ DATE OF BIRTH ___________
CO-APP DATE OF BIRTH ___________
NATIONAL INSURANCE NUMBER ______ DRIVER'S LICENCE ___________
CO-APP'S NI NUMBER _______________ DRIVER'S LICENCE ___________

NAME AND AGES OF ALL PERSONS TO RESIDE IN PROPERTY
____

EMPLOYMENT HISTORY LAST 5 YEARS (USE REVERSE IF NECESSARY)
PRESENT EMPLOYER _________________ TELEPHONE _____________
ADDRESS ____
GROSS SALARY ____ JOB TITLE _____________ DATE EMPLOYED ____
FORMER EMPLOYER ________________________________ TEL__________
ADDRESS ____
GROSS SALARY __________ PERIOD EMPLOYED FROM ______ TO ______
CO-APPLICANT'S EMPLOYER _________________ TEL ______________
ADDRESS ____
GROSS SALARY ______ JOB TITLE ___________ DATE EMPLOYED ____

OTHER INCOME
____

CAR Year ____ Make ____________ Colour __________
HOW MANY PETS DO YOU HAVE? ______ WHAT TYPE? _____________

Have you or any proposed occupant listed above ever:
Received a County Court Judgement against you? ________________________
Been evicted or asked to vacate a property? ___________________________
Broken a lease or rental agreement? ________ Been declared bankrupt? ________
Been sued for damage to rental property? ______________________________
If yes to any of the above, please indicate year, location and details ______________
____

IN CASE OF EMERGENCY NOTIFY _______________ Relationship ________
ADDRESS ____
TELEPHONE __________________________________

LAST THREE PLACES OF RESIDENCE (MANDATORY)
1. Date from /to ________ Address ____________________________
Landlord's name ______________________ Telephone _____________________
2. Date from /to ________ Address ____________________________
Landlord's name ______________________ Telephone _____________________
3. Date from /to ________ Address ____________________________
Landlord's name ______________________ Telephone _____________________

1

Form 7-3: Rental Application (Page 1 of 2).

CREDIT REFERENCES
Bank name ____________________ Branch ____________________________
Account name ________________________ Account no ___________________
Sort code ____________ How long have you been with this bank? ____________

Co-applicants bank ________________ Branch ________________________
Account name __________________ Account no ______________________
Sort code ______________ How long have you been with this bank? __________

PERSONAL REFERENCE (this should be someone who is not related to you but knows you well and can vouch for your character)
NAME _________________________ JOB TITLE ______________________
TELEPHONE ____________________________________

Falsification or unverifiable information will be grounds for denial of rental application, Applicant states that all of the above information is true and correct and hereby authorises verification of the above items including, but not limited to, the obtaining of a credit report, and agrees to furnish additional credit references on request.
Applicant agrees that the Landlord shall not be liable for any delay in the date said property is ready for occupancy. The first month's rent and deposit, equal to a month's rent, must be paid by BACS transfer to Landlord's account prior to moving in.

SIGNED:

LANDLORD
NAME ________________________
SIGNED ______________________
DATE ________________________

APPLICANT ONE Name ____________________
SIGNED __________________________
DATE __________________________

APPLICANT TWO Name ______________________
SIGNED ______________________________
DATE ________________________

2

Form 7-3: Rental Application (Page 2 of 2).

You may be asked by the prospective tenant – or you may determine on your own – to go over the rental application with him and assist in providing the information. If you do so, be very careful to ask only questions that are part of the rental application. Avoid asking questions that may directly or indirectly discriminate. Do not ask the rental applicant about his birthplace, religion, marital status or children, or a physical or mental condition. You can ask him if he has ever been convicted of a crime and whether he is at least 18 years of age, however.

Holding a deposit

Some prospective tenants are willing to make a firm commitment, but they will not or cannot give you the full deposit and first month's rent. Maybe they just don't have the funds at the time or maybe they want to keep your property as a standby while they continue looking for a better one. In these situations, you may want to ask for a holding deposit to allow you to take the property off the market for a limited period of time while you obtain a credit check or verify other information on the rental application.

Don't allow the prospective tenant to reserve your rental property with a small deposit for more than a couple of days. A couple of days gives you more than enough time to screen him, and any additional time the property is off the market often translates into rent that you will never see. After you approve the prospective tenant, you should ask him to sign the tenancy agreement. If he still insists that he needs more time, he should agree to pay the daily rental rate, or you should refund his holding deposit and continue your leasing efforts.

By taking the property off the market, you're losing the ability to rent it to someone else. If the prospective tenant fails to go on and rent your property for any reason, you will have potentially lost revenue while the property has been vacant and reserved. On the other hand, prospective tenants don't want to pay rent while you're running them through your tenant screening process. The solution is to use a written holding deposit agreement and receipt, like the one shown in Form 7-4, which outlines the understanding between you and the prospective tenant.

If you use a holding deposit you must have a written agreement or you are very likely to encounter a misunderstanding or even legal action.

Holding Deposit Agreement and Receipt

On the date below ________________________ (Owner) received £________ from ______________________________ (Applicant) as a Holding Deposit for the premises located at ________________________________ (Property address) on the terms and conditions set forth herein.

1. Rent of £____ per month shall be payable in advance on the first of each month. The tenancy will begin on the ____ day of ____________, 20__, but subject to any present tenant vacating or the unavailability of the property.
2. Of the total funds hereby received by Owner, the sum of £,,,,. is an Application Fee that the Applicant understands and agrees is non-refundable. The Application Fee represents the estimated costs incurred by the Owner in obtaining and verifying the credit information, employment and references of the Applicant and similar tenant screening functions.
3. Of the total funds hereby received by the Owner, the sum of £____ represents a Holding Deposit.
4. The Applicant has paid the Application Fee and Holding Deposit to the Owner in the form of cash, cheque, or banker's draft. Owner is free to deposit all funds received herein and shall maintain this Holding Deposit in liquid funds subject to review by Owner or its agents of the Applicant's rental application.
5. Applicant shall be entitled to a full refund of the Holding Deposit within ____ days if the Owner determines that:
   a) The Owner does not approve the Applicant's rental application; and/or
   b) The premises are not available on the agreed date
6. Upon notification by the Owner to the Applicant that their rental application has been accepted, the Applicant agrees to execute all lease or rental agreement and related documents and pay any balance still due for the first month's rent and full deposit. Applicant understands that once their rental application has been approved, the rental property is taken off the market and reserved for the Applicant and any or all other potential Applicants will be turned away.
7. If after acceptance of the Applicant's rental application, the Applicant fails to comply, the Owner may immediately deduct from the amount received the sum of £___ per day (daily rate) for each day the rental property is vacant from the date the Applicant's tenancy was to begin through to the date the rental property is let to another tenant, but not in any event to exceed 30 days. It is agreed that the daily rate is calculated as an amount equal to 1/30th of the above monthly rental rate. In addition, the Owner shall be entitled to retain reasonable administrative fees and advertising expenses associated with remarketing the rental property. The Applicant agrees that the daily rate plus the actual incurred administrative expenses and advertising costs are reasonable and liquidated damages since the actual damages would be difficult or impossible to ascertain.

1

Form 7-4: Holding Deposit Agreement (Page 1 of 2).

8. The Owner, within ____ days after the rental property is re-let, shall return to the Applicant, to the Applicant's address shown below, any remaining balance of the Holding Deposit and shall include an itemisation of the Owner's losses.
9. If any legal action or proceeding is brought by either party to enforce any part of this agreement, the prevailing party shall recover, in addition to all other relief, reasonable solicitor's fees and costs. By signing below, both the Owner and Applicant acknowledge and accept all terms contained herein.

______________________ Applicant's Signature	______________________ Applicant's Signature
______________________ Applicant's Name (print)	______________________ Applicant's Name (Print)
______________________ ______________________ Applicant's Address	______________________ ______________________ Applicant's Address
______________________ Date	______________________ Owner/Agent

2

Form 7-4: Holding Deposit Agreement (Page 2 of 2).

Using waiting lists

If you have several suitable prospective tenants who are interested in your property, you're only going to be able to rent to one of them. Use the tenant selection criteria covered in Chapter 8 to select the best tenant.

If you have other suitable tenants, you may have other properties nearby that would interest them. If those other properties aren't available immediately, instead of turning away the suitable applicant, you may be able to offer them a spot on your *waiting list,* which is just a way for you to keep track of suitable prospective tenants for whom you simply don't yet have available properties. Being in this situation is a dream come true for many landlords.

If potential tenants express a desire to rent your property at a future date, and if you know that other properties are available in the area, it may be because your rents are lower than the market rate. (Otherwise, they would simply find another comparable property somewhere else instead of having to wait.) If you have a long waiting list, make sure it's just because your property is desirable – not because you're charging too little rent.

Some prospective tenants are simply looking for a great property several months in advance. Although you can't keep your property vacant and off the market until they're ready to rent, you can lock them in to one of your other properties that may be available in the future at the time they are prepared to move. This situation is especially typical for prospective tenants who are moving from another town or city and make a trip to look for a property a few weeks or months before they officially make the move. You may be able to pre-rent your properties even before they become vacant (and that's a great position for any landlord to be in).

When you create a priority waiting list, don't just write the prospective tenants' names on a piece of paper, because this gives you no commitment, and the chances of that applicant returning to rent from you are slim. However, prospective tenants' level of commitment will increase if you confirm that they are suitable applicants, take a partially refundable deposit, and give them a written confirmation that they are on your priority waiting list. You may even want to offer that you will charge a specific amount of rent if they become one of your tenants within a certain period of time.

Be sure to let your prospective tenants know where they are on the waiting list. Also be sure to let them know that you can't guarantee that a certain property will be available, because you can't control when your current tenants will actually vacate. Give prospective tenants the right to cancel, and let them know that their deposit is fully refundable at any time.

As with all rental policies, you need to apply them uniformly to all prospective tenants. So if you have a priority waiting list, be sure to let all prospective tenants know about it and do not restrict anyone from being added to the list. Otherwise, you could be accused of discrimination.

Handling Hazardous Materials and Environmental Issues

One of the major challenges to being a successful landlord is keeping abreast of the constantly evolving health and safety requirements that affect rental properties. In addition to providing your tenants with a clean and habitable property, you need to take precautions to ensure that it is a safe and healthy environment.

Although legal implications and substantial liability occur for failing to meet required laws, most landlords would not want to see their tenants get sick or injured anyway. In the following sections, we cover some of the most common issues facing rental property owners today.

New legislation is constantly under consideration, and rental property owners must stay-up to-date with all requirements or face serious consequences. Ignorance is not an adequate legal defence.

Lead-based paint

Although lead-based paint is not a hazard when in good condition, it can be a serious problem (particularly for young children) when it cracks, peels, or turns to dust due to age. The UK banned the use of white lead in paint in the 1960s so older rental properties, such as period houses, may still contain lead paint underneath more recent decoration unless it has previously been stripped down to the bare wood and repainted with modern paint which is lead-free. You cannot tell whether paint contains lead just by looking at it; a special lead test of each different painted surface in your property by a professional is the only way to verify the existence of lead.

DIY lead-testing kits are available but studies have shown that they can be inaccurate and unreliable in detecting lead paint. Laboratory analysis is the most accurate way to test for lead paint.

In older properties, lead is usually found on:

- Exterior painted surfaces
- Interior trim
- Windows, windowsills, and horizontal painted surfaces
- Doors and frames, railings, and banisters

If you are buying a property built before the 1960s which has paint in thick layers, a chance exists that it contains a lead-based paint. Left to deteriorate, it is dangerous because lead dust can be created by activities such as opening a window, removing wallpaper, or repainting. Nearly all cases of acute lead poisoning in adults and children are attributed to unsafe home renovations and maintenance.

Lead-based paint is not easy to remove and must be done very carefully. Lead dust and fumes are particularly dangerous, and we recommend you hire an expert to remove the paint for you. Your local Yellow Pages lists licensed contractors who specialise in paint stripping services and will be able to address your concerns about lead. Unfortunately, the removal of lead can be quite expensive, but it is well worth making sure you do it right to avoid problems later on.

Asbestos

Asbestos has received a lot of media coverage over the past 20 years and is now banned by law in the UK because breathing it in can cause cancer. However, asbestos was frequently used in the construction of many older properties – so you may find that you have some in your property. Because asbestos was not banned in the UK until 1999, an awful lot of it is around. Products containing asbestos are quite often not labelled either. It has been used extensively in over 3,000 commercially manufactured products. Hence many areas of a rental property could potentially include asbestos, such as pipe and boiler insulation, fire door insulation, roof and wall cladding, vinyl flooring, paints and sealants, and textiles.

Left alone asbestos is safe. But the concern in most rental properties is that asbestos-containing materials will be disturbed. If disturbed or damaged, asbestos-containing material may release asbestos fibres, which can be inhaled into the lungs. The fibres can remain there for a long time, increasing the risk of disease.

If you have asbestos-containing substances in your rental property and the material is in good condition, leave it alone. If the material is damaged, you may want to have the material repaired or removed. Always seek the advice of a professional contractor to evaluate and recommend the best course of action concerning asbestos.

Repair usually involves either sealing or covering asbestos material:

- Sealing is also commonly referred to as *encapsulation* and involves coating materials so that the asbestos is sealed in. Encapsulation is only effective for undamaged asbestos-containing material. If materials are soft, crumbly, or otherwise damaged, sealing is not appropriate.
- Covering involves placing something over or around the material that contains asbestos to prevent the release of fibres.

If sealing or covering isn't an option, you have to have the asbestos removed. The removal of asbestos-containing materials is an expensive and hazardous process and should be a last resort. Removal is complex and requires special training, tools, and techniques. A licensed contractor who specialises in asbestos-containing materials should be used, because improper removal could very easily increase the health risks to the workers, yourself, and your future tenants.

Asbestos is a very dangerous material if disturbed. Do not attempt to test for asbestos on your own. Hire a professional environmental testing firm because the act of breaking open potentially asbestos-containing material to obtain test samples could release asbestos into the air and create a very dangerous situation.

All about asbestos

Asbestos is a mineral fibre that historically was added to a variety of products to strengthen them and to provide heat insulation and fire resistance. In most products, asbestos is combined with a binding material so that it isn't released into the air. As long as the material remains bonded so that fibres aren't released, asbestos doesn't pose a health risk. Several types of asbestos exist, including white, blue, and brown asbestos, and the type can be positively identified only by using a special type of microscope.

The risk of lung cancer and *mesothelioma,* a cancer of the lining of the chest and the abdominal cavity, increases when a high amount of asbestos is inhaled. The risk of lung cancer from inhaling asbestos fibres is also greater if you smoke. People who get asbestosis have usually been exposed to high levels of asbestos for a long time. The symptoms of these diseases do not usually appear until about 20 to 30 years after the first exposure to asbestos.

Radon

Radon is a radioactive gas, known to cause cancer and found in soil and rock. It is formed as a by-product of the natural decay of the radioactive materials radium and uranium. Radon gas is invisible; it has no odour or taste. However, most radon found in buildings poses no direct threat to human life because its concentration is generally low.

As a landlord, you should be aware of radon levels in your rental properties, and check with your local authority for more information about the prevalence and appropriate precautions that should be taken to avoid radon exposure.

Although radon may be found in all types of homes and buildings, it is more likely to occur in the lower levels of tightly-sealed, energy-efficient buildings where ventilation is poor. According to the Building Research Establishment (BRE), the UK authority on radon in buildings, the principal areas of the country in which radon is a problem are the granite areas of Cornwall and Devon, and the limestone areas of Derbyshire, Northamptonshire, North Oxfordshire, Lincolnshire, and Somerset.

The Radiation Protection Division of the Health Protection Agency (HPA) recommends that radon levels should be reduced in homes where the average is more than 200 Becquerels per cubic metre. The Government endorses this recommendation. For more information about radon, go to `www.hpa.org.uk/radiation`.

The only reliable guide to monitoring the level of radon in a building is a simple process taking three months to complete. For a fee of around £40 payable to the HPA you get a radon detector pack, subsequent analysis and their report of the result. If your tests reveal dangerous levels of radon the cost of rectifying the problem will depend on the work carried out. The most effective way to reduce high levels is by using a radon sump, which can cost several hundred pounds.

If you want to find out whether the rental property you are interested in buying is in a radon-affected area, you can get hold of a report from the HPA on a building's radon potential. The service covers the whole of England and is based on published data.

Chapter 8

Eenie, Meenie, Miney, Mo: Selecting Your Tenants

In This Chapter

- Setting up written criteria for your tenant screening process
- Verifying your applicants' information
- Knowing the anti-discrimination laws

Most landlords are paranoid about whether their tenants are going to be able to pay the rent. Bad tenants who don't pay their rent or pay it late every month and trash your property are the type of tenants you don't want. So ensuring you pick the tenants most likely to pay the rent and treat your property with respect is fundamental to your success as a landlord. This means that one of your most important tasks is screening and selecting tenants. You can't prevent your tenant defaulting on the rent, but you can reduce the risk of this happening as much as possible.

Because the process of screening tenants is time-consuming, you need to have a system in place for doing it efficiently, so this chapter is here to help you navigate these unfamiliar waters with ease.

Actually tenant selection and screening can be summed up very simply:

- Develop and use objective, written tenant selection criteria.
- Consistently screen all prospective tenants against these minimum criteria.
- Select the most suitable tenant based on your review.

With a good system in place, tenant screening really isn't that difficult; it just requires assertiveness, diligence, and patience.

Another critical part of choosing your tenants is making sure you handle the selection process without bias or discrimination. This can be a murky issue, but it's an important one, and one you need to pay attention to no matter what your situation, to ensure that you don't end up with an embarrassing and costly court judgement against you. This chapter also tells you how to avoid these problems.

Understanding the Importance of Screening

If you're like many landlords, you may be thinking, 'Screening? Isn't that just a waste of time? After all, I trust my gut instinct when I meet people. I know which ones are good and which are just trouble.' But even people who've been managing your rental properties for many years aren't able to just look at a prospective tenant and instantly know whether the applicant is suitable. At first glance, the answer to the question 'Would I want this person to live in my house?' might be 'yes', but you also have to check the tenant's references, credit history, employment income, job stability, and history as a tenant. You can't simply rely on gut instinct, which is very inaccurate and arbitrary.

Although verifying all the information on your prospective tenant's rental application does take time, it's time well spent. Remember: Selecting a bad tenant is much worse than having a vacant rental property – and is likely to cost you more money in the long term. So take the time to choose your tenants wisely (as explained in this and the following sections), and you'll profit in the long run.

In order to increase your chance of finding a long-term, stable tenant, and in order to avoid charges of discrimination, your tenant selection criteria and screening process should be clear, systematic, and objective. Put it in writing to ensure that the process is applied consistently and fairly to *all* applicants.

Setting up a systematic screening process is critical if you only have a few rental properties. Here's why: Tenants who go from property to property damaging it or not paying their rent are experienced and shrewd. They know that the large, professionally managed rental properties have detailed and thorough screening procedures that attempt to verify every single item on the rental application. If certain items don't check out, professional and experienced property managers don't just trust their feelings on the prospective tenant. They need to cover their own backs because the landlord hired them to do a professional job of finding a good tenant. These troublesome tenants, who always have something to hide, know that small-time landlords are easier targets because the novice property owner is more likely to bend the rules than the professional.

Sometimes the mere mention of the tenant screening process is enough to make the prospective tenant fidget and then shift into the classic 'I'm just looking' mode. Don't rush or allow a prospective tenant to hurry you through the tenant screening and selection process. The wrong decision can be financially devastating, particularly if you have just a couple of rental properties and have big mortgages to pay on them. If you have several properties and one tenant defaults on the rent, you can probably cover your mortgage payments on the property with the troublesome tenant by using the other rents for a short time. If, however, you have just one property and the tenant defaults on the rent, that strategy isn't possible, and you'll have to make the shortfall up out of your own pocket.

Establishing solid tenant-selection criteria and performing a thorough tenant screening process does not guarantee a good tenant, but it does significantly improve your odds of getting a tenant you'll be happy with.

Establishing Tenant Selection Criteria

Tenant selection criteria are written standards that you use to evaluate each prospective tenant's qualifications to live in your property. You should determine your exact minimum qualifications and adhere to them. Of course, your written criteria cannot be discriminatory or violate any anti-discrimination laws (see the section 'Avoiding Complaints of Discrimination' for details).

To establish your tenant selection criteria, review what you're looking for in a tenant. Your ideal tenant may be different from someone else's, but here are five important traits to look for:

- Someone who will be financially responsible and always pay his rent on time
- Someone who will respect and treat the property as if it were her own
- Someone who will be a good neighbour and not cause problems
- Someone who will be stable and likely to renew his lease
- Someone who will leave the premises in a condition the same as or better than she found it

To have the best results in selecting your tenants and make sure that prospective tenants understand your tenant-selection criteria, develop a *statement of rental policy,* which is a formal, written statement explaining your screening criteria.

Giving all prospective tenants an overview of your rental screening procedure and requirements up front lets them know exactly what you're looking for in a suitable tenant. Because these are the minimum standards you'll accept, prospective tenants will know why their rental application may be rejected.

If you make an exception for one applicant and not another, you could find yourself accused of discrimination in your tenant selection process.

Form 8-1 shows a sample statement of rental policy that you can develop for your rental property and provide to each and every prospective tenant over the age of 18. Your policy standards may be more or less stringent depending on the current rental market and experience. But no matter what, be sure that they comply with the law.

Statement of Rental Policy

We are glad that you are interested in our rental property. For your convenience, we have prepared this overview of our guidelines used in processing all rental applications. Please feel free to ask any questions.

We are an equal opportunities housing provider: It is our policy to rent our properties in full compliance with anti-discrimination laws. We do not discriminate against any person because of their race, colour, ethnic origin, religion, sex, age, marital or family status, physical disability, or sexual orientation.

Rental property availability: Rental properties only become available when they are completely ready to rent, including cleaning, painting, and the completion of all maintenance work and planned improvements. Rental property availability can change as properties become available during the day or are removed from the rental market based on finding tenants, cancellations, or maintenance issues.

Valid photo identification and written authorisation: You must be able to present current photo identification such as a driver's licence or passport so that we can verify your identity. If your rental application is approved, we will require a photocopy of your ID when you move into the property to be kept in your tenant file. You must authorise us to verify all information provided in your rental application from credit sources, credit agencies, current and previous landlords and employers, and character references.

Occupancy guidelines: In compliance with local authority guidelines there are restrictions on the total number of persons that may occupy a given rental property. Our guidelines allow two people per bedroom as long as that room is at least 10.2m square. Bedrooms of 6.5m square are suitable for one person. These guidelines are to prevent overcrowding and are in keeping with the limitations of the property. Occupancy will be limited to the persons indicated on the original rental application and lease only unless otherwise agreed in writing. Any proposed additional tenants must complete a rental application and be processed and approved through this same tenant-screening process prior to occupying the rental property.

Application process: All rental applications are evaluated in the same manner, and each adult applicant must voluntarily provide his or her national insurance number and other details which will enable us to conduct a consumer credit report. Every adult applicant must complete a separate rental application form and pay the non-refundable application fee in advance. Any false or incomplete information will result in the denial of your application. If discovered after you are approved and have moved in, we reserve the right to terminate your tenancy. We will verify the information provided on each rental application through our own screening efforts and/or with the assistance of an independent tenant-screening firm. A credit report, along with references from your employer and current landlord for each and every applicant in a given rental property will determine whether our rental criteria has been met. Unless we need to verify information by regular mail, we are usually able to process a rental application in a couple of days.

1

Form 8-1: Statement of Rental Policy (Page 1 of 2).

Rental Criteria

Income: The total combined monthly gross income of all rental applicants in a given rental property must be at least three times the monthly rental rate. Only income that can be verified will count. We expect rental applicants with income to prove at least one year of continuous employment. Full-time students are welcome if the total income of all applicants combined is sufficient or they have a guarantor. You must provide proof of a source of income if you are unemployed. Remember: all adult tenants are joint and severally liable, which means that each one can be held responsible for the payment of all funds due regardless of ability to pay.

Credit history: You must be able to demonstrate fiscal responsibility. If you have any unpaid debts or a pattern of late payments or county court judgements (CCJs) against you, your application may be denied.

Rental history: Each rental applicant must be able to demonstrate a pattern of meeting their rental obligations, leaving prior rental properties in good condition and not causing a barrage of complaints from neighbours. We will require satisfactory rental references from at least two previous landlords. If you have ever been evicted for violating a lease, your application may be denied.

Guarantors: If you do not meet one or more of the above criteria, you may be able to qualify to rent a property if you have a third party living in the UK who will guarantee your lease. The guarantor must pass the same application and screening process except that we will deduct the guarantor's own housing costs before comparing his or her income to our income criteria.

2

Form 8-1: Statement of Rental Policy (Page 2 of 2).

Developing your own statement of rental policy has several benefits:

- You have explained to the applicant that you're aware of and comply with anti-discrimination laws.
- You have outlined that your policy and your maintenance of good records can minimise accusations of discrimination.
- You have explained your process of evaluating prospective tenants so the applicant knows what to expect.
- Your objective tenant screening criteria show that all applicants are evaluated consistently and fairly.

Your statement of rental policy should be given to each and every applicant with the rental application. Insert the policy in a see-through, waterproof folder and place it in clear view on a worktop in the kitchen in the rental property or another surface where all prospective tenants can see it as they view the property.

Although you must offer all prospective tenants a rental application and process each one received, you aren't required to provide your prospective tenants with a copy of your written tenant selection criteria. You may want to, however, because there is a benefit to prospective tenants making their own decision not to apply to rent your property based on the criteria you've set up. The key is to follow the criteria without exception and have the information available if you're challenged.

Some landlords feel more comfortable discussing the tenant-selection criteria right from the first rental enquiry call; others wait and distribute copies only to those who actually apply. You need to decide which policy works best for you and then apply it consistently.

Always be very thorough when you perform tenant screening, and use the same process with all prospective tenants. You run the risk of a charge of discrimination if you deviate from your written standards for certain applicants. There are many legally acceptable reasons to deny a rental application. Be sure that your requirements are clearly understood and followed.

The fact that you carefully pre-screen all prospective tenants is a positive factor not only for you, but also for your rental applicants, your current tenants, and even the neighbours. In fact, you have a responsibility to your current tenants to weed out the unsuitable tenants with a track record of disrupting the neighbours everywhere they go, particularly if you rent out a couple of properties that are situated next door to each other. The good prospective tenants will appreciate the fact that their neighbours had to meet your high standards, too.

Over 90 per cent of your rental applicants will be good tenants, pay their rent on time, take good care of their homes, and treat you and their neighbours with respect. You just need to carefully guard against those few bad apples, and don't hesitate to deny applicants who cannot meet your standards.

Verifying Rental Applications

Bad tenants don't walk around with a helpful sign on their foreheads declaring that this is the case. The tenant screening process requires you to be a detective, and all good detectives verify each fact and take thorough notes. You want to ensure that the prospective tenant meets the minimum standards outlined in your statement of rental policy (see the preceding section for information on these criteria).

We recommend that you use a rental application verification form, like the one shown in Form 8-2, to collect and review the necessary information that allows you to properly evaluate the suitability of your prospective tenant. This document is very important because it enables you to collate all the information necessary in helping you decide whether you want this applicant as your tenant.

Ensure that your rental application form clearly informs the prospective tenant that credit checks and references will be made in accordance with the Data Protection Act. If you intend to charge a fee for the credit check, this should also be stated on the application form.

Keep copies of all rental applications, the corresponding rental application verification forms, credit reports, and all other documentation for both accepted *and* rejected applicants for at least three years. That way, if anyone ever makes a claim that you discriminated against him, your best defence will be your own records, which will clearly indicate that you had legal rental criteria and you applied it consistently.

Verifying the identity of all adults

The very first step to take in verifying a rental application is to personally meet each prospective adult tenant. You should require each prospective adult tenant to show you his or her current driver's licence or other similar (and official) photo ID such as a passport so that you can confirm that the applicant is providing you with the correct name and current address. Advise the prospective tenants that if their application is approved, you will need a photocopy of their ID to be kept in their tenant file. Initial the rental application to record that you did indeed verify this information.

Enquire about any discrepancies between the application and the ID provided. Even if the explanation seems reasonable, be sure to write down the new information so that it's there to check if any need should arise in the future. Maybe an old address appears on the photo ID; if so, making further checks through a credit reference agency is worth considering.

Having a photocopy of the ID for each adult tenant can be very important if a dispute concerning the tenant's identity arises in the future. In these situations, you want to be able to clearly show that you positively identified the tenant before he or she moved in.

Rental Application Verification Form

Name of Applicant ______________________________

Address of Property ______________________________

Rental History (*Note:* Use separate sheets to verify at least two previous landlords.)

Name and Phone Number of Prior Landlord ______________________________

Prior Address ______________________________

____

How much rent does the applicant pay each month? ______________________________

Are you related to the applicant? ______________________________

Is the applicant a lodger or guest? ______________________________

How long has the applicant been your tenant? ______________________________

Did the applicant pay their rent on time? ______________________________

If late, please provide details

____

Did you ever begin legal proceedings against the applicant or other occupants?

____

If yes, what was the outcome of these proceedings? ______________

Why is the applicant moving out? ______________________________

If the applicant is leaving voluntarily, have they given you proper notice? ________

How many days? __________

Did the applicant or other occupants damage the property (beyond normal wear and tear) or damage the common areas? ______________________________

If yes, please describe______________________________

____

Did the applicant pay for any damage? ______________________________

Has the applicant maintained the property in a clean and sanitary condition? ____

____

What type of pets does the applicant have? ______________________________

1

Form 8-2: Rental Application Verification Form (Page 1 of 3).

Were there any problems with the pets? ______________________

Would you rent to this applicant again? ________ Why or why not? __________

Other Comments ______________________________

____

Employment Verification

Contact Name ______________________________

Company ______________________________

Contact's Job Title ______________________________

Contact Telephone Number ______________________________

Date contacted ______________________________

Date joined Company ______________________________

Applicant's Job Title ______________________________

Salary ______________________________

Staff position/fixed term contract? ______________________________

Comments ______________________________

Credit History

Credit report obtained from ______________________________

Date of credit report ______________________________

Information consistent with rental application? ______________________

Summary of results ______________________________

____

Character reference

Contact Name ______________________________

Contact Telephone Number ______________ Date contacted ______________

Relationship to Applicant ______________________________

How long have you known applicant? ______________________

Comments ______________________________

2

Form 8-2: Rental Application Verification Form (Page 2 of 3).

Additional Information

____

____

Reason for Rejecting Applicant (if applicable)

____

____

3

Form 8-2: Rental Application Verification Form (Page 3 of 3).

Reviewing occupancy guidelines

Take a look at the rental application information provided by the tenant concerning the number of people that plan to occupy your rental property to ensure that the anticipated use is within your established occupancy guidelines.

One of the major concerns of landlords is excessive wear and tear of the rental property. Clearly, the greater the number of occupants packed into a rental property, and the longer they live in the property, the more possibility for wear and tear. Local authorities provide guidelines for houses in multiple occupation (HMOs), which are defined as those occupied by people who make up more than one household. This could be a house converted into bedsits, flats, or private rooms with common areas such as entrances, exits, bathrooms, and kitchen. It could apply to 20 people living in separate flats or as few as three people sharing a house.

The exact number of occupants needed for a house to be classed as an HMO varies from one local authority to another, so unfortunately universal guidelines as to how many people can occupy the property don't exist. You can contact the housing or environmental health department of your local council for information on the regulations concerning occupancy in your area and advice on the legal requirements.

A much stricter system exists in Scotland. If you let properties in Scotland, make sure you are well aware of the legal requirements.

Landlords need to ensure that layouts and facilities meet minimum standards and that the property is maintained in a safe and habitable condition. Occupancy must also be at an acceptable level.

Checking rental history

Contact the prospective tenant's current landlord and go through the questions on the rental history portion of the rental application verification form. When you first contact the previous landlord, you may want to listen to his initial reaction and let him tell you about the applicant. Some landlords welcome the opportunity to tell you all about your prospective tenant. Listen carefully.

Some prospective tenants provide you with letters of reference from their landlord or even a copy of their credit report. This is particularly true in many competitive rental markets where only the prepared tenants have a chance to get a good quality rental property. Although the more information you have, the better decision you can usually make, be very careful to evaluate the authenticity of any documents that the prospective tenant provides. Accept any documents that the prospective tenant provides, but always perform your complete tenant screening process to independently verify all information.

We've heard of instances where a prospective tenant provided a glowing written reference from a previous landlord when in fact it was written by her boyfriend. Make sure you double check all references.

If the information you receive about your applicant from the current landlord is primarily negative, you may decide that you've heard enough and not bother to check with any other former landlords before turning the applicant down. However, be wary that the current landlord may not be entirely honest; he could be upset with the tenant for leaving his property. Or he may not want to say anything bad about a problem tenant so that he can get the tenant out of his property and into yours. Not all landlords are going to be as honest as you!

Current or previous landlords may not be entirely forthcoming with answers to many of your questions. It is likely that they will be concerned that they be liable if they provide any negative or subjective information. Of course, it is unlikely that a tenant would actually follow up a bad reference and pursue the landlord for compensation, but many landlords simply don't want to take this risk.

When a current or previous landlord is not overly cooperative, try to gain his confidence by providing him with some information about yourself and your rental property. If you are still unable to build up a rapport, try to get him to at least answer the most important question of all – 'Would you rent to this applicant again?' He can simply give you a 'yes' or a 'no' without any details. Of course, silence can also tell you everything that you need to know.

Verifying employment and income

Although credit reference agencies may provide information on your prospective tenant's employment and income, they typically won't have all the information you need to properly evaluate this extremely important rental qualification criteria.

Independently verify the employer information and phone number the applicant puts on her application. You may have reason for concern if the employer is a major company and the telephone is not answered in a typical and customary business manner, for example. You also need to be careful that you confirm the sensitive questions of how much the prospective tenant earns and the stability of their employment only with an appropriate representative of the employer.

Occasionally, you may find that an employer, or the current or previous landlord, will not verify any information over the phone. So be prepared to send letters requesting the pertinent information and include a stamped, self-addressed envelope. Be sure to tell your prospective tenant that you may have a delay in providing her with the results of your tenant screening process.

In addition to your credit reference information and the results of your verification calls, your prospective tenant should provide you with proof of her employment and income with pay slips for the past three months. No matter how compelling the information is, you must still verify it directly with the employer or source of the income.

Always require written verification of all other sources of income that a prospective tenant is using to meet your income qualification requirements. If you cannot verify the income, you do not have to include it in your calculations to determine whether the applicant meets your minimum income requirements.

When you have a prospective tenant whose income relies on commission or bonuses, make sure you review at least six consecutive months of her most recent pay slips. Of course, the best policy is to require all applicants with any income other than a monthly salary to provide a copy of their signed self-assessment tax return for the last two years. Although you must be careful to ensure that it is an authentic document, we have yet to find a prospective tenant who overstates her annual income on her tax return.

As a detective, you need to pay close attention to applicants who seem to be overqualified or anxious to be approved and take possession of your rental property. Remember the old saying, 'If it sounds too good to be true, it probably is'? That definitely applies in the world of rental property, so keep it in mind at all times.

Be particularly careful of prospective tenants who seem to have plenty of cash to pay your deposit and first month's rent, but who do not have verifiable sources of income that seem consistent with their spending patterns. The applicant may be involved in an illegal activity, and you may need to evict her later at considerable expense and loss of income.

If it looks too good to be true, it probably is!

A friend owns a number of rental properties in Guildford, Surrey, ranging from 1-bedroom flats to 5-bedroom family houses. With so many properties on his books, he is quite often on the lookout for new tenants to fill them. He regularly visits the vacant properties to inspect their physical aspects and ensure they are ready for prospective tenants to view them. At the same time, he is aware of the importance of the rental procedures. One area of ongoing review is the new rental applications, which he ensures are properly completed and that the tenant screening process is applied uniformly.

One rental application he received was from a 23-year-old who was studying part-time for an MA at Surrey University. This applicant was looking to live on his own for the first time and required a 1-bedroom flat. He stated that his income was £400 per week. So with £1,600 a month in income, it appeared as if he was financially qualified to rent the property.

Having been in rental management for many years, our friend was curious about the weekly income given the young age of the applicant and he wondered how he had time to study as well as hold down such a well-paid job. So he took a closer look at the rental application and contacted the employer, a local manufacturing company. Sure enough, upon his subsequent enquiry of the employer and then the prospective tenant, it became apparent that the latter did indeed earn £400 per week. The only problem was that he did not work during term-time so this was only for five months of the year. Clearly, it's important to look at the income of an applicant over a long period of time.

Reviewing the applicant's credit history

You can and should check out an applicant's credit history by making a credit check. Information is held on all of us; this can include where we have lived, how we use our credit cards, and what our loan repayments are. You can also find out whether a tenant has been declared bankrupt or has county court judgments (CCJs) against him.

So what are you looking for with a credit check? You want someone with a pattern of financial responsibility and prudent or conservative spending. You want to avoid prospective tenants who seem to use excessive credit and live beyond their means. If they move into your rental property and have even a temporary loss of income due to illness or because they lose their job, you may be the one with an unexpected loss of income because of it!

What's in a name?

Identity theft is a growing problem in the UK. It occurs when someone's identity is stolen and used to apply for credit cards, loans, mortgages, and passports. It can also be used by someone trying to rent a property – in other words, the applicant interested in living in your 3-bedroom family home.

The case of Derek Bond, the 72-year-old British pensioner who was arrested on holiday with his wife in Durban, South Africa because the FBI thought he was Derek Sykes, a conman wanted for allegedly fleecing hundreds of Americans in an investment scam in the mid-1990s, shows how widespread identity theft is. Mr Sykes had been using Mr Bond's identity for years, but it wasn't until the FBI caught up with him that Mr Bond knew anything about it. And so hard was it to clear his name that Mr Bond spent nearly three weeks in jail until his innocence could be proved.

Unfortunately, identity theft on this scale is growing more common. Landlords also need to look out for cases of mistaken identity where several people share a name and subsequently get muddled up. When checking out applicants, make sure they are who they say they are. Photo identification in the form of a driving licence or passport should be your first port of call. But you must run checks to ensure as far as possible that that everything the applicant tells you adds up. Ensure you check their employer, landlord, and character references.

In some cases, perfectly good prospective tenants are turned down because their information is not carefully screened and verified and in some cases, is not information on the actual prospective tenant. In the US, you can find instances of some very responsible and qualified applicants being turned down when they submitted rental applications, because they have the same name as an individual with a very poor credit report. This problem occurred when certain tenant screening companies didn't cross check their information sufficiently to prevent such a mix up.

So what's the upshot of all this? It's to be sure to verify the applicant's name, National Insurance number, and several former addresses to ensure that you are using the correct information in your screening efforts.

Carefully compare the addresses contained on the credit check to the information provided on the rental application. If you find an inconsistency, ask the prospective tenant for an explanation. Maybe they were temporarily staying with a family member or they simply forgot about one of their residences. Of course, be sure to contact previous landlords and ask all the questions on the rental application verification form just to make sure that the applicant didn't tell you about that residence for a reason.

Information obtained through credit checks must be kept strictly confidential and cannot be given to any third parties. The prospective tenant is entitled to a copy of his own credit check upon request.

Credit checks can have their limitations. So make sure that you are reviewing the credit report of your actual applicant. People with poor credit or tenant histories have been known to steal the identity of others, particularly their own children if they are 16 or over, by using the child's national insurance number.

A number of credit reporting agencies offer a credit checking service and prices can vary significantly. Credit checks usually take a couple of days, and the tenant tends to bear the cost. Experian and Equifax, the two main credit reference agencies, offer a tenant verifier service – a credit checking service for landlords – but this tends to be cost-prohibitive for most small-time landlords. However, large managing agencies who have to check the references of hundreds of tenants tend to use it.

If you receive a large number of rental applications, review them first and then only run the credit check on the most suitable applicants. Be sure to return any unused credit check fees to those for whom you don't run the credit check.

The Internet is quickly changing the tenant screening procedures for many landlords. Credit reports and tenant history information are now available from your computer in a matter of hours, and often this capability enables you to approve your prospective tenant in a single day, which can be a strong competitive advantage. Many firms are entering this market, and all offer very impressive services designed to save you time and help you fill your vacancies faster. Using technology can improve the efficiency of the information collection for tenant screening and provide you with more information to make a better decision. However, don't rely just on what you find out online. You still need to personally contact past landlords, verify the applicant's income and employment, and consider your own dealings with your prospective tenant. Rental property ownership and management is still, and always will be, a people business.

Many types of applicant screening products are available to landlords. With the wide choice of tenant screening services, you may have a hard time deciding exactly what you need. So we recommend that you use a tenant selection service that offers a retail or consumer credit report, an eviction search or tenant history, an automated crosscheck of addresses, and an employment or reference verification.

Talking with all character references

Although you could expect that character references only give you glowing comments about how lucky you are to have the applicant as your new tenant, investing the time and making the calls is important for several reasons.

You will occasionally find someone who tells you that the prospective tenant is her best friend but she would never loan the applicant money or let him borrow her car. Plus, if you call the references given and find that the information is bogus, you can use this information as part of your overall screening of the applicant.

Dealing with guarantors

Just as parents often act as *guarantors* when their children are trying to get on the property ladder for the first time because they couldn't afford to do it otherwise, your prospective tenant might not meet the criteria outlined in your statement of rental policy but he is ready to offer a guarantor. The guarantor needs to sign a Guarantee of Tenancy Agreement form (shown in Form 8-3); however, you still need to screen the guarantor and make sure he or she is financially qualified, or the guarantee is worthless.

Make sure the guarantor completes a rental application, pays the application fee, and goes through the same tenant screening process as the applicant. Keep in mind that the guarantor will not actually be living at the rental property and thus will have his own housing costs. So in order to ensure that the guarantor can meet all of his own obligations and cover your tenant's rent in case of a default, you need to deduct the guarantor's cost of housing from his income before comparing it to your income requirements. For example, if the proposed guarantor has a gross monthly income of £4,000 with a £1,000 mortgage payment, he has an adjusted gross income of £3,000. So assuming you have an income standard that requires the tenant to earn three times the monthly rent (and assuming the guarantor meets all of your other screening criteria), the person could be the guarantor for your prospective tenant as long as the rent does not exceed £1,000 per month.

Although a guarantor can be very important and can give you the extra resources in the event of a rent default by your tenant, overseas guarantors are not as valuable as those living in the UK. Enforcing the guarantee against an overseas party can be very difficult or even financially unfeasible.

Guarantee of Tenancy Agreement

On the date below, in consideration of the execution of the Tenancy Agreement, dated

________________, 20__, for the premises located at:__________________

________________________________ (Rental property) by and between

________________________________ (Tenant)

________________________________ (Owner) and

________________________________ (Guarantor);

for valuable consideration, receipt of which is hereby acknowledged, the Guarantor does hereby guarantee unconditionally to Owner, Owner's agent, and/or including Owner's successor and assigns, the prompt payment by Tenant of any unpaid rent, property damage and cleaning and repair costs or any other sums which become due pursuant to said lease or rental agreement, a copy of which is attached hereto, including any and all court costs or solicitor's fees incurred in enforcing the Tenancy Agreement.

If Tenant assigns or sublets the Rental property, Guarantor shall remain liable under the terms of this Agreement for the performance of the assignee or sublessee, unless Owner relieves Guarantor by express written termination of the Agreement.

In the event of the breach of any terms of the Tenancy Agreement by the Tenant, Guarantor shall be liable for any damages, financial or physical, caused by the Tenant, including any and all legal fees incurred in enforcing the Tenancy Agreement. Owner or Owner's agent may immediately enforce this Guarantee upon any default by Tenant and an action against the Guarantor may be brought at any time without first seeking recourse against the Tenant.

The insolvency of Tenant or non-payment of any sums due from Tenant may be deemed a default, giving rise to action by Owner against Guarantor. This Guarantee does not confer a right to possession of the Rental property by Guarantor, and Owner is not required to serve Guarantor with any legal notices, including any demand for payment of rent, prior to Owner proceeding against Guarantor for Guarantor's obligation under this Guarantee.

Unless released in writing by the Owner, Guarantor shall remain obligated by the terms of this Guarantee for the entire period of the tenancy as provided by the Tenancy Agreement and for any extensions pursuant thereto. In the event Tenant and Owner modify the terms of said Tenancy Agreement, with or without the knowledge or consent of the Guarantor, Guarantor waives any and all rights to be released from the provisions of this Guarantee and Guarantor shall remain obligated by said additional modifications and terms of the Tenancy Agreement. Guarantor hereby consents and agrees in advance to any changes, modifications, additions, or deletions of the Tenancy Agreement made and agreed to by Owner and Tenant during the entire period of the tenancy.

1

Form 8-3: Guarantee of Tenancy Agreement (Page 1 of 2).

If any legal action or proceeding is brought by either party to enforce any part of this Agreement, the prevailing party shall recover, in addition to all other relief, reasonable solicitor's fees and legal costs. By signing below, Owner, Tenant and Guarantor acknowledge and accept all terms contained herein.

________________	________________	________________
Tenant's Signature	Guarantor's Signature	Owner's Signature
________________	________________	________________
Tenant's Name (print)	Guarantor's Name (print)	Owner's Name (print)
________________ ________________ ________________	________________ ________________ ________________	________________ ________________ ________________
Tenant's Address	Guarantor's Address	Owner's Address
________________	________________	________________
Daytime phone no	Daytime phone no	Daytime phone no
________________	________________	________________
Date	Date	Date

2

Form 8-3: Guarantee of Tenancy Agreement (Page 2 of 2).

Notifying the Applicant of Your Decision

Landlords are legally allowed to choose which tenant they want to live in their property as long as their decisions comply with anti-discrimination laws and are based on legitimate business criteria.

One of the most difficult tasks for the landlord is informing a prospective tenant that you have rejected his application. You obviously want to avoid an argument over the rejection, but even more importantly, you want to avoid being accused of discrimination based on the applicant's misunderstanding about the reasons for being turned down.

Regardless of whether you accept or reject the prospective tenant, be sure to notify the applicant promptly when the decision is made. If you have approved the applicant, contact him and arrange for a meeting and a viewing of the rental property prior to the move-in date. Do not notify the other qualified applicants that you have already rented the property until all legal documents have been signed and you've collected in full all funds due upon move-in.

If you reject an applicant, be prepared to account for the reasons why you have done so because they are bound to ask you. In fact, we recommend that you notify your rejected prospective tenant in writing, using the notice of denial to rent form (shown in Form 8-4). In addition to notifying the applicant of the denial, this form also helps you to document the various reasons for your rejection of the applicant.

If you notify the applicant only by phone, you may have difficulty giving all of the details and required disclosures. The written notice of denial to rent avoids a situation in which the applicant may unintentionally (or sometimes intentionally) form the opinion that you are denying his application in a discriminatory manner and make a complaint.

Although you need to carefully follow the law, never compromise your tenant screening criteria or allow yourself to be intimidated into accepting an unsuitable prospective tenant. Rejecting an applicant who doesn't meet your tenant screening criteria isn't discrimination.

NOTICE OF DENIAL TO RENT

To: ____

____

(Full Names of All Applicants Listed on Application)

Thank you for applying to rent at: ______________________________

We have carefully and thoroughly reviewed your rental application. We are hereby informing you of certain information as to why your application was unsuccessful. Based on the information currently in our files, your application has been denied for the following reason(s):

I. Rental History

____ Could not be verified __ Unpaid or missed payments __ Property damage reported
____ Disruptive behaviour reported ___ Prior eviction reported __ Other __________

II. Employment and Income

____ Employment could not be verified ____ Insufficient income

____ Irregular or temporary employment ____ Income could not be verified
_____ Other ____

III. Credit History

____ Could not be verified ______ Unsatisfactory payment history

____ Declared bankrupt ______ County court judgements (CCJs)

____ Other ____

IV. Character References

________ Could not be verified ______ Lack of non-related references

________ Negative reference __ Other ______________________

1

Form 8-4: Notice of Denial to Rent Form (Page 1 of 2).

V. Application

________ Application unsigned ________ Application incomplete

________ False information provided ______ Rental property let to prior qualified tenant ________ Other ____

The credit reporting agency (if used) that provided information to us was:

Name ____

Address ____

Telephone ____.

This agency only provided information about you and your credit history and was not involved in any way in making the decision to reject your rental application, nor can they explain why the decision was made. If you believe the information they provided is inaccurate or incomplete, you may call the credit reporting agency at the number listed above or communicate by post.

____
Signature of Owner or Agent for Owner

____
Name of Owner or Agent of Owner (print)

____
Date

2

Form 8-4: Notice of Denial to Rent Form (Page 2 of 2).

Avoiding Complaints of Discrimination

In the UK, suing landlords for discrimination is not a common occurrence but that doesn't mean you don't have to worry about being anti-discriminatory. It is all too easy to slip up, with problems arising when landlords are unaware that their policies or practices are discriminatory. For example, you may think that you are just being a courteous and caring landlord by only showing elderly prospective tenants your empty flat located on the ground floor because you think they wouldn't be able to cope with the flight of stairs at another property. But not giving all applicants the same treatment is a form of discrimination – even if that wasn't your intention.

What it is and what it isn't

Discrimination is a major issue for landlords and has serious legal consequences for the uninformed. If you don't know the law, you may be guilty of various forms of discrimination and not even realise it until you've been charged with discrimination. That's why knowing the law is so important, and it's up to you to make yourself familiar with the relevant aspects of it.

There are two types of discrimination:

- **Treating people differently.** For example, if you had two applicants with similar financial histories, tenant histories, and other screening criteria, but charged one applicant a larger deposit, you could be found guilty of discrimination or a complaint on the basis of different treatment.
- **Treating all prospective tenants equally, but having a different impact because of an individual's particular situation.** If your occupancy standard policy is two persons per bedroom, you may be accused of discriminating against applicants with children. Although you have set an occupancy standard policy that is applied equally to all tenants, your restrictive policy will discourage applicants with children. This policy has a *disparate impact* – the policy is the same for all applicants, but the policy has a much different effect on certain applicants and essentially creates an additional barrier to rental housing for families.

You are not allowed to discriminate on the basis of race, colour, religion, national origin, sex, age, familial status, or disability.

Here are some other practices that may result in discrimination and that you need to keep in mind:

- **Gender stereotypes:** Be careful that you don't inadvertently favour one sex as tenants. For example, some rental property owners may have the perception that male tenants aren't as clean or quiet as female tenants. Conversely, some owners with a rental property in a rough area may believe that male tenants are less susceptible to being victims of crime. Don't allow any stereotypes or assumptions to enter into your tenant selection criteria. Men and women make equally good tenants and should all be judged on their own merits.

  You cannot refuse to rent on the basis of gender, nor can you have special rules for tenants based on gender, such as limiting female tenants to upper-level flats only.
- **Ageism:** Be careful with the whole issue of age. Typically, you will be able to deny renting a property to applicants who are under 18 years of age. Applicants over the age of 18 cannot be turned down on an issue of age, however, as this would be discriminatory.
- **Other issues:** There are other issues that are not specifically protected under the law. Examples include marital status, sexual orientation, and source of income. But common sense should prevail: For example, you can't refuse to rent to a couple on the basis that they are not married but are cohabiting. This would be seen as being discriminatory.

Steering

Steering means to guide, or attempt to guide, a prospective tenant towards living where you think he should live based on his race, colour, religion, national origin, sex, age, familial status, or disability. Steering is not advisable because it deprives persons of their right to choose to rent a property where they want. Not showing or renting certain properties to minorities is one form of steering; however, so is the assigning of any person to a particular section or floor of a building, because of race, colour, religion, sex, handicap, familial status, or national origin.

Rental property owners often have only good intentions when they suggest that a prospective tenant with children see only rental properties on the ground floor or near a playground. However, the failure to offer such an applicant an opportunity to see *all* the available rental properties on your books is steering – and breaking the law.

Be very careful not to make suggestions or comments that could be misinterpreted as steering a prospective tenant. All prospective tenants should receive information on the full range of rental properties available and be able to decide which they want to see, making the choice themselves.

Children

No law says you must rent your property to adults with kids, but be very careful about discriminating against children. Rental property owners cannot cite moral reasons or concerns about additional wear and tear that children might cause, because it effectively discriminates against them.

Some rental property owners are concerned about renting to adults with children because there are hazards that may be dangerous to them. For example, the property may not have any safe areas for the children to play, particularly if it is a flat on the third-floor of an apartment building located next to a busy main road. Although you may truly only have the children's best interests in mind, it is up to the parents to decide whether the property is safe for their children. Of course, you do need to take steps to make your property as safe as possible by reminding parents to not let their children play in unsafe areas or to play while unattended.

Charging prospective tenants with children higher rents or higher deposits than applicants without children is also illegal, as is offering different rental terms, such as a shorter lease, fewer amenities, or different payment options because they have children. The property facilities must also be fully available for all tenants, regardless of age, unless there is a clear safety issue involved.

We always recommend that landlords openly accept tenants with children. Families tend to be more stable, and they are looking for a safe, crime-free, and drug-free environment in which to raise their children. They are unlikely to move around from property to property as much as single tenants because, in many cases, they have schooling needs to consider. Along with responsible pet-owners, who also have difficulty finding suitable rental properties, families with children can be excellent, long-term tenants. And typically, the longer your tenants stay, the better your cash flow and the easier life is for you.

Disabled tenants

Letting property to disabled people is governed by the Disability Discrimination Act. It makes it unlawful for landlords to discriminate against disabled people. Discrimination occurs when a disabled person is treated less favourably than someone else and the reason for this is related to the person's disability. Most rental premises, including houses and flats, are covered by the Act.

With residential housing, unlawful discrimination occurs when a landlord:

- Offers less favourable terms to a disabled person
- Refuses to let to a disabled person
- Offers different facilities to a disabled person

- Refuses a disabled person access
- Evicts a disabled person
- Refuses to give tenants consent to sub-let to a disabled person

However, certain circumstances are exempt under the Disability Discrimination Act. The Act says that it may sometimes be justifiable to treat disabled people differently from other people. It may be justifiable:

- To refuse a disabled person on health and safety grounds, for example, to refuse to rent to a disabled person
- To refuse a disabled person access to a facility, such as a shared kitchen or lounge, if allowing them access stops others from using it
- To give a disabled person different access to a facility, if this was necessary to allow others to gain access
- To refuse to rent to a disabled person who is not capable of entering into a legally enforceable agreement, or of giving informed consent

Landlords must not charge a disabled tenant a higher rent for the property or a higher deposit against damages. Both count as discrimination.

Don't forget your managing agent, if you use one. A landlord who lets their agents or other representatives discriminate against disabled people is acting unlawfully under the Disability Discrimination Act. But if you can show that you have taken reasonable steps to prevent your agent from acting unlawfully you won't be considered to have broken the law, even though your agent has.

Any landlord who discriminates against a disabled person can be taken to court. The disabled person may take action to seek damages to help make up for the loss or for injury to their feelings. Falling foul of the law can be costly, in terms of time and money, so take steps to ensure you don't make that mistake.

Reasonable accommodations

Landlords do not have to alter their premises in order to make them more accessible for disabled tenants. However, as a landlord, you should act in such a way as to make life easier for the disabled tenant and make accommodations where possible. Reasonable adjustments to your rules, procedures, or services should be considered upon request. Examples of reasonable accommodations that the landlord may be asked to offer might include:

- Providing a parking space that is wider and closer to the rental property of a wheelchair-bound tenant, in instances where the property has a parking space
- Arranging to read all management communications to a tenant with poor vision
- Adjusting the date when the rent is due to take into account when the tenant receives his or her disability benefit

Reasonable modifications

Landlords should think about allowing the disabled tenant the right to modify her living space at the tenant's own expense. The modifications can only be to the extent necessary to make the environment safe and comfortable, only as long as the modifications don't make the property unacceptable to the next tenant, or only if the tenant agrees to return the rental property to its original condition when she moves out. Alternatively, the tenant can pay the landlord to restore the property to its original condition at the end of the tenancy.

Reasonable modifications that tenants may request to make at their expense include:

- Ramps at the entry to the property where there are stairs that are difficult for the tenant to negotiate
- Lower light switches and removal of doors or widening of doorways to allow for wheelchair access
- Grab bars or call buttons in bathrooms

The modifications must be reasonable. You can ask the tenant to obtain your prior approval and ensure that the work will be done in a workmanlike manner, in line with any government or local authority guidelines. You can also ask the tenant to provide proof for the need for the modification from their GP. But you cannot ask about the specific handicap of the tenant that necessitates these changes.

Guide dogs

Many landlords include in the lease a clause preventing tenants from keeping pets in their rental property. But guide dogs for the blind or hard-of-hearing that assist tenants with daily life activities are exempt and must be allowed in all rental properties, regardless of any no-pet policies.

Sexual harassment

Sexual harassment, in the world of property management, occurs when you refuse to rent to a person who refuses your sexual advances or when you make life difficult for, or harass, a tenant who resists your unwanted advances. Most landlords understand this concern and find such behaviour unconscionable; however, the problem often arises when rental property owners hire someone to assist them with the leasing, rent collection, or maintenance requirements at their properties. The rental property owner is accountable, because these individuals are the employees or agents of the owner.

Make sure that you have a clear written policy against sexual harassment, provide an open-minded procedure for investigating complaints, and conduct thorough and unbiased investigations that lead to quick corrective action, if necessary.

Part III
The Brass Tacks of Managing Rentals

"I don't want three wishes – I just want my rent."

In this part . . .

Managing rental property involves a lot more than just managing the property itself. Working with tenants – from fielding the first call of a prospective tenant to having the paperwork in order when the tenant moves out – is what you'll spend a huge chunk of your time doing. So the chapters in this part take you through that relationship step by step. We show you how to help tenants at move-in and move-out times, how to increase the rent without losing your tenants, and how to retain the good tenants and deal with the bad. Chances are you'll find the answer to any question you may have about your tenants in this part.

Chapter 9

Moving in the Tenant

In This Chapter

- Agreeing on a move-in date
- Guiding your tenant through the policies and procedures of your property
- Noting the condition of the property before the move-in date
- Keeping all the paperwork organised
- Making your new tenants feel welcome in their new home

After you select your new tenants, you still have to complete one very important step to ensure that you establish a good tenant/landlord relationship: moving them in. In order to ensure that this goes smoothly, you need to hold a tenant orientation and rental property inspection meeting, which gives you the opportunity to present the rental property and your ownership and management skills in the best possible light. You also need to ensure that your new tenants understand and agree to the policies and rules you have established for the rental property.

Tenants are very excited and motivated to begin moving in to their new home, but moving is very stressful for most people. New tenants can remember a bad move-in experience for months; the memory may stay in their minds throughout their entire tenancy. Although you can't guarantee your new tenant a simple and painless move (many aspects of the tenant's move are beyond your control), you can take steps to ensure that you are organised and ready to handle any complaints or concerns about their new home. By being organised and prepared, you'll be able to quickly and efficiently handle the administrative steps to get the tenants into their new rental property, thus making this process smooth and pleasant for everyone.

In this chapter, we outline the important steps to ensure that your tenant/landlord relationship gets off to a good start, including scheduling the move-in date and the tenant orientation meeting; performing the pre-occupancy inspection and the inventory; and sharing important policies in the tenant information letter. We also offer creative ideas to welcome your tenants the day they move in.

Establishing the Move-In Date

When you have informed your prospective tenant that his rental application has been approved, you need to determine a mutually agreeable move-in date. You and the tenant may have discussed this during your initial telephone conversation or when you showed the rental property, but be sure to raise the issue again to make sure that you agree on the date.

After new tenants have been approved, some tenants suddenly stall on setting the move-in date. They may stall because they are still obligated under another tenancy agreement or 30-day notice at another rental property and they don't want to pay two lots of rent. Unless you're willing to suffer additional rent loss that you can never recover, insist that the tenant starts paying you rent on the originally scheduled move-in date. The time for your new tenant to negotiate the move-in date was *before* you approved him.

In some situations, your rental property may not be available at your mutually agreed move-in date. Perhaps the prior tenants didn't vacate as they said they would, maybe the property was in much worse condition than you anticipated, or maybe you just weren't able to complete the work required in time. If it becomes apparent that there will be a delay in getting the rental property ready as promised, you need to tell your new tenant immediately. Often, new tenants can adjust their move-in date as long as you give them reasonable notice. If they can't adjust their move-in date, communicate with them and try to work out other possible arrangements.

Sometimes new tenants ask if they can begin moving just a few items into the rental property before your pre-occupancy conference. Don't allow it! You will create a tenant/landlord relationship simply by letting the new tenants have access to the rental property without being there or by allowing them to store even a few items in the flat or house. If you need to cancel the tenancy agreement for any reason, you would then need to go through a formal legal eviction that could take several weeks.

Although the rental property should be in rent-ready condition before being shown to prospective tenants, the property can quickly get dirty or dusty if there is any delay between showing the property and the date when the new tenant actually moves in. So before meeting with your tenant prior to move-in (covered in the following section), make one last visit to the rental property and go through your rent-ready inspection checklist (covered in more detail in Chapter 4) again just to make sure that you won't encounter any surprises when move-in day arrives.

If at all possible, arrange to be on the premises while they are moving in so that you can answer any questions they may have.

Meeting with Your Tenant Prior to Move-In

After you and your tenant have decided on a move-in date, you need to get together to deal with some of the technicalities, like inspecting the property, signing some paperwork, and giving the tenant the keys. Getting together to do this is a very important step, and you need to do it before your new tenant actually moves in and takes possession of the rental property.

Schedule a meeting with the tenant either for the day that they move in or within just a few days before they move in.

At this meeting, you review your property policies and rules, review, and sign all the paperwork, collect the move-in funds, and conduct a thorough property inspection with your new tenant, including the completion of the inventory (covered later in this chapter).

Going over the rules with your new tenant

When you meet with your new tenant, start by giving him a copy of your house rules (see Form 9-1 for an example of this kind of document). Give him a chance to read over the rules and ask any questions, and provide clarification as necessary. Then ask for his signature, indicating that he has received and understands the rules and agrees to abide by them.

Many owners and managers with just one rental property or a small studio or flat to rent do not worry about detailed rules and regulations because they think the tenancy agreement covers it all. But setting up some basic rules that can easily be changed as necessary upon proper written notice to the tenants is a good idea. Doing so ensures that you and your tenants are on the same page and gives you flexibility as you manage your property.

Policies and Rules

We are proud of this Property and we hope that you enjoy living here. The support and cooperation of you, as our Tenant, is necessary for us to maintain our high standards.

This is your personal copy of our Policies and Rules. Please read it carefully as it is an integral part of your Tenancy Agreement. When you sign your Tenancy Agreement, you agree to abide by the policies and rules for this rental property, and they are considered legally binding provisions of your Tenancy Agreement. If you have any questions, please contact us and we will be glad to help.

This document is an addendum and is part of the Tenancy Agreement, dated __________________, by and between ________________________, (Owner), and ______________ (Tenant), for the Property located at:________________________
____

New policies and rules or amendments to this document may be adopted by Owner upon giving 30 days written notice to Tenant.

Guests: Tenant is responsible for their own proper conduct and that of all guests, including the responsibility for understanding and observing all policies and rules.

Noise: Although the Property is well constructed, it is not completely soundproof and reasonable consideration for neighbours is important. Either inside or outside of the Property, no Tenant or their guest shall use, or allow to be used, any sound-emitting device at sound level that may annoy, disturb, or otherwise interfere with the rights, comforts or conveniences of the neighbours. Particular care must be taken between the hours of 9:00 pm and 9:00 am.

Parking: No vehicle belonging to a Tenant shall be parked in such a manner as to impede passage in the street or prevent access to the Property. Tenant shall only use assigned and designated parking spaces, for their own use and not sub-let them. Tenant shall ensure that all posted disabled or other no parking areas remain clear of vehicles at all times. Vehicles parked in unauthorised areas or in another tenant's designated parking space may be towed away at the vehicle owner's expense. No trucks, commercial vehicles, boats, caravans, or trailers are allowed anywhere on the Property without advance written approval of the Owner. Tenants shall ensure that their guests abide by all of these parking policies and rules.

Balconies, Patios, and Hallways: Balconies and patios are restricted to patio-type furniture and are to be kept clean and orderly. No barbecues or similar cooking devices are to be used at the Property without advance written approval. No items, such as washing or flags, may be hung from the Property's walls, windows, or balconies at any time, and all hallways and paths must be kept free from items that

1

Form 9-1: Policies and Rules (Page 1 of 3).

could be a hazard. Owner reserves the right that items that detract from the appearance of the Property be removed immediately upon request. No unauthorised storage is allowed at any time.

Wall Hangings: Pictures may be hung on a thin nail. Adhesives which mark the walls, such as Blu Tack, sellotape, and drawing pins should not be used for attaching posters to the walls. Mirrors, wall units, shelves, and hanging wall or light fixtures need special attention and professional installation. Please contact the Owner for approval in advance as damage to the Property will be the responsibility of the Tenant.

Rubbish: Tenant is responsible for keeping the inside and outside of the Property clean, sanitary, and free from objectional odours at all times. Tenant shall ensure that all rubbish is sealed in rubbish bags and placed in the wheelie bin or dustbin. No rubbish or other materials shall be allowed to accumulate so as to cause a hazard or be in violation of any health, fire, or safety regulation. Tenant shall refrain from disposing of any combustible or hazardous material and all rubbish shall be disposed of routinely per the local rubbish collection procedures.

Animals or Pets: No animals or pets may be kept or are allowed at the Property by the Tenant or their guests unless the Tenant and Owner have approved an Animal Agreement in advance.

Maintenance: Tenant agrees to promptly notify Owner of any items requiring repair at the Property. Requests for repairs or maintenances should be made by contacting the Owner or their agent during normal business hours, where possible. Emergencies involving any immediate health and safety matter should be handled by the appropriate agency (police, fire, ambulance) and the Owner shall be contacted as soon as practical thereafter. Costs for any repairs, including repair or clearance of blockages in waste pipes or drains, water pipes, or plumbing fixtures caused by the negligence of the Tenant or their guests are the responsibility of the Tenant.

Inclement Weather: Tenant shall close all windows, doors and other building openings tightly when leaving the Property to prevent damage from the elements to the Property. When the Tenant will be away from the Property during the winter, the thermostat will be placed at a minimum of 50 degrees to avoid freezing of pipes and other damage.

Keys: If you lose your key and need a new one, there will be a minimum replacement charge during normal business hours for the first request. Subsequent requests or after-hours lockout service will be handled at an additional charge of £20.

Key Release: Owner will not give a key to the Property to anyone unless their name is on the Tenancy Agreement. This is for the Tenant's protection. If you are expecting guests or relatives, please be sure they will have access to the Property.

2

Form 9-1: Policies and Rules (Page 2 of 3).

Insurance: The Owner's insurance cover offers no protection for the Tenant's personal property or any liability claims against the Tenant. The Tenant should obtain home contents insurance to cover damage against your personal belongings.

Right to Enter: Owner reserves the right to enter the Property with 24 hours' notice with or without the Tenant's permission at any reasonable hour for any lawful reason or without notice in the event of an emergency.

Safety/Security: Safety and security is the sole responsibility of each Tenant and their guests. Owner or their agent assumes no responsibility or liability, unless otherwise provided by law, for the safety or security of the Tenant or their guests, or for injury caused by the criminal acts of other persons. Tenant should ensure that all windows and doors are locked at all times, and Tenant must immediately notify Owner when leaving property unattended for an extended period. Tenant shall not smoke in bed or use or store any combustible materials at the Property.

3

Form 9-1: Policies and Rules (Page 3 of 3).

The term *rules and regulations* can sound rather imposing to most tenants. So we recommend using the term *policies and rules* or simply *house rules* whenever possible. Your policies and rules are separate from the tenancy agreement, which is drafted by a solicitor using lots of formal and hard-to-understand terminology. The rules you draft should be more informal and conversational in tone than your tenancy agreement. Be sure to use language that is clear, but not harsh or demeaning. Here are some tips regarding house rules:

- **Be clear, direct, and firm – but not condescending.** Review your rules with several of your friends and colleagues and see if there is a better way to say the same thing.
- **Try not to use too many negative expressions.** It is easy to be too blunt or negative when you are stating rules, such as 'No cash will be accepted for rent payments', 'No smoking in the bedrooms', 'No washing on your balcony', or 'Don't chain bikes to the front of the property'. Although each of these rules may be reasonable and important to the safe and efficient operation of your rental property, you can say the same thing in a much more positive way. For example, instead of saying, 'Don't chain bikes to the front of the property', you could say, 'Please put your bikes in the garage'. Or instead of saying, 'No cash will be accepted for rent payments', you can say, 'We gladly accept direct debits'. Phrasing the rules in a more positive tone and minimising the negative statements makes the rules – and you – seem friendlier to your tenants.
- **Make sure your policies and rules are reasonable and enforceable.** They must not discriminate against anyone because of their race, gender, ethnic origin, religion, and so on (see Chapter 8 for more details on this).

  Be particularly careful to review your house rules to avoid any reference to children unless the reference is related to health and safety issues. For example, if your rental property has a swimming pool, you can have a rule that states, 'Persons under 14 must be accompanied by an adult while using the pool', because unattended children in swimming pools pose legitimate safety concerns. But a rule that says, 'Children are not allowed to leave bicycles chained to the railings outside the property' is inappropriate, because it singles out children (implying that adults can leave bikes there if they want). A better way to handle this issue would be to use wording that isn't age specific, such as 'No one is allowed to leave bicycles chained to the railings at the front of the property.' Stated that way, the rule applies to everyone and doesn't discriminate based on age.
- **Regularly review and make improvements in your policies and rules based on situations that you've encountered.** But remember that you're not running a prison camp, and you don't want to alienate your tenants by harassing them with rules or controlling their day-to-day life. (Remember, you want your tenants to actually read and follow your rules, so try not to be too overbearing.)

And then there was light!

Tenants are usually not very anxious to begin paying for utilities, so you need to be sure that your procedures verify that your new tenants immediately contact the utility companies and put the utilities that are their responsibility in their name. These utilities could include electricity, gas, water, and telephone, depending on what's included in the rent. Most landlords let the utilities revert to their name when the rental property becomes vacant for the duration of rental showings. So if your new tenants don't change the utility billing information, you may end up paying for some of their electricity, gas, and water bills. Confirm that the tenants have dealt with the utilities soon after they have moved into the property.

Just to make sure that you don't end up paying your tenant's utility bills, you could immediately contact the utility company as part of your tenant orientation meeting. The new tenant can then establish the utilities in their name.

With the high cost of utilities, you need to make sure that you and your tenants are on the same page when it comes to who is responsible for paying for these. In properties with communal areas, such as a house divided up into three flats with communal stairs and hallways, the common area lighting is usually connected to the nearest flat to that light as the cost of such electricity is minimal. You could reduce this cost still further by installing a timer on the switch so that the light goes out after 20 seconds or so, leaving enough time for the tenant to unlock the door to their flat and enter. Replacing the light bulbs, however, is the landlord's responsibility. It's worth leaving a couple of spare bulbs with one of the tenants so that they can replace them when they burn out and don't bother you every time this happens.

As you revise your policies and rules, indicate the latest revision date in the lower left-hand corner of the document so that your tenants know which rules are the most recent. When you distribute the revised rules, be sure to remind your tenants that these policies and rules supersede any earlier versions. Get signatures from all of your tenants, indicating that they have received and will comply with the new rules.

Reviewing and signing documents

Tenants and landlords alike are usually aware of all the legal paperwork involved in renting a home. And although sifting through all those documents isn't fun for anyone, it is important. Landlords and tenants each have specific legal rights and responsibilities that are outlined in these documents, and being aware of what you're agreeing to – and being sure that your tenants know what they're agreeing to – is crucial.

In this section, we outline the documents you need to go over with your new tenant and which need his signature.

The tenancy agreement

Be sure that your tenant understands that, when he signs your tenancy agreement, he is entering into a business contract that has significant rights and responsibilities for both parties. Before your tenant signs the document, carefully and methodically review each clause of the tenancy agreement.

Certain clauses in the tenancy agreement are so important that you should have the tenant specifically initial them to indicate that he has read these points and understands his rights and responsibilities in relation to them. For example, the clause concerning the need for the tenant to obtain his own home contents insurance policy to protect his belongings should be initialled by the tenant.

Also get your new tenant to initial that he has received the keys for the rental property and acknowledge that you had the locks changed since the last tenant moved out.

Be sure to get the tenant to review and sign any other amendments to the tenancy agreement before taking possession of the rental property.

After the tenant has been given the keys and taken possession of the rental property, getting him to sign your required legal documents can be very difficult. Even if the tenant failed to sign the tenancy agreement, a verbal tenant/landlord relationship is established when you give the tenant the keys to the property – and when you're relying on verbal agreements, you and the tenant are likely to disagree on the terms. Regaining possession of your rental property can be a long and expensive process, so be sure that every adult occupant signs all documents prior to giving your new tenant the keys.

Gas safety certificate

All landlords have a duty to maintain gas appliances in their property through annual inspections and safety checks under the Gas Safety (Installation and Use) Regulations, 1994. A gas safety certificate, which you will have to pay for, must be obtained every 12 months from a fully qualified CORGI engineer (you can find an engineer registered with CORGI – the Council for Registered Gas Installers – in the phone book). The certification should cost in the region of about £60, although it varies from plumber to plumber. Keep a record of these inspections, and any remedial work, in a safe place and make this information available to the tenant on request.

Failure to comply with the regulations can result in a fine or imprisonment. The landlord must produce this record to the tenant when he moves in and within 28 days of each annual inspection. The record must be kept for a minimum of two years from the date of the inspection.

Carbon monoxide poisoning can kill

We know a landlord who had a bad experience letting his first property – so bad in fact that it put him off letting property for life. This cautionary tale is a solemn reminder to other landlords of the importance of ensuring that gas safety checks are carried out religiously every year.

Our friend bought a flat with some money he inherited. His plan was to let out the property to generate some extra income. He repainted and furnished the flat, and in no time at all, he found a young couple, both students, who wanted to rent the property. They moved in and paid their deposit and first month's rent upfront, and everything was going swimmingly.

However, the flat was rather draughty, and after the tenants complained to the landlord, he promised to get double-glazing installed. He also rang a CORGI-registered engineer to apply for a gas safety certificate. The engineer didn't turn up for his appointment, but the glazier did and the double-glazing was installed as promised. The trouble was this meant that, while the new windows kept the cold air out, they also trapped carbon monoxide fumes inside, which were leaking from a faulty boiler that nobody knew about.

Before long, the couple started complaining of drowsiness and feeling sick. It was only when the gas engineer finally showed up that the boiler was condemned. The tenants realised their symptoms were down to carbon monoxide poisoning. Luckily, the problem was detected in time before there were more serious repercussions, but the couple are now suing the landlord.

The moral? Don't forget to have your gas supply regularly checked. It could be the difference between life and death.

Smoke detector agreement

Inform your new tenant of the importance of smoke alarms. The Smoke Detectors Act 1991 states that any property built after June 1992 must have smoke detectors installed on each floor. You may even want to create a separate smoke detector agreement, like the one shown in Form 9-2, to be sure your tenants fully understand the importance of this vital safety equipment and realise that they must take an active role in ensuring that the smoke alarms remain in place, operate properly, and have electrical or battery power in order to protect them in case of smoke or fire.

Many tragic instances have occurred in which fires broke out and tenants had completely removed or disabled the smoke alarms because they were annoyed when they repeatedly went off, triggered by smoking or cooking. Some tenants fail to regularly test the smoke alarms or replace the batteries as needed. Your tenants need to understand that you can only address conditions brought to your attention, so the tenants must be actively involved in ongoing inspections of the rental property to ensure their own safety.

It can be easy for the tenant to forget to check their smoke alarms, so suggest that they test the alarms on the first day of every month. That way they are less likely to forget.

Smoke Detector Agreement

This document is part of the Tenancy Agreement, dated____________ by and between ____________________ (Owner/Agent), and _______________ (Tenant), for the Property located at: ____

In consideration of their mutual promises, Owner/Agent and Tenant agree as follows:

1. The Property is equipped with a smoke alarm/s.

2. Each Tenant acknowledges the smoke alarm/s have been tested and their operation explained by management in the presence of the Tenant at the time of initial occupancy and the alarm/s in the property was working properly at that time.

3. Please be aware that the Tenancy Agreement requires that you as Tenant/s ensure that the smoke alarm/s are operable at all times, to test for correct operation of the smoke alarm/s on a regular basis (perhaps weekly). Also Tenant must replace the batteries with new ones as and when required.

4. If after replacing the battery the smoke alarm does not work, inform the Owner or authorised Agent immediately in writing. Tenant(s) must inform the Owner or authorised Agent immediately in writing of any defect, malfunction or failure of a smoke alarm.

5. In accordance with the law, Tenant shall allow Owner or Agent access to the Property for the purpose of verifying that the required smoke alarm/s are in place and operating properly or to conduct maintenance service, repair, or replacement as needed.

________	__________________	________	______________
Date	Owner/Agent	Date	Tenant

Form 9-2: Smoke Detector Agreement.

Animal agreement

Marketing your rental property to tenants with pets can be very profitable, because you usually have lower turnover and higher rents. If your new tenant has pets, you need to get him to complete and sign an animal agreement, like the one shown in Form 9-3. The animal agreement outlines the policies and rules at your rental property for your tenant's animals or pets.

Dogs, cats, birds, and fish are not the only pets that people keep in their homes. With the broad variety of animals that tenants are known to keep, we have broadened the concept from merely pets to animals in general. A good pet or animal policy clearly outlines exactly which animals are acceptable. It may just be semantics, but you don't want to get to court only to hear your tenants argue that the large pot-bellied pig that trashed your rental property is not subject to your rules because it is not their 'pet'.

Keep current photos of each animal living on your property in the individual files of their owners. This may seem ridiculous, but no matter how large your deposit or how strict your rules, animals have the potential to cause significant damage. Determining the source of the problem can be difficult if you cannot accurately identify the guilty animal.

After they have moved in, tenants may be tempted to take advantage of your policy and bring in additional animals or pets. We have seen the goldfish in the small glass bowl be replaced by a 200-gallon aquarium. Your tenant may decide that the small poodle you agreed to is lonely and needs the company of a Great Dane in your studio flat! Often tenants have very good and heart-warming stories about how they've ended up adding new animals to the mix, but you need to retain control over the number, type, and size of the animals on your property. One way to do this is to actually meet and photograph the animal so there is no doubt as to what you have approved. Also, remember that small puppies can grow into large dogs. Make sure that your policies anticipate the animal at its *adult* size.

Pythons, and piglets, and goats, oh my!

When you have managed rental properties for several years, you will come across tenants who try to get all sorts of pets and animals past you and into your rental property. We know of one landlord who allowed his tenants to have pets but didn't impose any limitations on them. He eventually found out that one tenant had everything from the usual dogs and cats to a large Burmese python and a pot-bellied pig. Another tenant even had two goats living on his small patio. Be sure to strictly define exactly which animals are acceptable – or you could be in for a big, unwelcome surprise.

Animal Agreement

This document is an addendum and is part of the Tenancy Agreement, dated ________________ by and between ________________, (Owner/Agent) and ______________ (Tenant), for the Property located at:
____

In consideration of their mutual promises, Owner/Agent and Tenant agree as follows:

1. The Tenancy Agreement provides that without Owner/Agent prior written consent, no animals whatsoever shall be allowed in or about the Property. Tenant shall not keep or feed stray animals in their rental Property or anywhere in the grounds. Tenant may not allow an animal to be in their rental Property even temporarily. Tenant must advise their guests of this policy prohibiting animals or secure advance approval of the Owner/Agent.

2. Tenant desires to keep the following described animal (see attached photo), herein after referred to as Pet, and represents it as a domesticated dog, cat, bird, fish, or _____________
Said Pet is: Breed: ___________________; Size (Current and Adult Height//Weight): _______________; Colour: _____________
Tenant represents to Owner/Agent that said Pet is not vicious and has not bitten, attacked, harmed or menaced anyone in the past.

3. Tenant agrees to comply with all applicable regulations and laws governing pets. If Pet is a cat, it must be spayed or neutered and Veterinary proof is required. Tenant must provide and maintain an appropriate litter tray, where required, placed in a safe location in the Property. Pet shall not be fed directly on the carpet or any floor covering in the Property. Tenant shall prevent any fleas or other infestation of the Property.

4. Tenant acknowledges and agrees that Owner/Agent may, at any time and in Owner/Agent's sole and absolute discretion, revoke its consent by giving Tenant thirty (30) days' written notice, if Owner/Agent receives complaints from neighbours about Pet, or if Owner/Agent, in their sole discretion, determines that Pet has disturbed the rights, comfort, convenience, or safety of neighbours. Tenant shall permanently remove Pet from Owner's Property upon Owner/Agent's written notice that consent is revoked.

5. If any rule or provision of this Animal Agreement is violated, Owner/Agent shall have the right to demand removal of Pet from the Property upon three (3) days' written notice. Any refusal by Tenant to comply with such a demand shall be deemed to be a material breach of the Tenancy Agreement, in which Owner/Agent shall be entitled to all the rights and remedies set forth in the Tenancy Agreement for violations thereof, including but not limited to, eviction, damages, and solicitor's fees.

6. Tenant agrees that Pet will not be permitted outside Property unless restrained by a lead, cage, or other appropriate animal restraint. Tenant shall not tie Pet to any object outside the Property. Use of the grounds or garden for any sanitary purposes is prohibited and Tenant agrees to promptly clean up after Pet, if necessary.

__________	__________________	__________	__________________
Date	Owner/Agent	Date	Tenant

Form 9-3: Animal Agreement.

Collecting the money

In your meeting with the tenant just before he or she moves in, be sure to get the first month's rent and the deposit, equal to at least one month's rent. You need to collect this money *before* you give the tenants the keys to the rental property. Be sure to give your tenants a receipt for their payments.

Before giving the keys to your new tenant and allowing him to take possession of your property, you need to insist on having the cash in hand through *good funds* (as opposed to *insufficient funds,* where a person writes a cheque and doesn't have the money to cover it in his account). Most owners do this by requiring cash, a banker's draft, or building society cheque. The banker's draft or building society cheque are superior to personal cheques because they represent good funds and, at the very least, won't be returned to you because there was no money to cover them. Consider these bits of advice:

- **Although cash is legal tender, have a firm policy *against* accepting cash, and only accept cash when the tenant moves in or for the monthly rent payment when absolutely necessary.** Regularly collecting cash for your rent can make you a target for crime. Because you will often have tenants moving in on the weekends and in the evenings, you don't want to have cash on you or at your home until you can get to the bank. Cash is also harder to keep track of.
- **Payment of the deposit and first month's rent should be in the form of a banker's draft or building society cheque.** Don't accept a personal cheque because you have no way of knowing whether the cheque will clear. (You also may prefer to insist on a direct debit paid directly to your bank account each month because then the tenant is less likely to forget to pay his rent on time and – unlike cheques – direct debits don't bounce. Either way, be sure to let your tenant know whether your rent collection policy allows him to pay his future monthly rent payments with a personal cheque.)
- **If, despite our advice, your tenant persuades you to accept a personal cheque, then at least don't give him access to the property until you have called and verified with his bank that the cheque will be honoured.** Your best bet is to take the cheque to the tenant's bank and cash it or at least have it certified. If the bank certifies the cheque, it is guaranteeing that sufficient funds are available. In addition, the bank will also put a hold on the funds. Of course, cashing the cheque is the only way you can be certain of collecting your funds, because a devious tenant can always stop payment even on a certified personal cheque.

You can't judge a book by its cover

We know a landlord who has been in the rental management business for many years. He has probably rented to literally hundreds of tenants over the years, enjoying very high occupancy and rarely any uncollected rent. He used to tell us how, over the years, he began to feel as though he could read a person and had even developed a sort of sixth sense to weed out bad applicants as he reviewed their rental applications.

One Saturday afternoon, a very well-dressed woman in her 30s came in to see a flat in a large development in Chester. She drove a sports car and was dripping in expensive jewellery. She looked at a couple of flats our landlord friend owned in the block and then said she would take the larger flat at the back of the property away from the road, because she preferred privacy. She said that she had just arrived in the area and had been staying at a nice hotel nearby, but she was anxious to get settled and wanted to know if she could move in the next day, on a Sunday afternoon. The woman was quite charming and very smooth. So charming, in fact, that this seasoned landlord didn't wait for the results of the credit screening and accepted a personal cheque for all of her move-in funds, even though it was clearly against his policy. Unfortunately, her personal cheque bounced, and it took over two months to evict this lady from the rental property. When the landlord finally got possession of the flat after a lengthy eviction action, he found that this individual was quite a saleswoman – she had installed over a dozen phone lines in her flat for her telemarketing operations.

Inspecting the property with your tenant before the move-in

The number one source of tenant/landlord disputes is the deposit. Many of these potential problems can be resolved with proper procedures even before the tenant takes possession of the rental property by using an inventory, like the one shown in Form 9-4. This form is an excellent tool to protect you and your tenant when the tenant moves out and wants the deposit returned.

The first column of the inventory is where you can note the condition of the property before the tenant actually moves in. The last two columns are for use when the tenant moves out and you inspect the property with the tenant again. Often, you won't immediately know the estimated cost of repair or replacement, so you can complete that portion of the inventory later and then include a copy when you send your tenant the remainder of his deposit.

Inventory

Tenant Name(s) ____

Property Address

____

Move-In Date _______________ Move-Out Date _______________

Tenants have inspected the entire premises both inside and outside, including but not limited to, each item listed on this form. The condition of each item is clean, undamaged, in good working order and adequate for usual and customary residential use unless otherwise noted. Tenants understand and agree that the Condition on Arrival versus the Condition on Departure comments will be compared and that all Tenants will be joint and severally liable for all discrepancies in an item's condition. Tenants also understand that when they move out of the property, the Owner/Manager may make deductions from the deposit for cleaning, repairing, or restoring said items to their move-in condition except for damage caused by ordinary wear and tear. Tenants note that the property must be returned completely clean and that cleaning is not subject to allowance for normal wear and tear. Cross out items that are not applicable. Use additional sheets for bedrooms and bathrooms as necessary.

	Condition on Arrival	Condition on Departure	Estimated Cost Of Repair/Replacement
Kitchen			
Floor covering			
Walls & ceiling			
Windows/locks/blind			
Door			
Light fixtures/bulbs			
Cupboards			
Drawers/worktops			
Sink/taps			
Shelves/drawers			
Stove/oven			
Fridge freezer			
Dishwasher			
Washing machine			
Electric kettle			
Toaster			
Iron			
Ironing board			
4 glass tumblers			
4 mugs			
4 soup bowls			
4 side plates			
4 dinner plates			
4 knives, forks, and spoons			
4 teaspoons			
Wooden spoon			

Form 9-4: Inventory (Page 1 of 5).

Spatula
Sieve
Tin opener
3 saucepans with lids
Frying pan

Living Room
Floors/floor covering
Walls & ceiling
Windows/locks
Curtains
Doors
Light fixtures/bulbs
Cupboards/shelves
Fireplace
Coffee table
Two-seater sofa
Armchair

Dining room
Floor/floor covering
Walls & ceiling
Windows/locks
Curtains/blinds
Light fixtures/bulbs
Cupboards/shelves
Table and chairs
Other

Hallway/Stairs
Floors/floor covering
Walls & ceiling
Windows/locks
Curtains/blinds
Light fixtures/bulbs
Mirror
Rug
Cupboard/shelves
Other

Front entry/Porch
Light fixtures/bulbs
Doorbell
Other

Garage
Floor type/condition
Doors/locks
Light fixtures/bulbs

Form 9-4: Inventory (Page 2 of 5).

Cupboards/shelves
Other

Storage
Exterior
Interior
Loft/basement
Other

Garden
Lawn/trees
Flower beds
Sprinklers/hose
Path
Driveway
Patio
Swimming pool
Spa
Other

Bedroom 1
Floors/floor covering
Walls & ceiling
Windows/locks
Curtains
Cupboards/shelves
Double bed
Bedside table
Chest of drawers
Light fixtures

Bedroom 2
Floors/floor covering
Walls & ceiling
Windows/locks
Curtains
Cupboards/shelves
Wardrobe
Double bed
Bedside table
Chest of drawers
Light fixtures

Bathroom
Floors/floor covering
Walls/tiles/ceiling
Blind
Doors/locks
Light fixtures

Form 9-4: Inventory (Page 3 of 5).

Extractor fan
Cupboards/shelves
Mirrors/cabinets
Power shower
Bath
Sink/toilet
Toilet paper holder
Lavatory brush
Shower curtain
Towel rail
Other

Other items
Boiler
Heating thermostat
Cable TV/TV aerial
Telephone/intercom
Fire extinguishers
Other

Keys/Alarms	**Received**	**Returned**	**Charge for missing key**
Door			
Garage			

Additional items/comments

____
____
____

Move-in comments

____
____
____

Move-out comments

____
____
____

Smoke Alarm(s)

____ By initialling here, Tenants acknowledge that all smoke alarms were tested in their presence and found to be in proper working order. Tenants have been advised as to the proper testing procedure and agree to test the smoke alarm(s) at least once a month and to immediately report any problems to the Owner in writing. Tenants agree not to remove, disable, or remove the batteries from the smoke alarm(s) for any reason and Tenants agree to immediately replace/install all smoke alarm batteries as necessary.

Form 9-4: Inventory (Page 4 of 5).

Burglar Alarm

___ By initialling here, Tenants acknowledge that the alarm system was tested in their presence and found to be in proper working order. Tenants have been advised as to the proper operating instructions and testing procedure and will immediately contact the Owner if there is any malfunction of the system. Tenants have also been given an instruction manual that they have and will read.

Inventory completed upon **move-in** on ____________ at ______, and approved by:
Date Time

____________________________ and ______________________
Owner/Manager

____
Tenants

Inventory completed upon **move-out** on ____________ at ________ and approved by:
Date Time

____________________________ and ______________________
Owner/Manager

____________________________ ______________________
____________________________ Tenants
Tenant's Forwarding Address(es)

Form 9-4: Inventory (Page 5 of 5).

When properly completed, the inventory clearly documents the condition of the rental property upon acceptance and move-in by the tenants and serves as a standard for the entire tenancy. If the tenant withholds rent or tries to break the lease claiming the property needs substantial repairs, you may need to be able to prove the condition of the rental property when they moved in. When the tenants move out, you'll be able to clearly note the items that were damaged or were not left clean by the vacating tenants so you can deduct the necessary money from their deposit.

The inventory is just as important as your tenancy agreement. The purpose of the inspection is not to find all the items that you forgot to check, because you should have already been through the rental property looking carefully to ensure that it met your high standards. The purpose of the inspection is to clearly demonstrate to the tenant's satisfaction that the rental property is in good condition except for any noted items.

The inventory is unique in that you will use the form throughout the entire tenancy – upon initial move-in, during the tenancy (if there are any repairs or upgrades to the rental property), and when the tenant finally vacates the rental property. Be sure to give your tenants a copy of the completed and signed form for their records.

Noting the condition of things

You need to physically inspect all aspects of the rental property with your new tenants and guide them through the inventory. Let the tenants tell you the conditions they observe and make sure that your wording of the noted conditions and comments are detailed and that they accurately describe the conditions. As you note the condition of each item, follow these guidelines:

- **Print legibly and be as detailed and specific as possible.** This may sound obvious, but you'll want to be able to read what you wrote at a later date, and if you're scribbling down things in a hurry, your writing may be difficult to decipher several months later. Try to give as much information as possible for each item, so there is no doubt as to its condition.

- **Note any items that are dirty, scratched, broken, or in poor condition.** Be particularly careful to note any and all mildew, mould, pest, or rodent problems, because these are health issues that must be addressed immediately before the tenant takes possession of the property. If the problems persist after the tenants have moved in, consult with the appropriate licensed professional to evaluate any potential health risk to the tenants and for the necessary response and remedial action.
- **Be sure to indicate which items are in new, excellent, or very good condition.** If the linoleum flooring in the kitchen is new, be sure to indicate that on the form.

Many disputes can be resolved if the inventory specifically notes the condition of the item. If you only comment on dirty or damaged items, a court may conclude that you didn't inspect or forgot to record the condition of a component of the rental property that you are now claiming was damaged by the tenant. You may think that everyone knows and agrees that all items without any notation are in average or okay condition, but the tenant is likely to tell the court that the item was at the very least rather dirty or damaged and that you should not be able to charge her for that item.

- **Be sure to note the condition of the carpets and floor coverings.** This is one of the most common areas of dispute with tenants when they move out of the property. Although tenants should not be charged for ordinary wear and tear, if they destroy the carpet, they should pay for the damage. Indicate the age of the carpet and whether you've had it professionally cleaned as part of your rental turnover process. When a tenant leaves after only six months and has destroyed the carpet, you can be sure that their memory will be that the carpet was old, dirty, and threadbare. The tenant's selective memory will not recall that the carpet was actually brand new or at least in very good condition and professionally cleaned upon move-in!
- **Be specific.** Rather than generally indicate that the oven is 'broken', for example, note that the 'built-in timer doesn't work'. The oven works fine, but the tenants know that they need to use a separate timer and that they will not be held responsible for this specific item when they move out.

You and the tenant should go through the inventory *together* before they move in or as they move out of the property. If it is impossible for you to do this with your tenant, you should complete the inventory and ask all the adult tenants to review and sign the form as soon as possible once they move in.

When used properly, your inventory not only proves the existence of damage in the rental property, but it can also pinpoint when the damage occurred. Don't fall for one of the oldest tenant ploys in the book. Tenants often try to avoid inspecting the rental property with you when they move in because they want to wait and be able to avoid charges for damage that occurs while they are actually moving in. You must ensure that the tenants do check the property and agree that all items are in clean and undamaged condition *before* they start moving in their boxes and furnishings.

If you discover any problems while you are checking the inventory, note them on the form and take steps to have them corrected, unless doing so is not economically feasible. You may, for example, have a hairline crack along the edge of one of the kitchen worktops. If you have decided that refinishing or replacing the worktop would be too costly, just note the condition on the inventory so that your tenants are not charged in error when they move out.

Be sure that your inventory reflects any repairs or improvements made after the initial property inspection. For example, if you and your tenants noted on the form that the bathroom door didn't lock properly, you would have that item repaired; then you would update the inspection form and get your tenants to initial the change. Or you may install new carpeting or make other improvements to the property that should be reflected on the form.

Another excellent way to avoid disputes over deposits is for you to take photos or video the rental property before the tenant moves in. In addition to your inspection form you will have some photos to help refresh the tenant's memory or show the court if the matter ends up there. Here are some suggestions for such a video:

- Be sure to get the tenant on the tape stating the date and time. If your tenant is not present, bring a copy of that day's newspaper and include it in your video.
- With all detailed photography, it's not always easy to understand exactly what the picture is showing unless specifically stated. So be sure to include a caption or descriptions with all still photos and provide a running detailed narrative with the video.

Explaining basic use and care of appliances and utilities

Do not assume that your tenants are familiar with the appliances and how they work. Provide your tenants with photocopies of the appliance manuals as in our experience the originals often go missing.

Part of your new tenant orientation should include showing your tenants exactly where and how to shut off the water at the mains in case of a leak. You should also point out the fuse box, in case a fuse blows. If they smell gas at any time, you should remind them to contact the gas board; they will find the emergency telephone number in the phone book.

Giving your tenant an informational letter

The key to success in managing rental properties is to develop an efficient system that reduces the time you spend managing those properties. A good way to minimise your phone calls from tenants is to provide them with a Tenant Information Letter (see Form 9-5) outlining all your policies and procedures that are too detailed to include in your tenancy agreement. You can also attach information on the proper operation and care of appliances, plus other important information that they should know about the rental property.

Customise the letter to present the policies and procedures you have implemented for each rental property. Although the letter should be customised for each property, here are some of the items to include:

- Property manager's name and contact number, where relevant
- Procedures to follow in case of emergency
- Rent collection information, including when rent is due, how payment is to be made, landlord's bank account details for direct debits, and how late fees and other charges are handled
- Requirements for ending tenancy, including notice requirement
- Procedures for the return of the tenant's deposit
- Handling of new or departing flat- or housemates
- Proper procedure for requesting maintenance and repairs
- Charges for lost keys
- Tenant's home contents insurance requirements
- Guest occupancy policy
- Annual safety inspection information
- Utility shut-off locations, including a separate diagram for the individual property
- Rubbish collection and recycling programme information, where applicable
- Parking policies

Distributing the keys

Key control is a very serious issue, with significant liability for landlords and managers. A problem in key control can allow access to a tenant's rental property, and theft or worse can occur. Keys require careful handling and should be stored only in a safe, if possible.

As the landlord, you're responsible for ensuring that the rental property can be properly secured. Include a five-lever mortice lock and a rim-mounted lock to British Standard BS3621 on the front door. Peepholes should be provided on the main or primary exterior entry door as well.

Tenant Information Letter

Tenant Name (s)____
Property address:

____

Dear ______________________________

We are very pleased that you have selected our property to be your home. We hope that you enjoy living here and would like to share some additional information that will explain what you can expect from us and what we will be asking from you.

1. Owner/Manager:

2. Rent Collection:

3. Notice to End Tenancy:

4. Deposit:

5. Maintenance and Repair Requests:

6. Lockout procedure/Lost Keys

7. Home Contents Insurance:

8. Guest Occupancy Policy:

9. Animal Safety Inspection:

10. Utility shut-off locations:

11. Rubbish collection or recycling programmes:

12. Parking:

Form 9-5: Tenant Information Letter (Page 1 of 2).

Please let us know if you have any questions.
Sincerely,

______________________ ________
Owner/Manager Date

I have read and received a copy of this move-in letter.

______________________ ________
Tenant Date

______________________ ________
Tenant Date

Form 9-5: Tenant Information Letter (Page 2 of 2).

Windows should have locks, particularly if the property is a ground floor flat or a house. However, we recommend that you provide locks for all windows that can be opened. Although not legally required, we recommend installing window locks on upper level windows as a safety device and to minimise the chance that young, unsupervised children could fall from an open window.

For the convenience of your tenants, have a single key that works all entry locks for their particular property.

One of the least desirable aspects of managing rental property is handling calls from tenants who have locked themselves out of the property. When this happens, you usually have to go round to the property to rescue them. The problem is that tenants rarely seem to get locked out of their rental property during the day – for some reason, it always seems to happen at 3:00 a.m. on a Sunday morning. To minimise disputes, inform your new tenants about your policies and charges for when they are locked out or have lost their keys. Set up a policy that acknowledges the difference between being locked out during reasonable business hours and non-working hours. For example, you could charge the tenant £15 for getting locked out between Monday and Friday from 9:00 a.m. to 6:00 p.m. and £25 for all other times.

Changing the locks between tenants is extremely important. Previous tenants may have retained copies of the keys and could return to steal or commit some other crime. You can purchase and install an entirely new lock, or, if you have several rental properties, you may decide for economic reasons to substitute the existing lock set with a spare lock set. Keep several extra lock sets so that you can rotate locks between properties upon turnover. Your new tenant should sign a statement indicating that they are aware that the locks have been changed since the previous tenant vacated the property. Give them a copy of the locksmith's receipt for their records.

The importance of changing locks between tenants

Some stories you hear are truly amazing. One tenant we know lived in a small studio flat in a large block of flats. He was shocked to find out that another tenant had a key to his rental property. Apparently, one of the tenants in the block had loaned his key to his sister who got confused and inadvertently entered the studio flat of our friend. When our friend confronted his landlord, the landlord was not very concerned at all and didn't understand or share the concern of the tenants. He stated that he always used the same locks so that he didn't have to carry around extra keys if he needed access to a rental property in case of emergency!

If you have a master key system for your rental properties, be extremely careful with it. Don't have any extra copies or loan the master key to anyone whom you don't trust implicitly. Although locksmiths are not supposed to duplicate certain keys, remember that an individual who wants a copy of your key to commit a crime is not likely to be concerned that he is illegally copying the key.

Setting Up the Tenant File

You need to be able to immediately access important written records, and one way of doing that is to have an organised filing system to ensure that you don't waste time searching aimlessly for a lost or misplaced document. The best way to accomplish this goal is to immediately set up a new tenant folder for tenants when they move into one of your properties.

Set up a file folder for each rental property with individual files for each tenant. Your tenant file should include the following:

- Rental application
- Rental application verification form
- Credit report
- Background information
- Holding deposit agreement and receipt

- Signed tenancy agreement
- Annual gas safety certificate
- Smoke alarm agreement
- Inventory
- Photos or videos of the unit, taken when the tenant moves in

You'll continue to turn to this file throughout the tenancy, adding to it all new documents such as rent increases, notices of entry, maintenance requests, and correspondence. Keep tenant files for three years after the tenant vacates the property in case of later problems.

Preparing a Welcome Pack for Your New Tenant

Tenant satisfaction and retention are critical to success in rental management. One way to make a positive first impression is to provide your new tenants with a move-in pack. Move-in packs can be very elaborate or just a few inexpensive but thoughtful items.

Give your new tenants a simple move-in pack with a few useful items that they will need. For example, a couple of bottles of mineral water in the fridge, a bar of soap and paper towels in the kitchen, change of address forms, a pad of paper and a pen by the telephone, and a roll of toilet paper in the bathroom can be very handy in the first couple of days when your new tenants have everything packed away in boxes. Menus from the local takeaway pizza place or Indian restaurant can also be useful for tenants who haven't yet unpacked their pots and pans.

Another simple idea that really impresses new tenants is to offer them one or two hours of free maintenance assistance when they first move in. Every new tenant needs to hang a few pictures or install a paper towel holder or some other minor maintenance work that makes him feel at home.

All your efforts to make a great first impression can backfire if there is not a clear understanding of the limitations of your offer or if the handyman you get to do the job is rude, does not provide quality work, or doesn't even show up when he says he will. Provide your new tenants with a list of suggested items for your handyman and make sure you get your tenants to sign a simple disclaimer form waiving their right to sue you or make a claim if your handyman accidentally damages their favourite picture while hanging it on the wall.

Although tenants can usually handle many straightforward plumbing problems, such as a blocked toilet, make sure you instruct your tenant to call you immediately if there is a bigger problem, such as sewage overflow, because this can be a significant health and safety risk. If blockages in the pipes become common, you should immediately call out a professional to correct the problem at your expense.

Chapter 10

Collecting and Increasing Rent

In This Chapter

- Establishing a rent collection policy
- Handling late payments
- Knowing what's involved with pursuing legal action
- Increasing the rent without losing your tenants

If location is the most important element when buying a property, then collecting rent in full and on time is the most important element in managing a buy-to-let investment. But how can you make sure that your tenants will pay their rent on time every month? The reality is that most people who rent do not have significant cash resources, and many live from payday to payday. So if a tenant's pay cheque is delayed or her car breaks down or she has an unexpected major expense, then her ability to pay the rent in full and on time is in jeopardy. And since the tenant's funds are likely to be so tightly budgeted, when she falls even one month behind on rent, catching up again is even more difficult.

However, you can take some steps to increase the likelihood of getting your rent money in full and on time. The key to success in rent collection is establishing policies and procedures and being firm with your enforcement of collecting your rent.

You can begin laying the foundation for successful rent collection even before your property is rented. The best preventive measures you can take to ensure that your tenants have the ability to pay rent include targeting your advertising to responsible tenants (see Chapter 6) and establishing a thorough and careful tenant screening and selection process (covered in Chapter 8).

Review your rent collection procedures with each adult tenant renting your property. Make rent collection a featured topic of your meeting with the tenants prior to the move-in date, when they review and sign the tenancy agreement. Include your rent collection procedures in the informational letter you give to all new tenants as well. This way you can at least be sure the tenant is informed.

Collecting the rent is a key part of property management, as is keeping the rent competitive in your market. Raising the rent to reflect the trends in your area is a necessary part of managing rental properties. Many property owners hesitate to raise the rent for existing tenants, but it can be done well, without risking the loss of your tenants.

In this chapter, we fill you in on what you can do to ensure that you're getting paid on time and that your rent is competitive in your area.

Creating a Written Rent Collection Policy

The fundamentals of property management are very straightforward: you provide the tenants with a clean and comfortable place to live; and they pay the rent, live quietly, and keep the property clean. Problems and confusion can arise, however, if you and your tenant do not understand the rights and responsibilities that come with the tenant/landlord relationship.

Establishing a successful rent collection policy, putting it in writing, and giving it to your tenants in the tenant information letter is the best way to avoid confusion. No single rent collection policy works for *all* landlords, but every policy should cover certain key issues, which we outline in the following sections.

When rent is due

We recommend that you require your tenants to pay the full monthly rent, in advance, on or before the first day of each month. This method is the most common.

Although rent is traditionally paid in full at one time, it is perfectly legal for you and your tenant to agree that the rent is divided up and paid twice a month, every week, or in any other mutually agreed timeframe. Generally, however, try to avoid accepting more frequent payments, because your goal is efficiency, and handling the rent collection process only once each month is definitely more efficient.

You and your tenant can agree that the monthly rent is paid on any mutually agreeable date during the month; rent does not have to be paid on the first of the month. This may make sense if your tenant receives his salary, maintenance payments, or income support on certain dates. For example, you may have a tenant who gets paid on the 10th of each month, so you set the monthly rent due date for the 15th of each month.

Think about the ramifications of accepting rent based on the tenant's scheduled receipt of income rather than your usual rent due date. By accommodating the tenant, you are tacitly acknowledging that the tenant needs that payment in order to afford the rent. But one of the most fundamental issues in the management of buy-to-let property is to avoid tenants who cannot afford the rent. If your tenant needs that income in order to pay your rent that month, no safety net is in place if the tenant's cheque is lost in the post, or his car breaks down, or he is temporarily laid off from his job. To avoid surprises and missed rent cheques, you don't want your tenants to have their finances so tight that they need this month's income to pay this month's rent. Your tenant screening process should provide you with the information so that you can effectively select tenants with enough financial cushion that they are paying this month's rent from cash already on hand as of the first of each month.

Some owners make the rent payable each month on the date the tenant first moved in. If, for example, the tenant moves in on the 25th of the month, her rent is due on the 25th of each future month. This policy is legal and may be acceptable if you have only a few tenants and are willing to keep track of each due date. But having all of your rents due on a single date makes life simpler and avoids confusion or the chance of making an error on legal notices for non-payment of rent.

If your rent due date falls on a Saturday, Sunday, or a Bank Holiday, the tenant should be allowed to pay it by the next business day.

Pro rata rents

Life would be simpler if all your tenants moved in and out only on the first of the month, but they won't. If your tenant's occupancy begins in the middle of the month and you have a rent collection policy that all rents are due on the first of each month, then you need to calculate the pro rata rent from the date she moves in. There are two basic ways to work out the pro rata rent at the beginning of your new tenant's occupancy.

If your tenant moves in towards the end of a month, collect a full month's rent (for the next month), plus the rent due for the additional pro rata portion of the current month. For example, if your tenant takes occupancy on July 25, upon move-in collect seven days' rent for the period of July 25 to July 31 *plus* a full month's rent for the month of August. Your new tenant will usually be glad to do this if there are only a few days pro rata.

However, if your tenant moves in early in a month, expecting him to pay a full month's rent plus the pro rata rent upon move-in may be unreasonable. If your tenant moves in on July 10, for example, he will most likely baulk at your request for payment of seven weeks' rent upon move-in. In these situations, collect a full month's rent prior to move-in and then collect the balance due for the pro rata rent on the first of the next month. For example, prior to your tenant taking occupancy, collect a full month's rent covering the period of July 10 through August 9. Then on August 1, collect the balance of the rent due for August 10 through to August 31, or 22 days. By September 1, the tenant is on track to pay his full rent on the first of each month.

Unless otherwise agreed, rent is normally uniformly apportioned from day-to-day using a 30-day month. Take your monthly rental rate and divide it by 30 to determine the daily rental rate. This formula applies to February as well.

Providing a grace period

Many landlords allow for a grace period that provides tenants with a few extra days to make the monthly rent payment in full before incurring late charges. And most tenants incorrectly believe that if they pay rent within the grace period, their payment is legally on time. However, the rent is due on or before the rent due date and is late from a legal perspective regardless of the terms of the grace period.

Make sure that the tenancy agreement and the tenant information letter are very clear and unambiguous about the fact that the rent is due on or before the first of the month and is technically late even if paid during the grace period.

Grace periods are optional and can be any number of days in length. We recommend that your grace period runs for 7 days after the rent due date, allowing time for any administrative errors with standing orders or direct debits to be corrected or for a missing rent cheque to be reissued.

You do not have to wait until the grace period expires to begin your collection efforts. Rent arrears need immediate action so that the tenant knows he cannot get away with it and you can take appropriate steps at an early stage. Contact tenants who are regularly late paying their rent.

How rent is paid

Your tenancy agreement should clearly indicate how rent is to be paid: by standing order or direct debit, cheque, or cash. Tenants who pay by cash are likely to require a receipt; those paying by cheque, standing order, or direct debit are much less likely to request one.

Standing order or direct debit

Paying rent these days is far easier than in the past when the landlord collected the cash in person or the tenant had to remember to write out a cheque and post it each month. Most tenants pay by standing order or direct debit with a pre-authorised amount deducted from their bank account on a set date each month. The money is transferred directly into your account with the minimum amount of fuss and hassle. And because cancelling a standing order requires some effort on the part of the tenant, he is less likely to try dodging out of his rent payments.

Once a direct debit or standing order is set up, payment is guaranteed (unless the tenant doesn't have money in his account). You are much more certain of getting paid than relying on the tenant to remember to put a cheque in the post.

If you opt for payment by standing order or direct debit, you must regularly monitor your bank account to ensure that rent has been paid on time because mistakes do happen. You don't have to visit your local branch to verify that a payment has been made; you can do it over the telephone or Internet. If you don't check on a regular basis, some time could pass before you realise a payment hasn't reached your account.

Cheques

Tenants can pay by cheque, but this method of payment isn't conducive to getting the rent on time because cheques can be delayed or go missing in the post. You must also go to the trouble of paying a cheque into your account and wait several working days for the funds to clear. Cheques place an additional burden on tenant and landlord when your goal is to simplify the rent collection process for everyone involved.

If you and the tenant agree that he will post the monthly rent to you, you may run into some questions about when the rent is actually considered paid. Is rent considered paid when it is postmarked or when it is received? Have a clear written agreement in your rent collection policy. We recommend that you consider the rent paid when the payment is postmarked. By posting the rent cheque on time, the tenant is acting in good faith, and you don't want to unfairly penalise your tenant if the post is delayed.

Payment by cheque is conditional. If the cheque is not honoured for any reason, it is as if the tenant never paid and late charges should apply.

Never accept second party cheques, such as a pay cheque. Have a policy that all rent payments made after the grace period must be in the form of a bank or building society cheque.

Cash

Avoid cash whenever possible. Turning down cash is always difficult, and your tenants may remind you that cash is legal tender. However, you have the legal right to refuse to accept cash. What's wrong with cash?

- **You become a target for robbery.** Even if you use a safe, you have an increased risk.
- **Accepting cash attracts tenants that may be involved in illegal businesses that deal primarily in cash.** These tenants don't want to have their activities tracked and prefer to rent properties where cash payments are allowed. Don't make your buy-to-let property more attractive to the criminally inclined.

Do not accept even small amounts of cash for rent or late charges. Clearly state in your tenancy agreement that cash is not accepted under any circumstances.

Clearly document all of your income and expenses. The Inland Revenue may become interested in auditing your tax returns if they become aware of frequent cash transactions in connection with an investment property.

Dealing with multiple rent cheques

When you have a number of tenants living in one of your properties, you may receive several cheques for portions of the total rent due. And you may not receive all the rent at the same time or for the proper amount. When you call the tenants, you may hear from one of them that he paid his share and you need to track down one of the other tenants for the money. How your tenants choose to divide the rent between them shouldn't be your problem, however.

Accommodating your tenants and accepting multiple cheques can cause administrative nightmares and lead tenants to erroneously believe that they are not responsible for the entire rent. If your tenants pay by cheque, we recommend that you have a firm policy of requiring one cheque for the entire month's rent.

Besides the administrative convenience for you, this policy has other benefits. Legally, each tenant in your rental property is 'joint and severally' liable for all lease or rental agreement obligations. This means that if one disappears, the others owe you the entire amount. If you allow them to pay separately, they may forget that they are each responsible for the entire amount.

You may also want to have your tenants assume responsibility and take the lead in getting the tardy tenant to pay their rent. Let the responsible tenant know that even if they have already paid a portion of the rent, they will be held responsible for the balance of the unpaid rent. After all, they are in a better position to track down their elusive flatmate than you are.

Dealing with Rent Collection Problems

As a landlord you're not in the banking business. So your tenants must always pay the entire rent due on or before the due date. However, you need to establish policies for the most common problems you will encounter in collecting rent.

These policies outline the specific penalties that are enforced for tenants whose cheques bounce, who fail to pay in full, or who occasionally pay after the due date and the expiration of the grace period, if any. We cover some of these key issues in the following sections.

Collecting late rent

One of the most difficult challenges for a landlord is dealing with a tenant when the rent is late. You don't want to overreact and begin serving threatening legal notices demanding rent, because that tactic will definitely create tension and hostility if a legitimate reason has caused the delay. On the other hand, late rent can be a very serious issue and demands immediate action.

If you are having trouble collecting rent on time, consider mailing your tenants a monthly payment reminder or an invoice.

You can also call your routinely slow rent payers and remind them that the rent is due on or before the first of the month. You can remind your tenants that you expect your rent to be their top priority among their various financial obligations. However, we don't recommend that you call and remind tenants indefinitely, because your time is too valuable to spend chasing your tenants. If they consistently fail to pay the full rent on or before the due date, you may have no alternative but to seek possession of the property if you want to avoid further losses.

The key to keeping your response in line with the magnitude of the problem is to communicate. You need to remain calm and businesslike and determine why the rent is late before taking any action.

The most effective way to collect rent and determine whether you should exercise a little patience is to contact your tenant directly. Simply posting a rent reminder or hanging a late notice on the front door typically doesn't get the job done. Your goal in personally contacting your tenant is not to harass them but to remind them or to work out an agreement to get your rent. Whatever agreement you reach, make sure that it is in writing and signed by the tenant.

Call your tenant at home and at his place of business. Although you may not want to bother the tenant at work, you have a right to know when to expect your rent. You can also go to the property and speak with your tenant directly. Don't be shy, or paying the rent will quickly become a low priority for your tenant.

If you're having trouble tracking down your tenant, check with the neighbours or call the emergency contact listed on their rental application. Check to see whether the utility company has been notified to cancel the utilities; maybe the tenant has done a runner and not notified you.

Charging late fees

Charging tenants late fees when they don't pay their rent on time is one of the most effective ways to encourage on-time payments. Although many landlords have late charges, they are often enforced inconsistently and therefore become ineffective. Other landlords have very long grace periods or set their fees so high that they are unenforceable if challenged in court, so they are often waived. If you institute a late fee, keep these things in mind:

- Late charges can be controversial, and most courts rule that excessive late fees are not enforceable. Implementing and enforcing a late charge policy makes sense, as long as the policy is reasonable and relates to your actual out-of-pocket costs or expenses incurred by the late payment.
- Don't allow tenants to form the impression that your late charge policy approves of late rent payments as long as the late charges are collected. Your late charges should be high enough to discourage habitual lateness, but not so high as to be unreasonable. Send a written warning to those tenants who regularly pay late (even if they pay the late charges) clearly indicating that their late payments are unacceptable and a legal violation of the terms.

Include a Non-Payment of Rent Clause in the tenancy agreement. This clause should allow for a charge if the tenant fails to pay their rent within seven days of the due date. You should also include further charges that will be incurred for subsequent reminder letters if the tenant still fails to pay the rent.

If the tenant's rent is not forthcoming, you should take action, depending on how late it is:

- **Seven days late:** If the rent is not paid within seven days of the due date, it is reasonable to charge £30 for the first letter you send, advising the tenant she will be charged £20 for any subsequent letters if she remains in arrears.
- **Fourteen days late:** You should send a second letter threatening legal proceedings.
- **Twenty-one days late:** Visit the property to persuade the tenant to pay, but be sure not to hassle her.
- **If the rent is still unpaid:** Send a final letter to the tenant reminding her that this is her last opportunity to pay before you begin legal proceedings. (Keep in mind, however, that a mandatory possession order is unlikely to be granted until she has been in rent arrears for at least two months.)

Take legal advice before constructing a reminder letter and deciding on charges for repeat letters.

Handling bounced cheques

Rent cheques that bounce can cause major problems for your collection efforts, so you need to charge tenants a fee when one of their cheques is returned from your bank.

Often, when you contact your tenant, he will have some excuse for the returned cheque and tell you that his cheque will now be accepted. We recommend that you don't try to redeposit the cheque, however. The best policy is to demand your tenant immediately replace a returned cheque with a bank or building society cheque.

If a tenant has a second returned cheque, regardless of the tenant's excuses, require all future payments be made only with a bank or building society cheque, which are guaranteed to have sufficient funds. But tenants can still request a stop-payment on a bank or building society cheque, claiming they were lost or stolen, so be sure to deposit the money straight away.

Like late charges, bounced cheque charges should be reasonable. Try setting the fee at £10 to £20 per cheque, or slightly higher than the amount your bank charges you for the cheque bouncing.

Unless the returned cheque is replaced before the end of your grace period, your tenant is also responsible for late charges.

Dealing with partial rental payments

Occasionally, a tenant won't be able to pay the full rent on time because he has lost his job or for some other reason. The tenant may offer to pay a portion of the rent that is due with a promise to catch up as the month proceeds. Your written rental collection policy should not allow partial payments of rent, and deviating from this policy is generally not a good idea.

However, in some instances, allowing for partial rent payments may make sense. If your tenant has had an excellent rental payment history and you can verify that this is a one-off, then you are probably safe in accepting a partial rent payment. Of course, you need to be careful and watch for the tenant who is delaying the inevitable and stalling you from pursuing your legal options.

If you do come to a mutually acceptable arrangement of accepting smaller rent payments with additional amounts, which increase over time to pay off the arrears over a period, you need to set out a plan of action in writing. Include timescales for payments and back payments of arrears.

In most cases, the acceptance of a partial payment voids any prior legal notices for non-payment of rent. If your tenant is causing trouble besides the late rent, do not accept any partial payments, or you'll have to begin your eviction proceedings from scratch – and you can be sure that they will be difficult to serve again.

Try to establish what is likely to happen in the future. If the tenant's situation is likely to be temporary, you may decide that it's worth seeing it out. But if you think your tenant's situation is unlikely to improve, you may want to cut your losses and seek possession of the property in order to avoid larger losses further down the line.

Advise your tenant to seek assistance if she has difficulty paying her rent. The Citizens' Advice Bureau is a good place to start for advice as to whether she qualifies for Housing Benefit, Council Tax Benefit, Jobseekers Allowance, or Income Support.

Be sure to apply your rent collection policies, including your late charges, partial payment, and bounced cheque policies, consistently with all your tenants if a number of them are living in the same property. If you don't, you could be accused of discrimination by simply allowing some tenants to pay late or by accepting multiple cheques from some tenants and not from others.

Housing Benefit

Housing Benefit enables people on low incomes to pay their rent and is not directly linked to whether they are working or receiving Jobseekers Allowance. Many landlords prefer not to take on tenants who receive Housing Benefit. But there is an advantage to letting your property to a tenant receiving Housing Benefit because the local authority can arrange for this money to be paid directly to you, with the tenant's consent.

The amount of Housing Benefit a tenant receives depends on his or her income and savings. A rent officer may also assess the rent you are charging to compare it with prices charged by landlords with similar properties in the area.

A rent officer from the Housing Benefit department will carry out a pre-tenancy determination if you want to find out the maximum amount of rent that will be met by Housing Benefit.

Serving legal notices

If you're having trouble collecting rent from one of your tenants, you may need to pursue legal action. If your tenant is on an assured shorthold tenancy agreement with a term of six months, it may be possible, depending on how long he has lived in the property, to wait until the mandatory possession notice can be served in the normal way.

Mandatory possession is possible where the tenant is a full two months in arrears both at the time of service of the notice and at the actual court hearing. In the case of a weekly tenancy, the tenant must be a full 13 weeks in arrears.

Increasing the Rent

Raising the rent is one of the most difficult challenges landlords face. If you need to raise the rent, you may be worried that the tenant will leave, or you may not even know how much to increase the rent by.

Even if you're raising the rent for the first time in several years, most tenants will naturally have a very negative reaction to the rent increase. So you need to do your homework and make sure that your rent increase is reasonable and justified. When the rental market is tight, you should adjust your rents by small amounts with greater frequency rather than a very large increase more sporadically. Most tenants won't leave over a small rent increase.

Deciding when and how much

You can review the rent as often as specified in the tenancy agreement. If the agreement is for a fixed term, say 6 or 12 months, the rent usually remains the same for the duration of the contract. But you can review the rent at regular intervals during the tenancy, as long as you have a clause in the tenancy agreement stating this.

Normally, you can raise the rent as much and as often as your good business judgement and the competitive rental market allows. Of course, don't be too aggressive, or you'll lose your best tenants. Trying to get that extra £50 a month over and above what is reasonable could frighten off your tenant, leaving you with significant turnover costs plus lost rent while you hunt for a new one.

The best policy is to regularly review and survey the rental market to determine the current market rate for comparable rental properties – ones that are of similar size and condition and that have the same features and amenities. Turn to Chapter 5 for more information on evaluating the competitive rental market and setting rents.

Many wise landlords intentionally keep their rents slightly below the maximum the competitive rental market allows as a policy to retain the best tenants. Unless planning a major upgrade of your property with more upmarket tenants and much higher rents, tenant turnover is usually bad business.

Be careful when raising the rent so that you are not accused of imposing rent increases out of spite in response to something the tenant did or because you want to encourage the tenant to leave the property. As always, your best defence is to have a sensible rent increase policy, keep good records, and be consistently fair and equitable with all of your tenants.

Informing the tenant

The tenant must receive a month's notice of any increase in rent. If the tenant agrees to the increase, she should start paying it from the date specified at the end of the notice period. If the tenant doesn't agree to the increase, she must apply to a rent assessment committee, who decide what the rent should be. This application must be made before the date on which the new level of rent is due.

Rent assessment committees are independent of central and local governments and usually comprise three people, including a chairperson, surveyor, and someone who doesn't have any specialist knowledge of the market. They decide what the maximum rent should be, using comparable properties in the area and documents provided by you and your tenant. The committee may agree that the proposed rent is fair or suggest a lower or higher rate. The rate set by the committee is the legal maximum you can charge your tenant and restricts you from increasing the rent for another year.

Although you are legally required to give only a month's notice of a rent increase (if the rent is paid on a monthly basis), we recommend a minimum rental increase notice of 45 days. If the rent increase is significant (10 per cent or more), a 60-day written notice is advisable. Some owners fear that giving their tenant notice of a rent increase also gives them plenty of time to find another property. However, if you've set your increased rent properly you want your tenant to have the opportunity to compare the new rental rate to the market conditions rather than just overreact with a notice to vacate. If possible, inform your tenant personally of the pending rent increase and be sure to follow up by legally serving a formal written notice and keeping a copy in the tenant's file. The letter doesn't have to be a literary work, but you may consider attaching any market information obtained from your market survey so that your tenant can see that you have made an informed decision.

Sweetening the pill

Before increasing the rent, be sure to determine whether you will make improvements to the property to sweeten the pill. We suggest that you set a budget equivalent to three to six months of the rent increase and plan on making an immediate upgrade to the tenant's property. Often, just painting and cleaning or replacing the carpet can help your tenant accept the rent increase. Installing new light fixtures are usually appreciated as well and needn't cost too much money.

Chapter 11

Keeping Good Tenants – and Your Sanity

In This Chapter

- Retaining your tenants by knowing what they want and making sure they get it
- Knowing whether renewing a tenancy agreement is the best option for you and your tenant

The key to your success as a landlord is an occupied rental property. But this basic fact is something many landlords quickly forget.

Although advertising your vacancy, having a well-polished presentation, knowing all the latest sales-closing techniques, implementing a thorough tenant-screening programme, and moving in your prized tenant with amazing efficiency are all important parts of your job, the reality is that the day your tenant moves in is the day your most important job – keeping your good tenants satisfied and happy – begins.

Your goal is to have your tenants stay and pay. If you offer a quality rental property at a reasonable price, you'll have lower turnover than other rental properties in your area.

You can retain your quality tenants and have a lower turnover rate by treating tenants with the same personal attention and courtesy you demonstrated when you first spoke to them on the phone or gave them a tour of the empty property.

Knowing what your customers want is really the key to success in any business, and as a landlord, your tenants are your customers. In this chapter, we let you know what most tenants are looking for when renting a property so you can make sure you're meeting those needs. We also give you some tips on getting to the point where your tenants not only enjoy their experience at your property but also want to renew their tenancy agreement and stay longer.

What Tenants Want

If you're trying to raise your level of tenant satisfaction (and that should always be your goal), you need to determine what your tenants want and work out how to make sure they get it. Your tenants are basically looking for the following:

- Timely and effective communication
- Professional maintenance of the interior and common areas
- Respect for their privacy
- Fair and consistent policies and rules, as well as equal enforcement of them
- Reasonable rent in relation to what they're getting for their money

These crucial demands are covered in the following sections.

Timely and effective communication

A variety of issues concern most tenants – and those issues are usually fairly obvious. Good tenants don't like loud or noisy neighbours, unkempt common areas, broken or unserviceable items in their rental property, or unsubstantiated rent increases on a regular basis. But the good news is that most of these problems can be solved if you communicate well with your tenants.

The one problem that tenants will not ignore is a landlord's apathy. If you seem uncaring or nonchalant about your tenant's concerns, he will get the message that you don't value his business. The perception of apathy is often created by an unwillingness or failure to communicate. If you give your tenants the impression that you only care about them when their rent is late, you're headed straight down that apathy path.

Keep your tenants informed. No one likes surprises, and tenants are no different. If the pest control company cancels its routine appointment to check the property, let your tenant know right away. If the handyman you have employed to fix a broken shower door can only visit the property earlier in the day than previously arranged, call, or e-mail your tenant to avoid an unwelcome and inconvenient surprise. Common courtesy goes a long way.

Quick responses to maintenance requests

One way to set *your* rental property apart from your competition is to handle tenant maintenance requests quickly and professionally. Promptly resolving your tenants' problems will keep them happy.

Speed is of the essence

After a new tenant moves in, if he notes any problems, don't view these complaints as negatives. Instead, think of them as opportunities to let your tenant know that you care. By quickly and professionally addressing the problem, you actually improve your tenant relations. Successful landlords don't have to be perfect; they just need to admit the mistake or problem, communicate openly and candidly, and take the necessary steps to resolve it.

Rental property owners often also overlook punctuality when it comes to making repairs. Undoubtedly, you're a very busy person, but it's easy to lose sight of the fact that your tenants are busy, too. If you tell your tenants that you will call or meet them at a certain time, be sure to be there when you said you would – or at the very least, call and let them know if you're running late. Ensure that your letting agent, handyman, or contractors treat your tenants with the same level of respect as well.

Treating your tenants as important customers can be the best decision you ever make. When trying to solve a tenant's concern or complaint, try to ask yourself how you would want to be treated. Treating your tenants as you want to be treated makes your tenant relations much more pleasant, and you dramatically decrease your tenant turnover and improve your net income – a win-win situation for all!

The appliance of science

One of the most common complaints about landlords is that they are unwilling to maintain, and especially upgrade, their rental properties for the current tenants. In our experience, tenants have a valid complaint. Refusing to repaint, recarpet, or upgrade the appliances for a great tenant makes no sense. Because if you don't do it for the great tenant you already have, and that tenant is frustrated with your lack of effort and moves out, you'll have to do the work anyway in order to be competitive in the rental market and attract a new unproven tenant.

Respect for your tenants' privacy

One of the biggest complaints most tenants have is a landlord who fails to respect the tenant's privacy.

You can only enter the premises with advance written notice or the tenant's permission, except in case of an emergency. Although you only need to give tenants a minimum of 24 hours notice for access to the property, that isn't enough to maintain a positive and mutually respectful relationship with your tenants. Even though you own the rental property, the last thing you want your tenant to feel is that their home isn't really theirs. If you don't respect the privacy of your tenants in their own home they will be less likely to show respect for you or your rental property during or at the end of their tenancy.

If possible, you should only enter the property during normal business hours. We recommend limiting your request for entry to Monday to Saturday from 8:00 a.m. to 7:00 p.m., unless the tenant requests or voluntarily agrees to a different time.

Enforcement of house rules

A frequent source of tenant complaints is the landlord's failure to enforce reasonable policies and rules.

Good tenants actually *want* and *appreciate* fair and reasonable policies and rules. They know that, if they are quiet and respectful of their neighbours, their neighbours are more likely to treat them the same way. Establishing standard policies and house rules for your rental properties and enforcing them fairly is all part of the job of managing rental property.

Tenants talk to one another, and if you have several properties in the same block or area, they will quickly discover if you have different rules for different tenants. Inconsistent or selective enforcement of rules has legal implications as it can be seen as a form of discrimination. For example, you may think that waiving a late fee for a tenant you've known for years but charging the late fee to a new tenant in similar circumstances is okay. After all, you've known the first tenant longer, and you're willing to forgive that oversight once in a while, right? Wrong. You can't have different interpretations of the rules, because the legal consequences you may face are severe. You can find out more about discrimination and legal matters in Chapter 8.

Fair rent and increases

Rent increases are always unpopular, and if you don't handle them properly, they can easily lead to increased tension and tenant dissatisfaction. No one likes to pay more, but we all know that the good things in life aren't cheap. Most tenants don't mind paying a fair and competitive rent as long as they're sure you're not plaguing them with unnecessary rent hikes. As long as the increase keeps your rent in line with that charged by landlords with similar properties in your area, your tenants probably won't object. If you are raising it by more than the rent charged on similar properties, you should think of a couple of sweeteners such as repairs or improvements, to justify the increase.

Although they may initially be upset with the increase, your tenants may be thinking to themselves that you will now finally be able to address the peeling paint and faded curtains. And if your rental property has peeling paint and old, tatty curtains and you've just increased the rent, you'd better be sure to address those problems right away, not months down the road, if you want your tenants to be satisfied.

There is nothing wrong with increasing your price – after all, you're running a business, not a charity. But common sense and prudence dictate that you explain to your tenants the reasons for the rent increase and what benefits are in it for them.

Renewing Tenancy Agreements

Tenancy agreement renewals are a sign that you're doing a good job at keeping your tenants satisfied and meeting their needs. Of course, renewing tenancy agreements is also one of your most productive activities as a landlord.

Tempting your tenant to stay

Give your tenant a list of items or property upgrades and let the tenant choose which upgrade she wants. These could include a new carpet in the lounge, a new microwave or replacing the old tiling in the bathroom. This way, you send the message that you value her input and strive to reward her business.

In a competitive rental market with increasing rents, most tenants who intend to stay will be glad to renew their current tenancy agreement or even sign a new one at a higher, but still reasonable, rent. Renewing a tenancy agreement in a strong rental market may not be in your best interest, however, because it prevents you from raising the rent or changing any terms during the period covered by the new agreement. Plus, with a tenancy agreement in place, evicting a problem tenant is much more difficult.

Unless your tenancy agreement contains an automatic renewal clause, it expires on the date specified. If you want your tenant to stay, don't be afraid to approach her and ask her to sign another tenancy agreement effective from when the current one expires. Contact your tenant at least a couple of months before the tenancy agreement expires.

If the tenant moves out, you'll incur extensive turnover costs for maintenance, painting, and cleaning, plus you'll lose rent for every day the rental property is empty. So why not make a few upgrades to the rental property a couple of months before the tenancy agreement expires, just as a reminder that you care about the tenant's satisfaction.

Better the devil you know

Of course, not all tenants are good candidates for tenancy agreement renewal, but renewing an agreement with a current tenant clearly has an additional benefit over taking on a new tenant. After all, you have a track record with your current tenant; you know her rent payment history and whether she treats the property and her neighbours with respect. And you can never be 100 per cent sure of that kind of information when you're starting from scratch with someone new.

Plus, your tenant knows what to expect from you as a landlord. She knows your standards for maintaining the property, your interest in and response to her requests, your policies and rules (and whether they're fairly enforced), and the level of courtesy and respect you have for her privacy. Your tenant is familiar with you, and as long as you're willing to be competitive with the rent you charge, staying is in her best interests.

House buying – the end of the rental line

One of the most common reasons tenants leave or don't renew their tenancy agreement is their intention to purchase a home. Although home ownership is a very worthy goal, you may want to advise your tenants about other options and whether, given their particular overall financial situation, they'd be better off renting rather than buying. Letting your tenants know about their options – without discouraging them from buying if that's really best for them – makes sense.

Chapter 12

Dealing with Problem Tenants

In This Chapter

- Knowing how to handle common tenant problems
- Using mediation or arbitration to resolve conflicts with your tenants
- Handling the eviction process
- Being prepared for everything – from tenant bankruptcy to tenant death

Although the proper tenant screening and selection techniques greatly improve your success in picking good tenants, they aren't a guarantee. As a landlord you are eventually going to come across a problem tenant or two. Some tenants don't pay their rent, disturb the neighbours, damage the property inside and out, or keep a growing collection of old bangers on the front lawn, and you need to take immediate steps to remove them from the rental property and replace them with someone else. But other tenants – like the one who pays his rent a few days late every single month, or the one who sneaks in an animal even though pets aren't allowed – are more subtle in the problems they present, and their behaviour may not warrant eviction.

In this chapter, we give you tips for handling some common tenant problems and let you know about valuable alternatives to evictions. Plus, we prepare you for some unusual situations that you may encounter with your tenants and let you know how to deal with them.

Recognising and Responding to Common Tenant Problems

The level of response you have toward a problem tenant depends on how severe the problem is and how frequently it occurs. Some issues – including non-payment of rent, additional occupants not on the tenancy agreement, noise or disturbances, and threats of violence or intimidation – are breaches of the tenancy agreement and clearly call for action. You should document non-payment of rent along with other breaches of the tenancy agreement in writing, using a Tenancy Agreement Violation Letter, like the one shown in Form 12-1.

Whenever you have a problem with a tenant, documenting the problem is critical. Even minor problems are worth documenting, because over time, they may add up or increase in severity. If you find yourself needing to evict a tenant, having written proof of how long the problem has dragged on is necessary, especially if the matter comes to court.

Tenancy Agreement Violation Letter

____
Date

____
Name
____
____
Address

Dear ______________________________________

This is a formal reminder that your Tenancy Agreement does not allow:
____
____

It has come to our attention that recently or beginning _____________________ and continuing to the present, you have broken one or more terms of your Tenancy by:
____
____
____
____

It is our sincere desire that you will enjoy living in our rental property. To make sure this happens, we enforce the Policies and Rules and all terms and conditions of your Tenancy Agreement. So please immediately:
____
____
____
____

If you are unable to promptly resolve this matter, we will exercise our legal right to begin eviction proceedings.

Please feel free to contact us if you would like to discuss this issue.

Sincerely,

____
Owner/Manager

Form 12-1: Tenancy Agreement Violation Letter.

Late payment of rent

One of the toughest issues you'll encounter is how to deal with a tenant who is consistently late in paying her rent. In other respects, the tenant may not create any problems, but she just can't seem to get the rent in on time. You may have even had to serve a Notice of Non-payment of Rent in order to get the tenant to pay – and even then, she may have not included the late charge. In our experience, this nagging problem won't go away unless you put a stop to it; check out Chapter 10 for more information on dealing with rent collection problems.

When you're faced with a tenant who just can't seem to pay her rent on time, you have many factors to consider (such as whether the tenant is creating any other problems for you). But the strength of the rental market is usually the most important issue. If it's a tenant's market and you know that finding another tenant to rent the property will be difficult, you may be willing to be more flexible and tolerant.

Even if you know you'd have trouble finding another tenant, you shouldn't ignore the problem of a tenant who consistently pays late. Clearly inform the tenant in writing that she has breached the tenancy agreement – and be sure to do so each and every time she pays late. If you fail to enforce your late charges, the tenant can later argue that you've waived your rights to collect future late charges. Be sure to let the tenant know in writing that very late payments are grounds for eviction – even if you're not necessarily willing to go that route just yet.

Additional occupants

Tenants frequently abuse the guest policy by moving additional occupants into their rental property for extended periods of time. But you may have trouble determining the difference between a temporary guest and a new full-time live-in occupant.

If you suspect that your tenant has moved an additional occupant into his rental property, your first step should be to talk to your tenant to find out what's going on. Get your tenant's story before jumping to any conclusions. This policy is sound not only because it's considerate, but also because you need to be careful to avoid claims of discrimination, particularly if the additional occupants are children.

If you find that the tenant is not in compliance with your guest policy, immediately send him a Tenancy Agreement Violation Letter in which you should indicate that he must ensure the additional occupant leaves as soon as possible or be formally added to the tenancy agreement as a tenant, as long as the property has room for another tenant. If the new occupant is an adult, that person must complete a rental application, go through the tenant screening process, and sign the tenancy agreement if approved. If the tenant fails to co-operate, you may need to take legal action.

Inappropriate noise levels

You usually hear about a noisy tenant from one of the tenant's neighbours. Some landlords we know who live near their rental properties often ask the neighbouring tenants to call them when the problem tenant is generating unacceptable noise levels and then go round themselves to investigate. The advantage of this policy is that you are witnessing first-hand the extent of the problem – information which can be useful when speaking to the noisy tenant. In such a scenario, it is also quite useful to knock on the tenant's door to have a word with them while the music is blaring because the tenant will find it harder to deny that the noise is excessive. If the problem continues, you should issue a written warning.

Most local councils have a special unit known as a *noise patrol.* You can find details of this out-of-hours service in your telephone directory. The noise patrol is responsible for coming out and checking complaints about excessive noise levels. If the tenants continue to cause problems with loud music or continual parties late into the night, the neighbouring tenants may well have to call out the noise patrol to monitor the level of noise, particularly if talking to the noisy tenants about the problem doesn't make any difference.

Encourage tenants to air any grievances they may have about their neighbours, who are also your tenants, in the first instance by writing to you. Neighbours usually don't want to go to court to testify; they just want you to quickly solve the problem and allow them to keep their anonymity. But if the noisy tenant disputes the charges, the courts are usually reluctant to accept your unsubstantiated testimony – and the neighbour's testimony becomes critical. Evidence from your local council's noise patrol, if they have to be called in, and a written complaint made at the same time by a neighbour, carry a lot of weight.

Unsupervised children

Tales of young children being left home alone while the parents go off on a two-week holiday or simply being left all day while the parents go to work, are, sadly, becoming all too common. If your tenants have children, one of the toughest dilemmas you'll face is dealing with a tenant's young child who may be left unsupervised at your rental property. While the general rule for landlords is not to interfere with how their tenants lead their lives as long as they pay the rent on time and look after your property, the issue of unsupervised children is a difficult one.

If the child is unsupervised and you have been alerted to the fact but don't do anything and the young child gets hurt, you could be in trouble for failing to take reasonable action. Yet if you don't handle the matter properly, the tenant may claim that you're discriminating against families with children, and you'll need to be able to prove that you acted reasonably and consistently.

If you become aware of an unsupervised child at your rental property, immediately contact the child's parents. If you can't get hold of them, call social services. If you do get hold of the parents but the problem occurs again, send a letter to your tenants warning them of the seriousness of the matter. If the written notice isn't effective, you can always call the police or social services while advising your tenant in writing that an eviction may be warranted.

If your tenants fail to properly supervise their children and the children damage your rental property, don't just talk to the children about the problem. Immediately contact the tenants and officially advise them of the problem, stressing the fact that property damage by tenants of any age is unacceptable. This kind of action is usually sufficient, but if the damage is severe or continues, notify the tenants in writing and bill them for the damage; also warn them that any continued problems will result in eviction.

Exploring Alternatives to Eviction

Evictions are not only expensive but emotionally draining as well. They can be costly in terms of lost rent, legal fees, property damage, and turnover expenses. And they can earn a negative reputation for your rental property with good tenants in the area. So be sure to evaluate each situation carefully and only turn to eviction as a last resort.

When you're looking for an alternative to evicting a problem tenant, don't underestimate the importance of communicating with your tenant. And for your records, make a note of any conversations you have or agreements you reach.

If the most likely outcome of a problem with a tenant is an expensive and time-consuming eviction, do your best to minimise or cut your losses. A County Court Judgement (CCJ) against a tenant without any assets won't help your cash flow, but a non-paying or bad tenant is much worse than no tenant at all. Your primary goal should be to regain possession of the rental property and find a new tenant as quickly as possible.

Negotiating a voluntary move-out

You may be able to negotiate an agreement with your tenant whereby she voluntarily moves out of the rental property. Some landlords have negotiated agreements with their problem tenants, in which they (the landlords) forget about the unpaid rent if the tenant agrees to leave by a mutually agreed upon date. Other owners have agreed to refund the tenant's full deposit immediately after the tenant has vacated the property (as long as no significant damage has been done to the property). Although you may feel strongly that your tenant should keep her side of the tenancy agreement, a voluntary move-out may work to your advantage if you can avoid legal action and don't have to worry about the problem anymore.

While legal action may be daunting, don't be afraid to start legal proceedings against a tenant if that's the only solution left. You may well need to threaten legal proceedings at some stage in order to get what you want – if this is the case, you must be prepared to act on your threat otherwise you'll lose face, and you won't ever get your money.

Never count on a verbal agreement. Any voluntary agreement to move out must be in writing.

Using mediation or arbitration services

If you aren't able to reach an agreement with your tenant on moving out voluntarily, consider taking your dispute to a neutral third-party mediator or arbitration. *Mediation* is an informal opportunity for both parties to resolve their disputes with the assistance of a local mediation group at little or no cost. Often confused with mediation, *arbitration* is legally binding and enforceable and can be a relatively quick and inexpensive alternative to legal action. Mediation typically involves only the parties to the dispute (you and your tenant), whereas arbitration often uses solicitors, witnesses, and experts. Many organisations offer both mediation and arbitration services, so if mediation does not resolve the issue, you can always try arbitration.

Taking your tenant to court

Your nearest county court is the place to go if you have problems with tenants caused by non-payment of rent or if you want to evict a tenant. Speak to a court official who can explain the procedure to you; remember, though, that they can't give legal advice. Many cases relating to property rental are heard in the small claims court, which is part of your local county court. You should go to the small claims court if you're claiming £5,000 or less.

Evicting a Tenant

Unfortunately, some tenants just don't pay their rent; others break the rules or are involved in criminal activities. In these situations, after you've explored your other options, you may have no other reasonable alternative but an eviction. The eviction process can be intimidating and costly, but keep in mind that allowing the tenant to stay only prolongs the problem.

Serving legal notices

The law states that non-paying or unsatisfactory tenants can be evicted after eight weeks of behaviour that directly defies their tenancy agreement. In order to evict a tenant, you have to instruct a solicitor to serve an eviction notice on your tenant, which must be handed to her in person. You have to pay for this service; be aware that you may not recover your money. If your tenant does not leave or pay up what she owes of her own accord, the next step is to take her to court, if you think doing so is worth it.

Taking a tenant to court is now a quick, simple, and straightforward process. County Court actions can even be conducted online these days at `www.moneyclaim.gov.uk/csmco2/index.jsp`. You don't need to be afraid: just tell yourself that you are owed money, and tenants who don't pay their rent or damage rented property shouldn't be allowed to get away with it.

Going to court

If your tenant has fallen into rent arrears, you may feel that an accelerated possession procedure (see "Accelerated possession" later in this chapter), is not for you if you want to recover outstanding rent as with this procedure you can only regain possession of the property and the costs of bringing the action. If the rent is late, write to the tenant immediately, saying that the rent doesn't seem to have been paid. It may be a simple mistake; perhaps the tenant just forgot to do it or she had a mix-up with her bank account. If the tenant puts the situation right immediately, that should be the end of the problem. But if you don't get a response, write to the tenant again, giving her 14 days to pay the amount in full and stating that, if she fails to do so, court proceedings will be instigated.

Nobody wants a CCJ (County Court Judgement) against them – see 'Exploring Alternatives to Eviction' earlier in this chapter if you're not sure what this is – because it makes renting another property or getting any form of credit very hard. Any right-minded tenant will want to avoid that scenario at all costs and may well pay the money owed before it comes to court.

If they don't, you must fill out a form, available from your local county court, detailing the amount you are owed in arrears, plus any damage to the property or goods stolen. You'll be charged a court fee, calculated on a sliding scale and depending on the amount owed. If you win your case, you get this money back from the tenant.

The court then sends the completed form to the tenant. He can either pay up there and then, counterclaim, or let the judge decide the outcome of the matter at a court hearing.

If the tenant simply can't afford to pay you, the courts say that there is no point in taking legal action in the first place to get back the money he owes you in unpaid rent. A judge can order the money to be paid, but it is up to you to enforce this judgement.

If you have started legal proceedings against a tenant, never discuss the matter with them in person or on the phone. The conversation could turn nasty or the tenant could try to emotionally blackmail you into giving more time or another chance. If you can, distance yourself from the conversation and tell the tenant that the court will decide on the outcome.

Accelerated possession

It doesn't have to end up in court. An *accelerated possession procedure* enables tenants to be evicted without a court hearing, purely on the basis of a written representation. Such a procedure does not include a claim for rent owed to you however, so if your tenant owes you a lot of money this procedure may not be the best solution for you. But it is a means whereby bad tenants can be evicted – and quickly.

You can use this procedure where the tenancy is of the Assured Shorthold kind, claiming possession under Section 21 of the Housing Act 1998. If your tenant has an Assured Tenancy dating back to before 1997 you can use this procedure under Section 8 of the Housing Act. Whichever tenancy agreement you have, you must supply reasonable grounds for taking the action. See Chapter 5 for more details on Assured Shorthold Tenancies.

Under Section 21, reasonable grounds include:

- The tenancy was for a fixed period, which has expired.
- The existing tenancy is for an unspecified period.
- You have given your tenant at least two months written notice under Section 21, informing him that you wanted possession of the rental property.

Claiming under Section 8 of the Housing Act 1988 is more complicated and more limited. Grounds include:

- The property is your main home and you want to reclaim it.
- You intend to live in the property as your main home.
- The tenancy was a holiday let, let to students, or is now needed as a residence by a minister of religion.

Where these grounds apply, you must give your tenants at least four months notice before the end of the tenancy. If he still fails to vacate the property, you then need to file your application to the court, along with all the papers required, including a copy of your tenancy agreement after the four months are up. The tenant is given 14 days to reply. If an order for possession is made, the tenant is normally told to leave the property within 14 days. The court may extend this period for up to six weeks maximum if the tenant can prove that to leave within this timeframe would cause exceptional hardship.

Because an accelerated possession procedure is carried out purely on written evidence, all of your documents must be in order. The tenancy agreement must be written and can't be verbal.

Enforcing County Court Judgements

If a CCJ is made against the tenant for non-payment of rent, the judge decides how much the tenant needs to pay you back. If the tenant doesn't pay, she could be paid a visit by a bailiff with the legal authority to remove the goods to sell to pay off the debt she owes you. Alternatively, the judge may decide that the debt should be deducted in instalments from the tenant's wages or benefit.

Knowing What to Do in Unusual Tenant Situations

After a year or so as a landlord, you may begin to think that you've seen it all, but there are always some new and interesting twists that keep a landlord's work challenging. Knowing how to handle these unusual, yet surprisingly common, situations, some of which we cover in the following sections, can make life much easier.

Bankruptcy

One last-ditch effort some tenants make when they're in financial trouble is to file for bankruptcy. Many landlords are dealt a severe financial blow when a tenant files for bankruptcy during the eviction process.

When the bankruptcy action has been filed, your court eviction proceeding cannot be filed or completed because the bankruptcy results in an automatic *stay* (halting) of the eviction. As soon as you become aware of the bankruptcy, you must stop any collection or eviction efforts. If you don't, you are subject to severe penalties. You will have to deal with the Official Receiver requesting permission to continue to proceed with the eviction. (The Official Receiver is a civil servant and an officer of the courts, appointed as an interim receiver or provisional liquidator to protect a debtor's property or take control of a company's affairs pending the hearing of the outcome of a bankruptcy petition.)

Even if you routinely handle your own legal work, instruct a solicitor to handle all tenant bankruptcy matters.

Sitting tenants

Another difficult challenge often faced by landlords is when a tenant fails to vacate the rental property as mutually agreed or at the end of the tenancy agreement. Unless you accept rent, tenants who continue to live at the property are referred to as *sitting tenants.* The eviction process can still go ahead in the usual manner, but it could take longer, particularly if the tenancy agreement was not correctly drafted.

If you accept rent, you have agreed to a continuation of the tenant's rental, generally on at least a month-to-month basis. So if your intention is to evict the tenant, you should not accept any rent that may be offered to you.

Broken tenancy agreements

Although you may occasionally be faced with a tenant who won't leave as agreed, you will certainly encounter a tenant who leaves before the expiration of his tenancy agreement and doesn't want to pay the balance of his financial obligation to you.

First confirm that the tenant has indeed given up his right of possession. Then take reasonable steps to mitigate or limit the ongoing rent and other charges to the departed tenant by preparing the rental property for re-renting. You should make a reasonable effort to promptly re-rent the property, including advertising or using other usual rental marketing methods, so that the tenant may be released from his obligation to pay the balance of rent owed under the tenancy agreement.

Handle the marketing of this rental property just like any other house or flat. You don't need to lower the rent, lower your tenant selection standards, or give this property priority over any other available one on your books. Of course, you shouldn't be vindictive and attempt to enrich yourself either, although you can charge the tenant for the cost of finding another tenant to replace them.

Tenants frequently dispute whether your efforts were reasonable in mitigating the former tenant's financial obligations. If challenged in court, you need to be able to show the court that you maintained detailed records clearly indicating the dates and actions you took to find another tenant, including copies of all documents. The tenant generally has the burden of proof, but the courts are often sympathetic to tenants who may be hard-up, so be prepared.

Tenants sometimes have legitimate reasons for breaking their tenancy agreements, and in these situations, they don't have any further obligations to you. These legitimate reasons can include the landlord harassing the tenant, a contravention of a significant provision of the tenancy agreement or a rental property that is uninhabitable.

Subletting

A tenant may approach you and request the right to sublet her room in the rental property. Tenants usually only do this because they must suddenly relocate for personal or professional reasons. Typically, tenancy agreements, like the one shown in Chapter 5, prohibit subletting because you, as the landlord, should have a direct relationship with the occupant (meaning that you screen them and approve their application).

Subletting needlessly complicates the tenant/landlord relationship and prevents you from directly taking legal action against the occupant of your premises. If the proposed occupant meets all your rental criteria, propose terminating the current tenancy agreement and entering into another one with the prospective new tenant.

Departing housemates

On occasion, you may receive a notice that a particular tenant or housemate will be leaving the rental property in the middle of a lease. The departing tenant will usually request a refund of a portion of the deposit, even though not all of the individuals on the tenancy agreement are moving out. But as discussed in Chapter 13, you should retain the entire deposit until all occupants on the tenancy agreement have vacated the property.

If one tenant chooses to move out early, then the tenants need to resolve any deposit issues between themselves. For example, if a new housemate is moving in, that individual can inspect the premises and pay the departing tenant an agreed amount for her share of the deposit. Or the remaining tenants can reach some other agreement with the departing tenant that they agree is fair and equitable.

If there is going to be a change in the tenancy agreement, make sure that the departing tenant completes a Deposit Assignment and Release Agreement (see Form 12-2). This will release you from liability.

Deposit Assignment and Release Agreement

This agreement is entered into on ____________________ (date), between

________________________ (Tenant) and ______________________(Owner).
WHEREAS, on or about ____________________ (date), Tenant delivered to Owner a written notice of termination stating an intention to vacate the Property located at:
____, effective from
_____________ (date).

In consideration for Owner releasing Tenant from the obligations under the Tenancy Agreement dated __________________, Tenant hereby assigns to
________________________________, any and right or claim to the deposit held by Owner for said rental property.

As further consideration for the execution of this Agreement by Owner, Tenant agrees to waive and release any and all right or claim to said deposit.

_____ ____________________
Date Owner/Agent

_____ ____________________
Date Tenant

Form 12-2: Deposit Assignment and Release Agreement.

Domestic problems

Another difficult challenge faced by landlords comes in the form of couples who rent the premises together and then have domestic disputes. Just as with disputes between neighbours or any housemates, you need to avoid getting involved. You lack the authority to side with one party or the other, so staying neutral, encouraging them to resolve the problems between themselves, and continuing to treat both parties fairly and equally is best.

Unfortunately, some disagreements between couples involve domestic violence, and you may receive a request from one member of the couple to change the locks or remove one of the co-tenants from the tenancy agreement. Do not agree to any such changes, regardless of the strength of the tenant's argument, without first seeking legal advice and requiring a copy of a restraining order or other appropriate court order. Ask for a verifiable letter or agreement and consent of the other party as well.

Death of a tenant

If you have reason to suspect the death of a tenant who lives alone, try calling the tenant or bang loudly on his door, check with the neighbours, and call the tenant's place of employment, as well as the emergency contact number on the rental application form. If you still aren't sure, exercise your right to inspect the rental property in an emergency or contact the police or fire brigade.

When the death has been confirmed and the body has been removed, you must immediately take reasonable steps to safeguard the deceased tenant's property, including refusing access except for obtaining personal effects for a funeral. Secure the property and only allow access to legally authorised persons or the police. If you have any doubts about the authority or actions of the tenant's relatives or friends, contact your solicitor for further advice.

If the tenant dies under suspicious circumstances, the property must remain as it was until the coroner has released it, which can take weeks.

In addition to the impact of your tenant's death, you may find yourself in the middle of a dispute as to who properly has access to the rental property. Although you should be sympathetic to the grieving relatives of your tenant, you need to make sure that you don't allow access to the rental property to an unauthorised person, or you may be held liable if anything goes missing.

Most tenancy agreements don't make provision for what happens if a tenant dies – but it does happen. There are clear legal rules to follow, however, if it does happen, and the landlord can demand full rent from the deceased's estate until the tenancy officially ends, although the deceased's solicitor might contest this.

If you take out rental insurance cover, make sure it covers the possibility of the tenant dying.

Chapter 13

Moving Out Tenants

In This Chapter

- Confirming the move-out with a Notice of Intent to Vacate form
- Setting up move-out procedures for your tenants
- Keeping your tenants informed of your policies and procedures
- Dealing with deposit disputes
- Knowing what to do when a tenant abandons your property

Although hanging on to your great tenants forever would be nice, the reality is that all tenants leave at some point. Your goal is to make the experience as straightforward and painless as possible, maintaining clear communication and having procedures in place to deal with every eventuality.

Don't assume that your tenants are familiar with the proper move-out procedures. You need to have a proactive plan that gets your tenants involved in the process of preparing the rental property for the next tenant.

This chapter covers the importance of written notice (the Move-Out Information Letter) and proper procedures in place for the return of the deposit. We also cover the definition of 'normal wear and tear'. And we help you handle special move-out situations.

Start preparing for your tenants eventual move-out when they first move in. The Tenant Information Letter (covered in more detail in Chapter 9) provides the tenants with the legal requirements of move-out as well as your expectations for giving proper notice. The inventory (also covered in Chapter 9) is completed upon move-in to establish the condition of all aspects of the rental property. Use this same detailed inventory to evaluate the condition of the property when the tenant moves out and calculate the appropriate charges, if any.

Requiring Written Notice

When giving notice that they plan to move, most tenants often just call or verbally mention it when they see you – even though your tenancy agreement is likely to contain clauses that require written notice.

Some tenants put their notice in writing by sending you a simple letter. Often these written notices are only one or two sentences and can be ambiguous, leaving out critical information or important details. Although any type of written notice from the tenant is usually legal, a proper notice should provide much more information.

To be sure that you're complying with the law in all regards, ask your tenants to use a Tenant's Notice of Intent to Vacate Rental Property (like the one shown in Form 13-1). This form contains important information, including the tenant's approval of your ability to enter upon reasonable notice to show the rental property to workers, contractors, and prospective tenants.

When you receive verbal or written notice, go ahead and honour the date of the notice but still ask the tenant to complete the form. Insisting that the tenant gives you a written Notice of Intent to Vacate is a good policy. If you don't have this information in writing, opportunities for misunderstandings can arise. You may not remember the move-out date and be caught by surprise, or you may schedule a new move-in only to find that the tenant won't be out until the following week. Surprises are not a good thing for landlords!

Time really is of the essence when it comes to a tenant moving out. In most cases, they need their deposit back so that they can pass it on to their next landlord. Or they might need the deposit to put towards some of the costs of buying their own home, if that's their next move. There is no legal deadline by which you must return the tenant's deposit (or what's left of it) to the tenant, but it should be within a reasonable period of time – usually within 30 days. This is especially the case if no deductions are made.

Tenant's Notice of Intent to Vacate Rental Property

____
Date

____
Owner/Manager

____
____
Property Address

Dear ________________________,

This is to notify you that the undersigned Tenant,

____

hereby give your written notice of intent to vacate the rental property at

____

___________________________________ on

____

I understand that my Tenancy Agreement requires a minimum of ___________ days' notice before I move. This Tenant's Notice of Intent to Vacate Rental Property actually provides _________ days' notice. I understand that I am responsible for paying rent through, the earlier of: (1) the end of the current Tenancy; (2) the end of the required notice period per the Tenancy Agreement; or (3) until another tenant approved by the Owner/Agent has moved in or begun paying rent.

(Optional Information)
We are sorry to learn that you are leaving. We would appreciate a moment of your time to tell us the reason for your move:

___ Moving to a larger property _____ Moving to a smaller property __ Buying a home

___ Moving out of area
___ Dissatisfied with rental property (explain)

____

___ Dissatisfied with management (explain)

____

___ Other (explain)

____

Is there anything we can do to encourage you to continue as our tenant?

____
____
____

Form 13-1: Tenant's Notice of Intent to Vacate Rental Property (Page 1 of 2).

Other comments

____

____

____

In accordance with our Tenancy Agreement, I agree to allow the Owner/Agent reasonable access with advance notice in order to show our rental property to prospective tenants, workmen, or contractors.

Sincerely,

____

Tenant

Form 13-1: Tenant's Notice of Intent to Vacate Rental Property (Page 2 of 2).

Giving Your Tenants a Move-Out Information Letter

Many tenants are afraid that you'll try to cheat them out of their deposit refund. Deposit disputes are the number one issue in many small claims courts. Just as the Tenant Information Letter (covered in Chapter 9) helps to get the tenant/landlord relationship off to a good start, the Move-Out Information Letter (shown in Form 13-2) can help end the relationship on a positive note.

Provide your tenants with a Move-Out Information Letter as soon as they give their written notice to vacate. This letter thanks your tenants for making your rental property their home and provides them with the procedures to follow to prepare the rental property for the final move-out inspection. It also informs them of your policies and method of returning their deposits after any legal deductions. Although your tenancy agreement may contain information on the deposit refund process, most tenants appreciate receiving this information so they know what to expect without having to search for their tenancy agreement while they're trying to pack.

The Move-Out Information Letter includes a reminder to the tenants that their deposit cannot be applied to the last month's rent and is only to be used as a contingency against any damages to the rental property or for other lawful charges. If no portion of the tenant's deposit was called 'last month's rent', you are not legally obliged to apply it in this way. Unless your tenancy agreement uses this wording don't allow your tenants to try to apply their deposit toward their final month's rent, or you may not have enough money on hand to cover any legally allowed charges.

If the tenant moving out is a good one, ask him if you can provide him with a letter of recommendation. A positive reference can be very helpful to tenants, whether they are moving to a new rental property or buying a home. This kind of offer is welcome and courteous – and one that most tenants have never received from prior landlords. If you make this kind of offer, the tenant will often work extra hard to make sure that the rental property is clean and undamaged in order to thank you for your positive comments and offer to provide that letter.

A good way to motivate your tenants to comply with your move-out procedures is to give them a simple reminder that they will have their deposit returned to them in full if they leave the rental property in clean condition, with no damage beyond normal wear and tear.

Move-Out Information Letter

Date _________________
Tenant Name (s) ____
Rental Property Address ____

Dear _____________________

We are pleased that you selected our property for your home and hope that you enjoyed living here. Although we are disappointed to lose you as a tenant, we wish you good luck in the future. We want your move-out to go smoothly and end our relationship on a positive note.

Moving time is always chaotic and you are likely to have many things on your mind, including getting the maximum amount of your deposit back. Contrary to some landlords, we want to be able to return your deposit promptly and in full. Your deposit is £ ______ Note that your deposit shall not be applied to your last month's rent as the deposit is to ensure the fulfilment of tenancy conditions and is to be used only as a contingency against any damages to the rental property.

This move-out letter describes how we expect your rental property to be left and what our procedures are for returning your deposit. Basically, we expect you to leave your rental property in the same condition it was when you moved in, except for normal wear and tear that occurred during your tenancy. To refresh your memory, a copy of your signed inventory is attached reflecting the condition of the rental property at the beginning of your tenancy. We will be using this same detailed inventory when we inspect your rental property upon move-out and will deduct the cost of any necessary cleaning and the costs of repairs, not considered normal wear and tear, from your deposit.

To maximise your chances of a full and prompt refund, we suggest that you go through the inventory line by line and make sure that all items are clean and free from damage, except for normal wear and tear. All cupboards, shelves, drawers, worktops, storage, fridge freezer, and exterior items should be completely free of items. Feel free to tick off completed items on this copy of the inventory, as we will use the original for your final inspection.

Some of our tenants prefer to let professionals complete these items. You can contact your own professional or, upon request, we will be glad to refer you to our service providers so that you can focus on other issues of your move. You will work directly with the service provider on costs and payment terms, knowing that you are working with someone who can prepare the property for the final inspection. Call us if you would like contact information or for any questions as to the type of cleaning we expect.

Please make sure you remove all personal possessions, including furniture, clothes, household items, food, plants, cleaning supplies, and any bags of rubbish or loose items that belong to you. Of course, please do not remove any appliances, fixtures, or other items installed or attached to your rental property unless you have our prior written approval.

Please contact the appropriate utility companies and arrange for the disconnection of the phone and utility services in your name.

Please contact us when all the conditions have been satisfied to arrange an inspection of your rental property during daylight hours. To avoid a key replacement charge, please return all your keys at the time you vacate the property.

You have listed ______________________ as the move-out date in your notice. Please be reminded that you will be charged £ ____ per day for each partial or full day after the above move-out date that you remain in the rental property or have possession of the keys. If you need to extend your tenancy for any reason, you must contact us immediately. Please be prepared to provide your forwarding address where we may post your deposit cheque.

It is our policy to return all deposits to an address you provide within ____________ days after you move out **and** return all keys. If any deductions are made for rent owed or other unpaid charges, for damages beyond normal wear and tear, or for failure to properly clean, an itemised explanation will be included with the deposit accounting.

If you have any questions, please contact us at ________________________________

Thank you again for making our property your home. It has been a pleasure to have you as our tenant(s) and please accept our best wishes and thanks for your co-operation. Should you need a reference for a future landlord please don't hesitate to contact us.

Yours sincerely,

____
Owner/Manager

Form 13-2: A Move-Out Information Letter.

Inspecting the Property's Condition at Move-Out

Try to schedule the move-out inspection with your vacating tenants just *after* they have removed all their furnishings and personal items, handed over all their keys, and had the utilities disconnected. The only way to determine the condition of some parts of the property is to wait until the rental property is vacant. Also, you want to make sure that the tenant doesn't do additional damage after the inspection while they're removing their possessions.

Unfortunately, you can't always arrange to do the inspection with the tenant at this time. If that's the case, conduct the move-out inspection as soon as possible and preferably with a witness present. If you wait too long to inspect the property and then discover damage, the tenant may claim that someone else must have caused the damage, and you may face an uphill battle in court.

Noting damages

Tenants have been known to show up for the final inspection but deny that they know anything about the damaged items you find. Refer to your inventory in these situations. If the item is clearly indicated on the inventory as being in good condition when the tenant moved in, the tenant doesn't stand much of a chance. However, if the inventory remarks are blank or vague, you may have some problems justifying a deduction. As you are the rental housing professional, the courts hold you to a higher standard and interpret your vague documents in favour of the tenant.

Although the tenant should be present for the move-out inspection, you may not know the actual charges for certain items until later, when the work is completed and you receive the final invoice from a contractor. Plus, damages are often not discovered until the rental property preparation work is being done. So just note that the item is damaged on the inventory and advise the tenant that you reserve the right to deduct the actual repair costs. When you know the actual charges, you can fill in the column on the inventory for the estimated cost of repair or replacement and include a copy of the completed inventory with your deposit itemisation.

Tenants are often counting on the return of their full deposit and will request the chance to do some more cleaning or make repairs if you indicate that deductions will be made. If they can act quickly and you feel that they are capable of the work, you may want to give them a second chance at cleaning or simple repairs. However, be wary of tenant repairs that could cost you more to correct later or that create liability issues. Even a simple touch-up to the paintwork by your tenants can become a disaster if they are sloppy decorators or mismatch the paint. When it comes to the majority of repairs, you're better off refusing the tenant's request to fix them himself.

Defining 'normal wear and tear'

Legally you are entitled to charge your tenant for damages beyond 'normal wear and tear'. But virtually all disputes over deposits revolve around this elusive definition. It's your job to be able to tell the difference between normal wear and tear and more serious damage that you can reasonably deduct from your tenant's deposit.

The standard definition of '*normal wear and tear* is deterioration or damage to the property expected to occur from normal usage. The problem then is what is considered to be 'normal usage'. Decisions vary from court to court. If you ask 100 small claims court judges, you are likely to get nearly 100 different interpretations of this definition.

The bottom line is that there are no hard and fast rules on what constitutes normal wear and tear and what the tenant can legally be charged. Table 13-1 gives you some room for comparison to help you determine what normal wear and tear is and what goes beyond normal into damage you can charge for.

Table 13-1 Normal Wear and Tear versus Damage

Normal Wear and Tear	*Damage beyond Normal Wear and Tear*
Smudges on the walls near light switches	Crayon marks on the walls or ceiling
Minor marks on the walls or doors	Large marks on, or holes in, the walls, or doors
A few small tack holes	Numerous nail-holes that require filling and/or painting
Faded, peeling, or cracked paint	Completely dirty or scuffed painted walls
Carpet worn thin from normal use	Carpet stained by bleach or dye
Carpet with moderate dirt or spots	Carpet that has been ripped or has pet stains
Carpet or curtains faded by the sun	Carpet or curtains with cigarette burns
Moderately dirty blinds	Damaged or missing blinds

Deducting repairs from the deposit

Many landlords see the tenant's deposit as a source of additional income that is theirs for the taking. However, as a business practice, the return of the full deposit is actually much better for the landlord. The only lawful deductions from the tenant's deposit are for unpaid rent, damages beyond normal wear and tear, keys, and cleaning.

If you make deductions from the deposit, make sure that your paperwork is accurate and detailed. Because property damage deductions are only for damages beyond normal wear and tear, you need to be sure that your description of the item explains why the damage exceeds that. If you merely indicate, 'Pet damage – £100' on the deposit itemisation form, you may very well be challenged. However, if you provide details like 'Steam cleaned carpeting in living room to remove extensive pet urine stains – £100', you greatly improve your chances if the matter gets to court or, better yet, of not even being challenged in the first place.

Excessive deductions almost always lead to acrimonious discussions with the former tenant that could end up in small claims court. Spending your day in court can be very counterproductive, particularly because the courts often seek a compromise that requires at least a partial return of the deposit to the aggrieved tenant. You may feel that there are no legal bases for a judge to find in the tenant's favour, but the court may rule merely to compensate the tenant for their time and costs of going to court.

Here are some guidelines to follow when listing the charges on your deposit itemisation form:

- **Indicate the specific item damaged.** List each damaged fixture, appliance, or piece of furniture separately.
- **Indicate the specific location of the damaged item.** Note the room and which wall, ceiling, or corner of the room the damaged item is located in. Use compass directions, if possible.
- **Note the type and extent of the damage.** Be sure to describe the damage in detail using appropriate adjectives, such as *substantial, excessive, minor, scratched, stained, ripped, cracked, burned,* or *chipped.*
- **Note the type and extent of repair done.** Describe the repair, using adjectives such as *patch, paint, steam-clean,* or *refinish.* Indicate if an item was so damaged that it had to be replaced and, if so, why.
- **Indicate the cost of the repair or replacement.** List exactly how much you actually spent or plan to spend based on a third-party estimate.

Some landlords give all vacating tenants a pricing chart with a list of prices that will be charged for different services or damaged items. These owners believe the pricing charts minimise disputes because the charges are predetermined and are given to the tenants in advance. Further, they argue that the tenants will see how expensive repairs are and will take care of some of the work on their own. There is some logic to this method, but it also poses some potential problems. For example, prices frequently change, and courts insist on actual, not estimated, charges. So the price chart would have to be consistently updated. Plus, many items can't possibly have preset prices for repair, and different contractors may charge different amounts. You can be assured that the tenant won't pay up if your actual charge turns out to be much higher than the preset charge indicated on your pricing chart. But if the tenant challenges your deductions and your actual invoice shows you paid less than what you charged the tenant, you'd better have your cheque book ready.

Deposit disputes are the number one problem in tenant/landlord relationships. Although proper use of the inventory eliminates many of these disputes, the definition of 'normal wear and tear' is one of life's greatest mysteries. You can minimise arguments with former tenants and avoid small claims courts by making only fair and reasonable deductions and providing the deposit accounting and any refund within reasonable time limits.

Using a Deposit Itemisation Form

After you have inspected the rental property and determined the proper charges, you need to prepare the Deposit Itemisation Form (shown in Form 13-3). You need to complete this form and give the vacating tenant a cheque for any balance due within a reasonable period of time. It shouldn't take much longer than 30 days to do this.

Send the deposit accounting and refund as soon as you are sure of the final charges. Tenants need this money, and the longer they wait the more impatient and upset they get – and the more likely they are to challenge your charges. Of course, you need to make sure that you have inspected the entire rental property carefully and found any tenant damage beyond ordinary wear and tear. In theory, you can always seek reimbursement for items discovered after you refund the deposit, but your chances of collecting would be slim.

Some tenants want to personally pick up the deposit as soon as possible; others won't even tell you where they can be reached. Generally, you post the Deposit Itemisation Form to the address provided by your tenants on their Tenant's Notice to Vacate Form. If you do not have your vacating tenant's forwarding address, send the deposit itemisation to their last known address, which may be your own rental property. There's a chance they've had their post forwarded to their new address; if not, the cheque will just be returned to you.

If your Deposit Itemisation Form and refund cheque are returned undeliverable, be sure to save the returned envelope in case the former tenant claims you never sent the legally required accounting. Also send the deposit via recorded mail in order to prove that you sent it and the date you sent it on.

Tenants, particularly housemates or married couples in the midst of a separation or divorce, may fight amongst themselves over the deposit. Legally, the deposit belongs equally to all tenants who signed the tenancy agreement, unless otherwise agreed in writing. If you arbitrarily split the cheque between the tenants, you can find yourself liable to the other party. So always make your deposit refund cheque payable jointly to all adult tenants; then post copies of your Deposit Itemisation Form to each of the tenants at their respective forwarding addresses. Include the deposit refund cheque to one of the tenants with a copy of the cheque to the others. Leave it up to the tenants to handle the endorsement of the cheque. However, if you have a court order or a written agreement or instructions signed by all tenants, you can handle the deposit as directed.

Unless the tenancy agreement states otherwise, the landlord should repay the deposit with interest, even if you do not keep it in an interest-earning account. The amount of interest is unlikely to be high, given that interest rates are so low, and although paying interest on the deposit may not be required by law, it is good practice to do so.

Handling Special Move-Out Situations

Although you may have worked very hard to make sure everything goes smoothly during your tenant's move-out, a few special situations inevitably arise. And the more you know as a landlord about how to handle these situations, the less likely they are to become significant problems.

When damage and unpaid rent exceed the deposit

As a landlord, you will probably encounter a situation in which a tenant's deposit is not sufficient to cover the unpaid rent and the damage caused by the tenant. You should first allocate the deposit to cover the damage and then to cover the unpaid rent – it makes sense to use the deposit to pay for items that would be more difficult to prove in court.

Deposit Itemisation Form

Deductions for unpaid rent, damages beyond normal wear and tear, and cleaning

____
Date

____
Name

____
____
____
Forwarding address

Rental property address: ____

Move-in date _________ Date that Notice to Vacate was received ______________

Actual date vacated _______________

Rent ____________ New tenant move-in date, if applicable ______________

1. Deposit received £ _______
2. Interest on deposit £ _______
3. Total credit (sum of 1+2) £ _______
4. Defaults in rent covered by any court judgement £ _______

____
____
____

5. Court judgement for rent, costs, solicitor fees £ _______
6. Itemised property damages and repairs £ _______

____
____
____

7. Necessary cleaning of property upon vacation £ _______
8. Other deductions £ _______
9. Total deductions (sum of 4 – 8) £ _______
10. Balance due

_____ Total amount Owner owes Tenant £ _______

_____ Total amount Tenant owes Tenant £ _______

Comments

____
____
____

Form 13-3: A Deposit Itemisation Form.

Tenancy Deposit Scheme

With deposits causing so many problems between landlord and tenant, the Government is introducing a compulsory Tenancy Deposit Scheme from October 2006. Under this scheme, landlords issuing tenants with new assured shorthold tenancy agreements must hand their deposits over to an independent private company (not yet appointed at the time of writing). This scheme will remove disputes over the repayment of a deposit and unscrupulous landlords will no longer be able to unreasonably refuse to repay the deposit to the tenant within a reasonable period of time.

The problem, as far as landlords are concerned, is that they will not be able to take any unpaid rent out of the deposit, as is currently the case. Instead, landlords will have to apply through the courts to get the tenant to cough up any unpaid rent. This is likely to be a pain for decent landlords, costing them effort and money.

For example, let's say you're holding a £500 deposit from a tenant when she vacates, owing £350 in unpaid rent. When you inspect her property, however, you find £400 in damage beyond ordinary wear and tear. The total of the rent owed and the damages done is £750, but you only have £500 in the form of a deposit. What should you do? First, apply the £500 deposit to cover the full £400 in damage, and allocate the remaining £100 toward the unpaid rent. You then can pursue the £250 rent balance with your records as evidence to clearly prove this amount is owed.

If, instead of resolving the costs for damages first, you choose to cover the unpaid rent and then bill the tenant for the £250 in damages, you can be assured the tenant will challenge the validity of the charges. And proving damages is harder than proving unpaid rent.

Be sure to always keep track of the actual costs for damages even if you don't intend to pursue the tenant for the balance owed. This way you can prove your expenses in court if you ever need to.

Even if your lawful deductions exceed the departing tenant's deposit charges, you must provide the tenant with a full accounting of the damages. This is true even if you file a small claims lawsuit for the balance due. So be sure to always follow the required procedures for the accounting of the deposit.

When disputes arise over the deposit

No matter how fair and reasonable you are with your deposit deductions, sooner or later you are bound to have a former tenant challenge your deductions. Even if your deductions were proper and you are sure that you're right, going to court over the deposit deduction may cost you more than the amount in dispute. Often, the actual disagreement is over a relatively small amount of money.

For example, you may have deducted £100 for touching up the paint work, but your former tenant may believe that the charge should be only £50. So you're only arguing over a £50 difference. Explore possible negotiations to resolve the matter before going to court. If you're sure that your charges were fair, be sure to always maintain that in your discussions with your former tenant, even if you want to see if a settlement is a possibility.

If you charge your tenants for damage to the rental property either during their tenancy or by deducting from the deposit, you need evidence to back up your claim in case your tenant disputes the damage. Videoing the damage can be an effective tool to resolve disputes with tenants or prove your position in court. Many courts now have video monitors that you can use to show your evidence. Be sure that you have possession of the property or have given proper legal notice before entering to videotape, however.

When the rental property is abandoned

Occasionally tenants will abandon your rental property without notice. This can be good news if you're taking legal action against the tenant, because you save lost rent days and you may be able to reduce your legal costs.

Determining whether the property is really abandoned

Abandonment is the voluntary surrender of a legal right, for example, an interest in land or property, such as a tenancy. Tenants sometimes leave their accommodation unoccupied for long periods of time, with the intention of coming back at some point. So the best way to know for sure whether the rental property has been abandoned or not is to contact the tenants and ask them for a statement in writing relinquishing their rights to possession of the rental property.

Have a clause in the tenancy agreement saying that your tenants must inform you if they are going to leave the property unoccupied for more than two weeks. This policy can be helpful in determining whether the property has been abandoned or the tenant is just on a long holiday.

If you think that the tenant has abandoned your property, but you have no written confirmation, consider whether the rent is still being paid, if the tenant has left the keys to the property, whether the neighbours know anything about it and if you can see the tenant's possessions through the windows. If these factors indicate abandonment and the property has been left insecure, you may have a case for entering the property and fitting a secure lock. A reliable independent witness should confirm the circumstances in writing.

If the property doesn't appear to be abandoned or there is some doubt, you need a court possession order before taking over the property or re-letting. When you have met the legal requirements, you can take possession of the rental property and begin your turnover work to put it back on the rental market.

Dealing with personal property left behind

One of a landlord's worst nightmares is discovering that one of their tenants has suddenly abandoned the rental property and left all of his furnishings and household items behind. More common, however, is finding that a tenant has moved out and returned the keys, but left behind a few items of personal property. Often these items are junk that even your favourite charity will refuse to accept.

The landlord is under a legal obligation to take care of the tenant's possessions. The law relating to this is the Torts (interference with Goods) Act 1977. Under this law, the landlord could suffer a financial loss for moving and transporting the uncollected goods, or disposing of the goods.

When you first discover that your tenant appears to have left abandoned personal property, immediately try to locate the tenant and ask her to reclaim her property. You should write to the tenant by registered post or recorded delivery, enclosing a legal notice that informs her that her goods are available for collection and will be kept for up to three months.

If the goods remain uncollected after three months, the original owner loses all rights to the goods, and you can sell them. Once you have covered your expenses for carrying out this process and any rent arrears, any remaining proceeds belong to the original owner or tenant. But this only applies if they turn up to claim them within six years.

Part IV
Techniques and Tools for Managing

"To make rent paying more pleasurable, I'm employing a singing rent collector."

In this part . . .

A big part of managing rental property has to do with people other than your tenants – everyone from employees you hire to contractors you work with. And just as owning your own home involves a lot of maintenance work, the same holds true for owning rental property. Plus, as a landlord, you have to be aware of the safety and security of your property – and your tenants. In this part, we cover all these issues, so that you have the information you need to successfully manage your rental property.

Chapter 14
Maintenance

In This Chapter

- Setting up a maintenance plan for your rental property
- Knowing what types of maintenance issues you're likely to face
- Responding to your tenants' maintenance requests professionally

Maintenance – the work required to keep something in proper condition or upkeep – is just part of the territory when you own rental property. Although maintenance is unlikely to be your favourite task, you can enhance your investment by making emergency repairs promptly and maintaining the property in the best possible physical condition.

Although owning and operating rental property clearly requires ongoing physical maintenance, many landlords are not prepared for the work involved. If you have a background and experience in maintenance and repairs, you may welcome the opportunity to do some of the work yourself. But maintenance requests do not always fit in with your schedule. And many repairs require special tools, skills, and training that only a professional would have.

Whether you do the maintenance work yourself or hire and oversee a handyman or tradesman to do it, take the time to know enough about basic maintenance that you can make sure they're doing a good job. Many fine books cover the specific repairs required in most rental properties, including *DIY & Home Maintenance For Dummies* edited by Jeff Howell (Wiley).

Besides the benefits in marketing and keeping your property fully occupied, you're required by law to properly maintain and repair your rental properties to meet all building, housing, and health and safety standards. This means that, from the day the tenant moves in until the day the tenant moves out, you must keep the rental property in a safe and habitable condition.

In this chapter, we cover the reasons why a good maintenance plan is essential for all rental properties, the most common types of maintenance, and some sound procedures for handling rental property maintenance and saving money.

Recognising the Importance of a Maintenance Plan

One of the most common reasons that dissatisfied tenants leave a rental property is the failure of the landlord to respond to the tenant's basic requests for maintenance. But you can use this to your advantage when you show your well-maintained rental property by informing your prospective tenants about your system for promptly addressing maintenance issues. If you have a solid maintenance plan in place, you will consistently get higher rents and have much lower turnover of tenants.

Plus, when you're working with a maintenance plan, you can control your expenses and keep them to a minimum. You greatly reduce the need for emergency repairs (which always cost more money). And you have the names of contractors and tradesmen on hand so that you can have the proper repair done the first time (instead of having to call someone else out to rectify a botched repair job).

Because long-term, satisfied tenants are the key to financial success in managing rental properties, you need to establish a responsive maintenance system that properly maintains the premises in order to avoid operating losses and potential legal problems. A poorly maintained property leads to higher tenant turnover and tenants of progressively lower calibre, who are willing to accept the poor condition of the property. A tenant can also use the poor condition of the property as an excuse to withhold rent, leave halfway through their tenancy, defend an eviction, or even take legal action against you.

Take a proactive approach to maintenance. At least once a year, conduct a safety inspection of the rental property. Most tenants will co-operate fully, but you must give proper notice of your intention to enter the property to carry out the inspection – usually 24 hours. In these cases, or as an additional tool to improve your tenant relations, you can send your tenant a non-intrusive note and maintenance checklist that allows a quick response. This standard policy will protect you from claims of poor maintenance, allow for repairs when problems are small, and keep your good tenants satisfied.

A good maintenance plan includes regularly scheduled exterior property inspections. A customised property inspection checklist for each rental property is a good management tool. The frequency of the inspections will vary, but they should be performed at least quarterly and when a tenant moves out.

Your tenant has a responsibility to maintain the premises in a clean and sanitary manner and to properly use the premises in a usual and customary fashion. You should always hold the tenant financially accountable for any damage caused to the property by their negligence or misuse of the property.

Being Prepared for the Different Types of Maintenance Issues

Maintenance isn't just a matter of fixing a leaky tap here and there – rental properties require several different types of maintenance, and you're sure to run into each of them at one time or another. Although each type of maintenance is critical, you need to respond to and handle each type in a unique way.

There is a saying in property management: 'To own is to maintain.' It's something worth keeping in mind when you find yourself having to do maintenance work on your rental property.

Emergency repairs

Part of being a landlord is being prepared for emergency maintenance requests at all hours of the day and night. Although your tenants should contact the appropriate authorities for safety issues where it is a matter of life and death, you will still receive more than your fair share of emergency maintenance requests.

When you get a maintenance call from a tenant, first you need to determine whether the urgent maintenance request really is an emergency. An emergency repair is work that must be done *immediately* in order to prevent further property damage or minimise the chance of endangering people. The most common maintenance emergencies typically involve plumbing or electrical problems.

In a maintenance emergency, immediately advise the tenant of what steps to take to limit any further damage. For example, if a pipe is leaking, tell the tenant to shut off the water at the stopcock under the kitchen sink; this can prevent further water damage. Instruct tenants not to use appliances or electrical systems that are malfunctioning until they have been inspected or repaired.

If a fire, flood, or gas leak ever occurs at your rental property, immediately shutting off the utilities may be imperative. Prepare charts and simple diagrams for each rental property, indicating where the tenant can find all utility shutoff locations and the tools necessary to operate them – as well as instructions letting tenants know which situations warrant shutting them off.

You may need to remind tenants that freezing outdoor temperatures can lead to water damage in unheated rental properties. Tenants may want to turn off the heating when they go to work or when they're away on holiday as a way of saving money, but turning the heating off completely or setting the thermostat too low can lead to the freezing and bursting of pipes. Make sure your tenancy agreement states that the heating must be kept on in winter, at least on a low heat, to prevent the pipes freezing and bursting, and send out a letter reminding the tenants of this when the weather starts to get colder.

Preventive maintenance

A sound preventive maintenance plan can increase your cash flow and reduce the number of maintenance emergencies at your property. *Preventive maintenance* is the regularly scheduled inspection and maintenance performed to extend the operating life of the building systems of a property. This often includes annual maintenance surveys or inspections of the interior of the rental property.

Preventive maintenance can often address problems when the conditions are still minor, thus saving significantly over future emergency repairs or replacement. The cost of maintenance labour is also reduced because maintenance personnel can work more efficiently by having all the necessary tools, parts, and supplies on hand.

For even further savings, schedule the preventive maintenance work when business is slow for the contractor.

Be sure to give all tenants written notice before beginning maintenance work that requires the discontinuance of any utility service. A temporary shutoff of utilities (particularly water) is often necessary in emergencies or while performing preventive maintenance and repairs at your rental property. Advising your tenants in advance can minimise the inconvenience for them. The necessary repairs should be made in a timely manner.

Corrective maintenance

Although planning and performing preventive maintenance work is usually cheaper than fixing or replacing items, the reality is that, if something breaks, it must be fixed or replaced in a timely manner. The most common maintenance requests from tenants are for corrective maintenance. If you respond professionally and quickly, you'll earn a reputation as a good landlord.

Even with the best preventive maintenance plan, corrective maintenance is inevitable. Anything in a rental property can, and eventually will, break or need attention in normal usage, including toilets and sinks that become blocked, doors that stick, and appliances that break down. The key to tenant satisfaction is often dependent upon whether you have a system for efficiently accepting and responding to tenant maintenance requests.

Although the telephone, a mobile or pager, or even an answering machine are still the best ways to communicate an urgent maintenance request, e-mail is becoming more popular with both landlords and tenants for many non-emergency maintenance situations. E-mail works well for landlords, who often prefer not being interrupted by a phone call at a potentially inconvenient time, and it works well for tenants, who appreciate being able to send the e-mail at any time of the day or night instead of having to wait until normal business hours to get hold of you. Upon receipt of the e-mail, you can reply with a confirmation or ask for more details. You can even forward the e-mail directly to the tradesman who will be handling the repair.

Custodial maintenance

Custodial maintenance is the regular day-to-day upkeep of the rental property and the most frequently occurring type of maintenance. The kerb appeal (see Chapter 6) and physical appearance of your property and grounds depend on regular patrolling and cleaning. In small family rental properties, the tenant typically handles this duty, and the specific responsibilities should be included in your tenancy agreement. If your rental property is a flat in a large block, a managing agent should be responsible for daily inspection and cleaning of the outside of the property. If you own several flats in one house, you are responsible for the upkeep of the communal areas, such as stairways and hallways.

Keep a list of routine maintenance items, including washing windows; hosing down parking areas, driveways and paths; and doing other tasks that will keep the interior and exterior of the rental property clean and presentable. Don't forget to keep the rubbish bin areas clean and free of litter as well.

The number one complaint of tenants, and the bane of all landlords, is deferred maintenance. Not really a type of maintenance at all, *deferred maintenance* is the result of obvious repairs that are not properly addressed in a timely manner. Common examples are peeling paint, broken doors, overgrown gardens, and minor roof leaks in the garage. Although every property has some deferred maintenance, your goal as an owner is to keep it to a minimum.

Cosmetic maintenance

Properties with great kerb appeal are easier to manage and generate higher returns on your investment. So if you're willing to spend money to improve and upgrade the appearance of your rental properties, you'll reap the rewards. Examples of cosmetic maintenance or upgrades include replacing old worktops in the kitchen, installing new light fixtures, repainting, fitting new curtains or blinds, and replacing old wallpaper.

One of the most common complaints tenants make is that their landlord refuses to paint the interior of the rental property every few years. The landlord is under no legal obligation to carry out improvements such as this. But if making these kinds of improvements means that your tenant is prepared to pay more rent or that you can more easily get a new tenant when the old one leaves, it may be in your best interests to get the work done anyway.

And what if I don't?

Landlords are under a direct statutory obligation to carry out repairs. This includes maintaining the structure and exterior of the property in a safe and watertight condition. It also means you must keep internal installations for water, gas, electrical services, heating, and hot water in a good safe condition.

However, if you don't fulfil these obligations, the Environmental Health department of your local authority has the powers to inspect private rental properties and serve enforcement notices on landlords where repairs are deemed necessary.

Your goal as a landlord should be to promptly respond to legitimate complaints about the rental property and to make sure that all maintenance work is done properly and for a reasonable cost. If the tenant has to resort to calling in Environmental Health Officers, it becomes a hassle you can do without. In other instances, the tenant may attempt to make the repair himself or herself or hire a contractor who is not skilled. Even worse, the tenant may hire a contractor who is very skilled but also quite expensive, and then have the bill sent to you.

The bottom line? Always make repairs in a timely manner and you won't have to face these problems to begin with.

Handling Rental Property Maintenance

Even though you may be assertive in properly maintaining your rental property through regular property inspections and diligent interior maintenance upon tenant turnover, there will always be an ongoing need to make repairs.

Responding to a tenant's request for repairs

Your first knowledge of a maintenance problem or needed repair is likely to be when your tenant contacts you. In many businesses, the companies with the best reputation and customer loyalty are those that are respected for the positive attitude and efficiency with which they address complaints. The rental property business is no different.

Typically, you will receive the request by telephone, and while you need to be respectful of your tenant's time, you also need to ask questions to gather a detailed description of the necessary maintenance and the precise location of the problem. This information allows you to make an informed decision as to the urgency of the problem and determine the proper person to handle the work. It also gives you the chance to make sure that the proper tools, equipment, and parts will be available when your handyman arrives to do the job, if possible.

Be sure that your tenants know that they cannot contact your handyman or any tradesmen directly. Tenants may think they're doing you a favour by directly contacting the plumber you use on a regular basis. Or they may remember another problem when your handyman is in their rental property working on something else. Either way, all service requests should be routed through you or your agent. Then, whenever a tenant contacts you with a maintenance problem, you can properly record all information in writing on a

Tenant's Maintenance Request Form (see Form 14-1), regardless of how insignificant the problem.

Having proof that the tenant gave permission to enter the rental property, either by signing the Maintenance Request Form in person or by giving approval on the telephone, is essential. If the tenant cannot sign the request in person, make a specific note indicating the date and time, and who gave permission to enter. If the tenant did not specifically give permission for a handyman or tradesman to enter the property, serve a Notice of Intent to Enter Rental Property (see Form 14-2).

Tenant's Maintenance Request Form

_______________ Maintenance Request No _____

Date

____

Tenant's Name

____

____

Property Address

_______________ _______________

Telephone (home) Telephone (day)

Service required (describe very specifically):

____

____

____

____

____

____

Best time to perform service (Day and time): _______________

Authorisation: Owner/Agent/Service personnel are authorised to enter rental property if Tenant is not present unless specific instructions have been given in advance to the contrary.

____

Signature of Tenant

If verbal approval received, given by: _______________ on _______________ (date)

Report of action taken:

____ Completed, by _______________ (Upon completion, describe problem/work done/materials used)

____

____

____ Unable to complete on _______________ (date), because _______________

____ Outside professional assistance required, because _______________

____ Will return to complete on _______________

Charge cost to Tenant: _____ Yes _____ No If yes, reason _______________

Comments:

____

____

Received: _______________ _______________

Date Owner/Agent

Form 14-1: Tenant's Maintenance Request Form.

Notice of Intent to Enter Rental Property

____

Date

____

Name of Tenant

____

____

Property Address

This notice is to inform all persons in the above Property that on ______________ (date), beginning approximately between the hour of _______ am/pm and until _________ am/pm, the Landlord, Landlord's Agent or tradespeople authorised by the Landlord, will enter the Property for the following reason:

_____ To perform or arrange for the following repairs or improvements:

____

____

____

_____ To show the property to:

_____ a prospective tenant

_____ a prospective or actual purchaser or lender

_____ workers or contractors regarding the above repair or improvement

_____ Other:

____

____

____

Naturally, you are welcome to be present. Please notify us if you have any questions or if the date or time is inconvenient.

Sincerely,

____

Landlord/Managing Agent

Form 14-2: Notice of Intent to Enter Rental Property.

All tenant maintenance requests should be entered in a master maintenance log in chronological order. (See Chapter 19 for more information on computer software and manual maintenance tracking systems that simplify the paperwork.) A good tenant maintenance tracking system does much more than just record the request for service and the fact that the tenant granted permission to enter. The system can provide proof that the repairs were actually made, record the parts and materials used in the repair, and serve as the basis of a billing record if the tenant caused the damage and will be charged for calling out a professional to deal with it.

Copies of Tenant Maintenance Request Forms should always be filed in the tenant file and in a separate permanent maintenance file for each rental property. If the tenant complains to your local authority about essential repairs not being carried out or alleges that you haven't carried out your legal obligations, such as annual gas safety checks, Tenant Maintenance Request Forms provide a repair history that you can use to document that tenant complaints were properly addressed.

Your maintenance personnel and tradesmen are key in giving your tenants a positive or negative impression, because they have direct contact with your tenant and are a reflection on you. Remind them that they are entering your tenant's home and they must immediately identify themselves with proper identification, such as a photo ID. They must always be well-groomed, respectful, and courteous, and they should never smoke in an occupied or unoccupied rental property. They must be businesslike and stick to the facts while keeping the tenant informed about the status of the service request. They should always clean up completely after themselves as well.

Although responding to tenant maintenance requests can lead to excellent tenant relations, some tenants may have excessive demands. The best way to handle these tenants is to remain calm and courteous and to address all legitimate health and safety issues or maintenance repairs that preserve your investment. When the tenant demands become unreasonable, politely explain that providing extra service calls or cosmetic upgrades will necessitate an increase in the tenant's rent to cover your additional expenditures.

Keeping tenants from fixing things themselves

Landlords cannot pass on their legal obligations to tenants for safety, such as gas checks, repairs, and maintenance. Even if your tenant is a qualified plumber or electrician, capable of handling many routine repairs, you should retain control of even the minor maintenance problems and hire your own tradesmen to rectify them.

Initially, allowing your tenant to handle certain minor repairs seems to offer significant savings in cost and aggravation. However, most tenants unfortunately lack the proper skills, training, special tools, or even motivation to do the job properly. They may be willing to ignore or live with a problem that can be resolved inexpensively. But that little problem may soon become a major problem – and a major expense – and you will be left with the responsibility to pay for it. And at the end of the day, it is the landlord's obligation, so it is up to you to see that the work is carried out.

One of the main advantages of renting is that someone else is responsible for the maintenance and repair of the property. Most tenants are relieved to know that you appreciate the opportunity to properly maintain the rental property and that they won't have to do a thing except alert you to problems when they come up.

Disabled tenants should be allowed to modify their living space at their own expense, where such modifications are practical, after obtaining your approval.

Purchasing maintenance parts and supplies

As a new landlord, you will suddenly find that you are interested in wandering through DIY stores looking for obscure parts or flipping through huge catalogues looking for bargains in the sale. Don't underestimate the importance of seeking out reliable stores with competitive pricing, because the ongoing maintenance and repair of a rental property will greatly exceed the original construction cost.

By visiting a DIY store frequented by tradesmen rather than one aimed at members of the general public who dabble in DIY at weekends, you should be able to get trade discounts. You may have to buy in bulk or volume – a sack of sand rather than a small bag – but it will be cheaper for what you're getting.

Don't fall into the trap of buying items in greater quantities than you immediately can use if the items don't have a long shelf life, regardless of the great savings offered at the time. A common mistake property owners make is buying the latest discontinued paint on sale, only to have to completely repaint their rental property when the tenants move out because the excess paint has gone off in storage. Instead, use the same standard colour on all your rental properties so that the colour will always be available. You can buy in bulk and do touch-ups when you need to.

Another growing trend is purchasing parts and supplies online. Web sites offer a wide variety of items, from appliances to plumbing and electrical fixtures to even tools and hardware parts. These sites make the purchasing process very easy and typically offer free delivery. If you own just a few rental properties, however, you may find that the savings are nominal unless you purchase in quantity.

All new appliances come with manufacturers warranties covering the cost of replacement or repairs if the appliance breaks down during the warranty period. Be sure to keep all appliance and equipment warranties, plus copies of all purchase receipts, in a readily accessible file for each rental property. Read the warranty before attempting a repair yourself, or you may inadvertently affect your rights to have the manufacturer replace or repair the appliance or equipment for free. After the basic warranty expires, many manufacturers offer extended warranties for an extra fee, but these can be expensive and generally aren't worth it as long as you have good quality appliances and a reliable service technician at your disposal.

Chapter 15

Safety, Security, and Insurance

In This Chapter

- Handling and preventing crime in and around your rental property
- Taking precautions to keep your tenants and your property safe
- Insuring yourself against loss and liability

As a landlord, you need to take an active role in implementing policies and security measures for the safety of your tenants and their guests. Even if your property is located next door to the local police station, you still need to implement proper building security measures. Crime can strike anywhere, even in seemingly respectable neighbourhoods. And even if crime is not a problem in your area, you may face potential safety challenges from Mother Nature. Take the lead in working with local experts and the Environment Agency if your rental property is in an area at risk from flooding.

Insurance is one of the major financial responsibilities you face as a landlord – from protecting your investment to ensuring you are covered if your tenants don't pay the rent or damage your property. This chapter makes sure you are prepared for all eventualities.

Tackling Crime in and around Your Rental Property

Crime is a fact of life for all of us, landlords or not. But part of your responsibility as a rental property owner is to make your property as safe as possible for your tenants and to alert your tenants to their responsibilities as well. In this section, we give you some tips for keeping crime to a minimum in your area and responding to it if and when it does occur.

Your local Crime Prevention Officer is the best source of crime prevention advice. Check your local telephone directory for the one nearest to you.

Participating in your local Neighbourhood Watch scheme

The Neighbourhood Watch scheme was set up in the UK in 1982 and has been an important part of local communities ever since. Neighbourhood Watch schemes help fight crime, improve home security, and increase the well-being of local citizens. However, not all areas are fortunate enough to be covered by a Neighbourhood Watch scheme. To find out if your rental property is located in an area where a scheme is in operation, log onto the Neighbourhood Watch Web site at `www.neighbourhoodwatch.net` for a list of schemes across the country.

Alternatively, your local Crime Prevention Officer can provide advice and information on whether your property is situated in an area covered by a Neighbourhood Watch scheme. She can also give you advice on how your tenants can join it. Joining can be advantageous for them as well as you; while you get tenants that are looking out for your property, they get to know the neighbours and feel more settled – and are therefore less likely to move on in six months time.

The Neighbourhood Watch Web site is also a great resource for tips on preventing crime in the home and how to improve the security in your rental property. You can find detailed advice and suggestions on using exterior lighting, securing front doors, ensuring rear gardens are safe and installing alarms in your rental property. Also included is information about things that can either attract or discourage criminals, plus a holiday checklist for when the property is empty.

Don't forget that, if your tenants are planning to be away for longer than two weeks, they should notify you (see Chapter 13). If left unattended for long stretches of time, your rental property is at risk.

Weekly crime incident reports are published on the Neighbourhood Watch site, although the number of regions covered is limited. Reported incidents range from garages broken into to cars stolen and houses ransacked. This site can be a useful resource for your tenants if your rental property is located in one of the areas covered by the scheme. If this is the case, make your tenants aware of the site.

You might also want your tenants to sign an agreement such as that in Form 15-1, to make your stance on crime and drug abuse clear to them.

Crime- and Drug-Free Housing Addendum

This document is an addendum and is part of the Tenancy Agreement, dated ________________

by and between ________________ (Landlord/Agent) and ________________ (Tenant),

for the property located at: ____

In consideration of the execution or renewal of a lease of the Property identified in the Tenancy Agreement, Management and Tenant agree as follows:

1. Tenant, any member of Tenant's household, or a guest or other person under the Tenant's control shall not engage in criminal activity, including drug-related criminal activity, in or near said Property. Drug-related criminal activity means the illegal manufacture, sale, distribution, use, or possession with intent to manufacture, sell, distribute, or use a controlled substance.

2. Tenant, any member of Tenant's household, or a guest or other person under Tenant's control shall not engage in any act intended to facilitate criminal activity, including drug-related criminal activity, in or near said Property.

3. Tenant or members of the household will not permit the Property to be used for, or to facilitate criminal activity, including drug-related criminal activity, regardless of whether the individual engaging in such activity is a member of the household or a guest.

4. Tenant or members of the household will not engage in the manufacture, sale, or distribution of illegal drugs at any location, whether in or near said Property or otherwise.

5. Tenant, or any member of Tenant's household, or a guest or other person under Tenant's control, shall not engage in acts of violence in or near said Property.

6. Violation of any of the above provisions shall be a material violation of the Tenancy Agreement and good cause for termination of the tenancy. A single violation of any of the provisions of this addendum shall be deemed a serious violation and a material non-compliance with the Tenancy Agreement. It is understood and agreed that a single violation shall be good cause for the termination of the Tenancy Agreement. Unless otherwise provided by law, proof of violation shall not require criminal conviction, but shall be by a preponderance of the evidence.

7. In case of conflict between the provisions of this addendum and any other provisions of the Tenancy Agreement, the provisions of the addendum shall govern.

____________ ____________________

Date Landlord/Agent

____________ ____________________

Date Tenant

Form 15-1: Crime- and Drug-Free Housing Addendum.

Paying attention to tenants' questions and complaints about safety-related issues

When tenants directly enquire about safety or security at your rental property, always provide an honest answer and inform them of any recent confirmed serious or violent criminal incidents. Also refer them to the local police station for specific information. (Landlords are not routinely advised or aware of crime in the area or often even in their own rental property.)

Although describing your building's security devices can be an effective marketing technique, you must take care to avoid inadvertently increasing your liability. The problem arises when you explicitly say or even imply that your rental property is safer and more secure than other properties. If you make those kinds of claims, your security measures had better live up to your statements. In reality, crime can happen anywhere, and no rental property is immune.

When discussing any building features, be sure to speak generically without embellishment. For example, if you happen to have a burglar alarm in your rental property, do not refer to it as a security protection system or add or imply that they will be safe and secure because of this or any other building feature.

Exclude the words *safe, secure, security,* or any variations from your vocabulary and all advertising and marketing materials. Don't use these words in your advertising, on the phone, or when showing your rental property. If you do and your tenant ever becomes a victim of crime, he can claim that your ads or comments gave him the expectation of security. Be honest with people, but be sure they understand that neither you nor the police can guarantee any level of safety or security for them, their family and guests, or their personal possessions or vehicles.

Make sure that you test any alarm and demonstrate the proper use of all security devices in the presence of your new tenants and ask them to sign an acknowledgement. Remind your tenants in writing to test these devices on a regular basis, because they can fail or malfunction, and to call you immediately for repairs or replacement if the devices don't seem to be working properly.

Some landlords put disclaimers in their tenancy agreements that say the owner isn't responsible if a tenant suffers damage or an injury, regardless of the cause. With such a disclaimer in place, landlords can get careless and slow in responding to tenant complaints about lights that need replacing or malfunctioning doors or window locks. But what they don't realise is that these disclaimers are almost certainly unenforceable. Most courts look unfavourably upon these broad clauses that attempt to shift the owner's duty to properly maintain the premises in order to avoid responsibility for a tenant's injuries or damage. However, it is a good idea to include language in your tenancy agreement informing tenants of the following:

- You have not promised security of any kind.
- The tenants acknowledge that you do not and cannot guarantee the safety or security of the tenants or their guests.
- You don't guarantee the effectiveness or operability of security devices.

Ask your solicitor for assistance in preparing the proper legal documentation.

Responding to crimes when they occur

If a serious or violent crime occurs in the block of flats in which your rental property is situated, be sure to give your tenants written notification as soon as possible, along with any warnings or safety tips provided by the police. Some landlords are concerned that telling tenants about crime at the property or in the immediate area will lead to increased vacancies. Although on occasion you may indeed lose a tenant this way, warning your tenants so that they can be more conscious of safety and security issues is important and can help prevent other, similar crimes from occurring.

There are no specific rules as to what crimes should be reported to your tenants. But you should notify them about any crime concerning physical attack or bodily injury, as well as any attempted or actual break-ins, burglaries, or robberies in neighbouring flats or houses. A random car break-in or minor isolated vandalism on the property usually doesn't warrant notification unless there are repeated incidents. You can use a letter or memo to inform tenants about criminal activity, but a quick phone call works equally well.

If you opt for written notification, the note should be dated and inform your tenants that a crime has occurred. Be sure to include any information, composite sketches, or safety tips provided by the police. Do not include the victim's name or address unless he or she has requested that you do so or unless you have advance approval. Remind tenants to be careful regarding security and safety and to call the police immediately if they suspect a crime. Also, remind tenants that security is their responsibility. And be extremely careful that you avoid making any statements that could be used against you in any future legal action.

You have highly sensitive personal information on your tenants, including where they live and work, what cars they drive, and all of their personal identification and financial information. You have a tremendous responsibility to keep this information confidential. Have a policy of not providing any information to anyone unless the tenant has specifically given you advance written authorisation to do so. You must also securely lock all of your property and tenant files in unlabelled drawers to prevent intruders from rifling through these documents to target vulnerable tenants.

You can protect your tenants' personal information in blocks of flats too, by ensuring that only the tenant's surname is indicated next to the entry buzzer – giving no indication of gender or full name.

Taking Security Precautions

One of the best ways to prevent crime from occurring at your rental property is to make security a top priority. In this section, we cover some important security issues worth considering, not only for the safety of your property but for your tenants' well-being, too.

You can't guarantee your tenants that their property will be safe. But you can and should do what you can to increase the likelihood that they'll be free of problems.

Keys

Rental property locks are useless as security devices when you don't have effective control over keys. Some properties have a master key system where one single key works on all locks. Although such a system is convenient, we strongly recommend against using a master key system, because one lost key can require you to change all the locks in the entire property. Instead, use a duplicate key system with different keys for each lock.

Rather than giving tradesmen and contractors a key, always arrange to have someone you know and trust let them into the rental property.

Keep all landlord or agent keys in a metal locking key cabinet or key safe. So that the keys can't be used easily if they're lost or stolen, don't label the keys with the tenant's address; instead code the keys so that you know which property they belong to. If a tenant reports a lost or missing key, change the lock instead of giving him a duplicate key, unless he is sure the key is irretrievably lost. Charge the tenant a reasonable fee to cover your costs of getting a new key cut or a new lock fitted.

Although you must always change all entry locks when a tenant moves out, some tenants want to change or install additional locks. This is fine as long as they give you a duplicate key so that you can enter the rental property during emergencies and to make previously agreed repairs. If you become aware that a lock has been added or changed, verbally explain your policy and request a copy of the key. If the tenant doesn't want to give you a copy of the new key, send a polite but firm letter informing him of your policy. Ultimately, you may need to consider eviction if you aren't able to get a copy of the key.

Use standard rental property security devices such as the following: A five-lever mortice deadlock (make sure it conforms to British Standard BS 3621). All wooden entry doors should be solid core and have wide-angle peepholes or door viewers. They should also be fitted with a safety chain. Key-operated window locks are also a must and are valuable security devices.

Make sure that any security devices you install are easy to operate and difficult to disable. A determined criminal can clearly break in to any rental property, but you want to make your flat or house a more difficult target. Also avoid installing security devices that create an illusion of security, because they can actually lower a tenant's guard and make him more vulnerable to crimes. For example, don't install fake closed-circuit television cameras (CCTV) in an attempt to deter criminal activity.

If your rental properties are large, expensive houses, regularly occupied by wealthy tenants with valuable belongings, you may want to consider installing an alarm, linked to your local police station. When activated, the police turn up at the property. A number of installation companies offer this service; ensure the one you pick is accredited in accordance with the provisions of the Association of Chief Police Officers Requirements for Security Services. This service is expensive, but the cost can be passed onto the tenants and reflected in the rent. If your tenants do have a lot of valuables, they're likely to welcome such a service and may even demand it.

Make sure that your tenant initials that all these security devices are operative on her inventory when she moves into the property and knows that she must contact you immediately if any locks or security devices are inoperative. Repair any broken locks or security devices immediately upon being notified.

Lighting

Outdoor lighting has many benefits. Proper lighting is an extremely cost-effective way to protect your property and your tenants. It can serve as a deterrent to vandalism while illuminating your building's paths and gardens to help prevent injuries to tenants and guests. The right lighting plan can also improve the appearance of your building and hence its kerb appeal.

Lighting is only effective if it is in good working order, properly located, and has the right type of fixture and light bulb for the intended purpose.

To keep your property well lit, opt for lights with built-in sensors so that they automatically detect movement. These types of lights reduce electricity costs because they don't need to be on during daylight hours and energy isn't wasted as they are only illuminated when you really need them. Such lights are also a good deterrent to burglars or other people up to no good because they're visible to people who approach the property.

Establish a regular schedule for inspecting exterior lighting and immediately repair broken fixtures and dead bulbs. The best time for inspecting and testing your lights is at night, when you can see that all fixtures are working properly and providing sufficient illumination in the correct locations. Be sure to log your lighting inspections and repairs or bulb replacement in your maintenance records.

Addressing Environmental Issues

Although crime is usually the first safety concern that comes to mind for landlords, important tenant safety topics also include fire protection, environmental challenges, and the potential for flooding or strong gales.

Fire safety

Fire safety is a critical issue for landlords. Every year, hundreds of people die in fires and many thousands more are injured. Fires can spread quickly and fully engulf a room or even an entire rental property in a matter of minutes. Fires also produce poisonous gases and smoke that are disorienting and can be deadly.

Unless your rental property is a House in Multiple Occupation (HMO), (see Chapter 8 for more information) there are no specific fire regulations for residential properties in the UK. However, regulations do apply to furniture and smoke alarms and you should make yourself familiar with these. Your Fire Prevention Officer, located at your local fire station, can help you with these.

Work with your local Fire Prevention Officer to develop an evacuation plan for your property. Think about means of emergency escape for tenants, particularly where sleeping accommodation is on second or third floors. You should also consider fire doors and emergency exits, along with other escape routes.

If you are really worried or just want to be on the safe side, ask for a fire inspection of your property; when your property is inspected you receive written notification of any deficiencies. You must address these noted items immediately and contact your local Fire Prevention Officer in writing to acknowledge that the items have been corrected and to request a re-inspection. Be sure to get written confirmation that all items have been satisfactorily corrected.

Fire extinguishers and blankets

No compulsory requirement exists to provide your tenants with a fire extinguisher or fire blanket, but doing so may be wise, particularly in the kitchen. If you do provide a fire extinguisher make sure to have it serviced every 12 months to ensure it's in good working order. These checks should be carried out by a company registered by the British Approvals for Fire Equipment (BAFE). Your fire extinguisher should also conform to the appropriate British Standard; look for the kitemark or special BAFE mark. Fire blankets should conform to British Standard BS 6575.

Evaluate your potential liability in the event of the fire extinguisher being defective, used improperly, or even improperly maintained by your tenant. If your tenant gets hurt because the fire extinguisher you provided wasn't working properly when she needed it, you could be held liable and sued. Your local Fire Prevention Officer can offer your tenants instruction on the proper use of extinguishers, and this could be a valuable lesson.

Smoke detectors

Fires are always serious, but the most dangerous fires are the ones that start while the tenants are asleep. That is one reason why landlords are legally obliged to install smoke detectors in all rental properties built after June 1992. The Smoke Detectors Act, 1991 requires that all properties built after this date must have smoke detectors installed on every floor. Even if your rental property was built before this date, we strongly recommend that you install smoke alarms in all hallways and near or preferably just inside all sleeping areas, in compliance with the manufacturer's specifications.

Always inspect and test smoke alarms according to the manufacturer's instructions when a tenant moves out and before a new one moves in. If a fire hurts a tenant because the smoke alarm wasn't working properly when he moved in, you could be sued and held responsible. So be sure to keep written records of your inspection and testing of the smoke detector and get your tenant to initial his tenancy agreement indicating that the smoke detector was tested in his presence and that he can perform his own tests. Remind him that the alarm should be tested on a regular basis to ensure that the battery is working – if he aims to do this on the first day of every month, it should be easy for him to remember.

Also, be sure to immediately address all tenant requests for smoke alarm inspections and repairs. Note these requests in your maintenance log along with the date that the smoke detector was repaired or replaced. If the tenant is present, get him to sign acknowledging that the smoke alarm now works properly. Smoke alarm complaints are always a top priority requiring immediate attention, so keep new smoke alarms on hand for this reason.

Carbon monoxide

Carbon monoxide is a colourless, odourless, and poisonous gas produced when fuel burns incompletely. It can build up in a rental property in just a few hours. If a leak occurs when the tenants are asleep, they could easily lose consciousness and suffer a serious injury before noticing anything was wrong, or even die.

Appliances such as Calor gas fires and oil-fired boilers, gas water-heaters, and wood-burning stoves and fireplaces can all emit carbon monoxide. When these appliances are working properly, the carbon monoxide is directed to the chimney or other air vent, and there's no danger. However, if the appliances or fireplace is not properly serviced and there is a blockage or malfunction, then carbon monoxide can build up.

Naturally, carbon monoxide poisoning is a particular concern for landlords with properties with a gas supply, particularly where tenants rely on Calor gas fires to heat their rental property. Carbon monoxide detectors are a good idea, and we strongly advise installing a carbon monoxide detector if your rental property has a fireplace or uses carbon monoxide-producing heating appliances.

Gas appliances in rented accommodation must abide by very strict legal requirements. The Gas Safety (Installation and Use) Regulations, 1994, require all landlords to maintain the gas appliances in their rental properties through annual inspections and safety checks. You cannot perform this check yourself; instead you must have a CORGI-registered engineer carry it out. Your tenant must receive a copy of this gas safety certificate each year. Failure to ensure that these annual checks are carried out could result in a fine or imprisonment.

If you have fireplaces, you need to employ a chimney cleaning company to periodically inspect your chimney, chimney connections, and insulation for cracks, blockages, or leaks. Have the recommended work done as soon as possible and quickly respond to any complaints from tenants about possible carbon monoxide poisoning.

Electromagnetic fields

Electromagnetic fields (EMFs) are a relatively new environmental hazard with varying scientific opinions regarding the potential danger to humans. Electric power-lines, electrical wiring, and even appliances all create some level of EMFs. Although the forces created by these sources is minimal when compared to even the normal electrical activity found within the human body, scientists cannot agree definitively as to whether exposure to EMFs can, or does, increase a person's chance of developing certain types of cancer, particularly childhood leukaemia.

This potential problem is well beyond your control, but although little conclusive scientific evidence that EMFs cause cancer exists, you should be aware of this issue in case you receive a tenant complaint. The bottom line is that, because you cannot insist that the electric utility remove its power lines and transmitters, the only viable solution for a tenant with legitimate concerns about EMFs is to move. Evaluate the legitimacy of your tenant's concerns to determine whether it's in your mutual best interest to release a tenant from his tenancy agreement.

The Health Protection Agency offers advice and information as to the risk of radiation around the country. If they are at all concerned, direct your tenants to its Web site at `www.hpa.org.uk/radiation` for more information.

Natural disasters

Although the UK is different to many other countries in that earthquakes and tornadoes are thankfully rare, we do have our own set of challenges from Mother Nature. Make sure that both you and your tenants are prepared for floods, if the property is situated on or near a flood plain, or severe gales. The Environment Agency offers advice and tips on ways in which you and your tenants can minimise flood risk, before any damage is done and an emergency occurs. For more information, log onto its Web site at `www.environment-agency.gov.uk`.

In winter, snow and ice accumulation can create dangerous conditions on paths and driveways. Landlords aren't responsible if a tenant slips and falls on natural accumulations of snow and ice. However, it may be worth supplying a shovel in the garden shed or garage, if your rental property has one of these, so that the tenant can remove any ice and snow if they want to before it builds up and becomes treacherous.

Cover Me, I'm Going In! Making Sure You Have the Insurance You Need

The thought of your property burning down or a tenant absconding owing you six months' rent are big enough fears to keep you awake at night. But if you have sound ownership and management policies combined with insurance cover that has been customised for your specific needs, you're probably okay.

Insurance buys you peace of mind. No law says that your property must be insured – although mortgage lenders insist that you have buildings insurance – and you'd be very foolish not to consider other forms of insurance as well.

The following sections explain what to think about when you're shopping for an insurance company and the types of coverage you'll need.

Choosing a company and getting the coverage you need

Some insurers cover you against any possible danger or loss in the world. And a sharp insurance salesperson is a master at describing all sorts of horrible problems that could befall your rental property. If you want to make sure you're covered at a reasonable cost, you need to sift through the sales pitch and decide which cover is right for you. Cover can be extended as required to include almost any conceivable eventuality when letting a property, but make sure the cover you get is essential. Your goal is to pay only for cover for events and losses that are most likely to occur at your property. The right insurance cover is worth a lot, but buying hurricane insurance in Chester doesn't make much sense.

Here are some tips to getting the cover you need at a competitive price:

- Be sure to shop around and use an insurance broker when sourcing the best insurance cover for your needs. The cover you can get as a landlord varies from insurer to insurer. The insurance broker can provide you with information on the kinds of policies worth considering. The Internet is also a good source of broker sites; most allow you to input your insurance requirements and then find you the best deal in a matter of seconds.
- When selecting an insurer, always use a reputable company. It is only when you come to make a claim that you are likely to find out how good your insurer is so think very carefully before making a selection.

- To ensure that you're receiving the cover you need at a competitive price, consult an insurance broker and contact a couple of insurance providers directly. But bear in mind that the lowest premium shouldn't be the determining factor in your decision. Going for the lowest premium may not always be the best policy for your needs. Ask a lot of questions.
- After you've chosen a policy and paid your premium, insist on evidence that the insurance company is actually providing you with cover. Your best proof of cover is a formal certificate of insurance, which should be carefully stored along with all policy documents.

You must notify your mortgage lender and insurer that you're letting the property. Not obtaining written consent from these parties beforehand may render your cover void in the event of a claim. If you decide to rent out your own home, immediately contact your insurance company and ask for your homeowner's policy to be converted to a landlord's policy. A landlord's policy covers the higher risk of having another person living in your home. Because of the increased liability risk for rental properties, your current insurance company may decline to offer you this cover. Certain insurance companies specialise in this business, however. Either way, make sure that you have proper landlord's cover for your rental property, or you could face the possibility of having your claim denied.

If you own several rental properties, you may be able to negotiate a discount with your insurance company in return for covering all of them. Using one insurance company for all your properties makes it easier to keep track of your insurance cover and know when the policies are up for renewal.

Understanding the types of insurance cover available

One of the first steps in getting the right insurance is understanding the different types of cover available. Insurance is broken down into two main types, outlined in the following sections:

- Buildings insurance
- Contents insurance

Good insurance cover protects you from losses caused by many perils, including fire, storms, burglary, and vandalism. A comprehensive policy also includes property owner's liability cover in case of injury, death, or damage to individuals (such as a postman or meter reader) on, or adjacent to, your property. You could also opt for legal expenses insurance covering all of your legal costs, solicitor's fees, and costs that arise from ending up in court with your tenants. Such policies usually cost less than £100 per annum – and given that the average cost of a possession hearing in 2001 was £785, according to the Association of Residential Letting Agents (Arla), that's money well spent.

Buildings insurance

Buildings insurance covers you in case anything happens to the building itself – if it burns to the ground, for example – and all mortgage lenders require that you have it. Landlords' buildings insurance should cover your property in the event of fire, lightning, explosion, smoke, impact, burst pipes, storm or flood damage, malicious damage, and subsidence and theft.

The property is covered for the cost of rebuilding the property – not the market value. Therefore, you must make sure you are adequately covered. Arla believes that 40 per cent of UK properties are under-insured, so if those property owners make a claim, their insurers will not pay the full amount of that claim.

Although most insurance companies supply quotes on the basis of information provided by you as to the size and age of the property, employ a qualified surveyor to calculate the rebuild cost of your rental property. Buildings insurance is index-linked to reflect the fact that building costs increase on an annual basis.

Some insurers won't offer you buildings cover if you are letting to tenants that they deem to be high risk. Such tenants include students, a group of single people living in a property together, or tenants receiving Housing Benefit. If your tenants fall into these categories, you may have to shop around a bit to find cover, and you'll probably end up paying more than you would for tenants who are considered to present a lower risk.

Contents insurance

Contents insurance covers a rental property's contents (as the name implies) rather than the property's structure. Two types of contents cover are available: a *full* policy or *limited* cover.

If you let your rental property either unfurnished or part-furnished, you may want to choose limited cover. *Limited* contents cover insures items such as carpets, curtains, light fixtures, and fittings in your rental property. The total you can claim on such a policy tends to be limited to around £5,000. These policies often include Employer's liability and Landlord's liability cover in relation to the rental property's contents. Such cover can be useful if your tenants or their guests are injured by tripping over a loose carpet or burn themselves on a faulty light fitting. Such accidents often result in expensive compensation claims. Upwards of £100,000 in compensation for modest injuries is not uncommon.

If your property is fully furnished, you should have full contents cover. With this type of cover, your insurer will ask you how much you want to insure the contents for. Specify a large enough sum to replace all the items on a new for old basis.

Even if you have hardly any furniture in your rental property, basic contents insurance and liability cover are well worth considering. Seriously consider how much replacing your rental property's furnishings would cost. Walk through the rental property, room by room, noting down all its contents. This is the best way of ensuring that you don't miss anything, which could happen if you rely solely on your memory.

Rent guarantee insurance

Some landlords who take out a buy-to-let mortgage to purchase a rental property think it makes a lot of sense to get a policy that guarantees the rent in case the tenant doesn't pay up. Not only are you guaranteed to receive the rent you expect from your property, enabling you to make your mortgage payments regardless of the tenant's ability to pay, but the premiums you pay for this type of insurance are also tax deductible.

If you rely on the rent to make the monthly payments to the mortgage lender, having rent guarantee insurance means you don't have to worry about finding the cash to make your payment if your tenant defaults on the rental payments.

Policies tend to guarantee rent for a fixed period, usually 6 or 12 months. Premiums are calculated in different ways, from a fixed cost policy to a percentage of the annual rent. The latter tends to be more common – usually 3 to 4 per cent.

Determining the right excess

Excess is the amount of money that you must pay out when you make an insurance claim. The higher the excess, the lower your premiums, so calculate what you can realistically afford to pay upfront when making a claim. Some insurers set the excess quite high – at around £300 or so, but for many landlords £100 is a more manageable amount. The amount you decide upon should depend on what you are personally comfortable with.

Evaluate the possibility of having a higher excess and using your savings on the premiums to purchase other important insurance cover.

Home contents insurance: Cover your tenants should buy

Home contents insurance is something your tenants should get and pay for themselves; it covers losses to the tenant's personal property as a result of fire, theft, water damage, or other loss. (Any item a tenant brings into the rental property is her responsibility to insure.)

A basic home contents insurance policy offers some protection for tenants' belongings against damage and theft. But specific tenant's contents insurance goes a lot further. Most policies cover tenants for accidental damage caused to the landlord's fixture and fittings, the building itself, and your furniture. Your tenancy agreement should make the tenant liable for damage such as red wine stains, and the cost of cleaning or replacing the carpet is usually deducted from their deposit at the end of the tenancy. If the damages are excessive, tenants are often not in a financial position to replace or pay for the cost of repair to items themselves, and such a loss could be devastating. If they take out tenant's contents insurance, they would be able to claim for such accidents on their policy.

Tenants often think they do not need home contents insurance because they have few valuables and because they have already shelled out a deposit, a month's rent, and administration fees when they first move into your rental property. When money is tight, insurance is often the last thing on tenants' minds. In addition, many tenants wrongly believe that the landlord has insured their personal possessions.

As a landlord, you benefit from tenant's contents insurance because it covers any claims in the event that the tenant starts a fire or flood. (As an added bonus, the tenant's premiums go up instead of yours.) So be sure to have a clause in your tenancy agreement that clearly points out that every tenant must have his or her own home contents insurance policy.

Handling potential claims

Immediately document all facts if an incident occurs at your rental property, particularly if it involves injury. Use the Incident Report Form (like the one shown in Form 15-2) to record all the facts. Be sure to immediately contact your insurance company or your insurance broker. Follow up with a written letter to ensure they were notified and have the information on file.

Incident Report

Date ________________ Time _________ Name of Reporting Person __________________________
Date of Incident _________ Time of Incident _________ Property __________________________
Specific Location of Incident ____

Type of Incident: Accident ______ Crime ____ Fire ____ Police ____ Ambulance _______
Mechanical _______ Theft ____ Flood ____ Other ______________________________

Details of what happened: ____
____
____
____

Details of injury/damage: ____
____
____
____

Names, addresses, phone numbers of people involved: ____
____
____

Names, addresses, phone numbers of witnesses: ____
____
____

Specific conditions at time of incident: ____
____
____
____

Name of insurance company ______________________________ Policy no ____________________
Name, address and phone number of insurance broker: ____
____
Date and time insurance company notified ______________ By phone ______ By mail _______

Request from/permission granted by insurance company to document incident: Yes or No
If yes, how: Photos _____ Video _____ Audio ______ Written statements ______________________

Date and time police/ambulance notified: ____
Time of police/ambulance arrival: __________________ Report number __________________

Follow-up required/taken: ____

Form 15-2: Incident Report Form

Part V
Money, Money, Money!

"I just hope our news of a £50 monthly rent rise won't come as too much of a shock for Madame Zara."

In this part . . .

Keeping track of your money is important no matter what business you're in, but it's especially important in property management. In the chapters in this part, we make two not-so-fun issues you'll have to deal with as a rental property owner – insurance and taxes – easy to understand. We also give you some great tips for keeping records and managing your finances. So for all issues monetary, read on.

Chapter 16

Raising the Cash to Buy Your Rental Property

In This Chapter

- Making sure you can afford a rental property
- Negotiating the buy-to-let mortgage maze to find the best deal for you
- Renting out your home in order to buy another property to live in
- Getting advice from a mortgage broker

Finding the right rental property is just the beginning. Financing your purchase is a big consideration, and there are many ways to go about it. Few of us are lucky enough to be in the position to have enough cash to buy a property outright – and even if you are, that might not be the best way of doing it. Luckily, scores of mortgage lenders now offer competitive buy-to-let loans specifically for this purpose. for investment landlords. But be warned: This can be a double-edged sword. Landlords are spoilt for choice: Deciding whether a fixed rate or discounted deal is best for you can be difficult, because much depends on the future movement of interest rates (which can be very difficult to predict). We recommend that you use an independent mortgage broker to help you source the best deal.

In this chapter, we look at the various ways that you can buy your rental properties and the different types of buy-to-let mortgages available. We also cover how to calculate whether your rental income will be good enough to pay the mortgage, and what criteria the lender judges you on. The financial side can be a bit of a pain to sort out, but to ensure it doesn't become a burden later on, you need to take a good look at your finances and plan your purchases very carefully.

More For Dummies house purchase help

Financing and purchasing a property is the sort of topic we could fill two books on, let alone the one chapter our editor is allowing us in this book. So Melanie has done just that – if you're looking for more details on property purchases or finding the right mortgage, take a look at Melanie's *Buying and Selling a Home For Dummies* and *Buying a Home on a Budget For Dummies* (both published by Wiley).

Making Sure You Can Afford to Buy a Rental Property

Buying property to rent out is a very fashionable step to take. Newspapers regularly feature tales of housewives and retired teachers who have made thousands of pounds speculating on the property market. These stories have great appeal because they are about ordinary people who, without much prior know-how, take the plunge and decide to become landlords.

Despite these media stories, property remains a big investment risk because so much money is involved. Becoming a landlord might be appealing, but you need to think carefully before taking the plunge. If you are in a lot of debt with a big overdraft, owe thousands of pounds on credit and store cards, have an outstanding personal loan or two, or a massive mortgage on your own home, think twice before buying a rental property.

Even with detailed tenant screening criteria (see Chapter 8), landlords can end up with tenants who don't pay their rent some months or with an empty property for a period of time because of a temporary shortage of suitable tenants. Ask yourself whether you could cover the rent and associated costs for several months if you had to. If the answer is no, you are likely to be over-stretching yourself – and buying a rental property might not be for you.

Buy-to-Let Mortgages

You must be between the ages of 18, 21, or 25 and 65 to 75 (depending on the lender and your particular circumstances) to qualify for a buy-to-let mortgage. The minimum term for borrowing tends to be five years, the maximum can be anything up to 40 years, as long as the landlord hasn't retired during that time

And the lender will also demand that the property is ready to rent before it lets you have a buy-to-let mortgage.

Many lenders offer a good range of competitive deals with rates of interest not that much higher than you'd typically pay on your main residence, rather than the commercial rates landlords paid in the past. In addition, buy-to-let lenders take into account the rental income of a property when deciding whether to lend you the money to purchase it, rather than your own income.

Before 1996, when the buy-to-let scheme was introduced, most landlords were cash buyers, as they weren't allowed to rent out a property on which they had an outstanding mortgage. Some lenders gave permission for the property to be rented out if there was a mortgage on the property – but certain conditions had to be satisfied first. But the buy-to-let mortgage scheme has changed all that.

Generating enough rental income

Buy-to-let loans are calculated differently to normal mortgages (where you might expect to borrow between three and four times your income). The lender decides whether or not to lend you the money to buy the property according to the likely rental income the property will generate, known as the *rental cover.*

The rental cover is the proportion of the mortgage payment that the lender requires the rent to cover. Because you are likely to have your own home already, you're probably already making payments on a mortgage based on your income. Thus you'll use the rental income from your tenants to pay the buy-to-let loan. For this reason, the lender needs to know that this amount will be enough to cover the mortgage.

The average minimum rental cover lenders require can be anything from 100 to 130 per cent. If we take the highest amount – 130 per cent – if the monthly mortgage payments on your rental property are likely to be £500, you should be looking at generating rent of £650 a month from your tenants.

When deciding whether to allow you a buy-to-let loan, some lenders still take your income into account, in addition to the potential rental income of a rental property. The amount you have to earn from a source other than your rental income varies from lender to lender.

You must calculate your rental income carefully. When you apply for a buy-to-let mortgage, most lenders ask for some evidence, in writing, of what the rental property is likely to generate. You can get an estimate of what rent the property can generate from a letting or estate agent who has some knowledge of the local rental market. Ask local agents with similar properties in the area on their books what rent you can expect from your prospective property. If agents estimate that the rent you can reasonably expect is much less than what you need, you may as well stop wasting your time and look for another rental property.

Raising a deposit

As with the purchase of your main residence, when you buy a rental property you need to put down a deposit. The deposit tends to be bigger than that required by the mortgage lender on your main residence, because the risks are thought to be that much greater. Most lenders require a deposit of at least 15 per cent.

The bigger the deposit, the smaller the mortgage. If you have, say, £60,000 in savings, you may be tempted to put this all down as a big deposit on one property. But ask yourself whether this strategy is the best way of doing things. Dividing this deposit between two rental properties may be better because, as long as the mortgage payments are adequately covered, how high they are doesn't really matter. Having two properties, rather than one may work out much better for you financially in the long run; in other words, put down the minimum deposit the lender requires from you and then keep the remainder until you see another rental property you like the look of. By following this strategy, you can grow a property portfolio and avoid putting all your eggs in one basket.

Think before committing your funds

We know one accountant who spends 90 per cent of his time dealing with clients who want to invest money for their retirement but don't want to use a pension to do this. Often they have thousands of pounds to invest and prefer to put it into property instead.

One client who came to visit him had £200,000 in cash. This client wanted to use this money to buy a rental property. He was convinced that the best course of action was to buy one large property outright because he didn't want to take on another mortgage.

But our accountant friend advised otherwise. He told his client that dividing the sum to pay four deposits on four rental properties was a much better use of his cash. He pointed out that taking out a buy-to-let mortgage on each property would not be increasing his risk, because the rental income would cover the mortgage payments. It could also work to his advantage because each property would generate a little bit of extra income and he could reduce his tax bill by offsetting his mortgage interest repayments against the rental income.

The client took his accountant's advice and ended up buying four properties with his cash, thereby spreading his risk and maximising his potential income. Think twice about how you invest the money you have before taking the plunge.

Extra fees

Don't forget that a valuation fee needs to be paid, based on the value of the property, but usually around £300. You also have to pay a fee of around £500, although this varies between lenders, for setting up the mortgage, which is added onto your loan on completion of the deal. If you use a broker, you may also have to pay a fee for their services.

Never invest money in a rental property that you may need in the short-term. Property is a very illiquid investment that you should plan to hold for the long term. There's no point overstretching yourself on the deposit if you haven't got enough spare cash in the bank to fix your car if it fails its MOT.

Finding the right buy-to-let mortgage

Getting the right deal can be the difference between making a go of your rental property business or not. Interest repayments that are too high will significantly eat into your profits.

Scores of mortgage lenders offer buy-to-let loans, and hundreds of different deals are available. Theoretically, you should be able to find a buy-to-let mortgage that's suitable for you. Finding the right one requires that you take the time to think about what you want from your mortgage – and what you don't.

You can find a wide choice of buy-to-let mortgages designed to fit all sorts of circumstances. Some are geared to the purchase of one property, others to the creation of a portfolio of up to five properties. Generally speaking, loans of £15,000 to £1m per investor are available, repayable over five to 40 years.

Some lenders offer *staged payment loans.* These types of loans are ideal if the rental property needs a lot of work before you can rent it to tenants. The lender's surveyor agrees to the value of a fully refurbished property, and the mortgage offer is based on this value. A proportion of the loan is made available up front to buy the property, with the rest of the cash paid in stages as work progresses. In other cases, the lender holds back a chunk of the money until the landlord has completed essential work, such as employing a tree surgeon to remove a tree growing close to the property whose roots could affect the foundations. In such cases, you have to ensure you have enough cash on hand to cover the required work until the lender releases the funds.

Some buy-to-let mortgages allow you to buy up to five properties with one loan. This option can be the simplest way of extending your property portfolio, so ask your mortgage lender or broker for more details.

Decision 1: Interest-only or repayment mortgage

As a prospective landlord you first have to choose between an interest-only and a repayment mortgage.

The following sections explain the features of each type of mortgage.

Interest-only mortgages

Interest-only buy-to-let mortgages are the most popular among landlords, with nearly two-thirds opting for this type of loan, according to the Association of Residential Letting Agents (Arla).

Interest-only loans do exactly what they say on the tin: You pay only the interest on the loan each month. At the end of the mortgage term, you still owe the mortgage lender the capital you borrowed in the first place. The onus is on you to set up an investment vehicle into which you save enough cash each month to repay the capital at the end of the loan period.

Landlords don't need to take out an investment product to back an interest-only loan on a rental property. This is because you are likely to already have a main residence and aren't relying on your rental property to provide a roof over your head once you retire. You can plough the money you would have put into an investment vehicle into other rental properties – the idea being that when you need to repay the capital on one of your rental properties, you can simply sell one to pay back the lender what you owe.

All of your monthly mortgage payments can be offset against the rental income of the property for tax purposes. If you opt for a repayment loan, it is possible to claim the interest part against the rental income for tax purposes, but not the capital portion.

Repayment mortgages

Repayment mortgages are less popular than interest-only mortgages for buy-to-let purposes, but may still be worth considering. With a repayment mortgage, you pay not only the interest on the loan each month, but also a slice of the capital. The idea is that at the end of the mortgage term you will have paid off the loan in full and the property will be yours.

Of course, your monthly repayments are higher than if you had opted for an interest-only deal. The calculation as to what percentage of the monthly repayment is interest and what is capital needs to be done when offsetting rental income against your mortgage repayments on your self-assessment tax return. Your mortgage lender should provide you with these figures.

Decision 2: To fix, discount, track, or be flexible?

Once you've decided to opt for an interest-only or repayment deal, you must choose between the various types of mortgage available: fixed rate, discount flexible, or tracker. The following sections explain.

Think very carefully about what sort of mortgage would best suit your requirements before signing on the dotted line. What suits one landlord quite often doesn't suit another. Consult an independent mortgage broker for more advice.

Tracker mortgages

Many landlords opt for tracker rate mortgages with no penalties at any time for switching because they like their flexibility. Their mortgage repayments track interest rate movements – the Bank of England base rate or LIBOR (the rate of interest at which banks borrow funds from other banks).

The advantage of tracking a rate of interest is that if your mortgage rate is one per cent above it, you always pay one per cent more than that rate – no more and no less. While the rate your mortgage is tracking can fluctuate, you are not at the whim of your mortgage lender. Instead of dictating rate movements as, and when, it likes, the lender is instead committed to following the movement of the rate being tracked.

Fixed rate mortgages

An increasing number of landlords opt for fixed rate buy-to-let mortgages because rates on these have fallen at the time of writing. They also bring peace of mind: You can't guarantee that your tenant is going to pay the rent on time every month, no matter how good your tenant screening criteria is (although you should make sure that your tenant screening *is* good anyway – see Chapter 8) but if you fix your mortgage rate, you at least know exactly how much you have to pay the mortgage lender each month.

The most useful fixed rate deals for your purposes are likely to be *short term* – of three or five years' duration. You can get fixed rate deals for one, two, ten, 15 and even 30 years, but it isn't much use if the fixed period is too short or indeed too long. You don't want to think about remortgaging in a year's time and a lot can happen in the next 30 years!

Discount mortgages

A discount mortgage is a popular choice for landlords. You need to be comfortable with the fact that interest rates can go up as well as down, so while you might be getting a discount of around 3 per cent off the standard variable rate, it could go the other way as well if the Bank of England decides to raise interest rates.

Discount mortgages can work out cheaper than fixed rate deals if the base rate is low, but keep in mind that the rates go up as well as down, and you have no protection against a rise in your mortgage repayments – unlike a fixed rate mortgage. Discount mortgages can be a good deal, but they also add an extra layer of risk that most landlords could do without.

Flexible mortgages

Many landlords choose a flexible mortgage because it actually helps them manage their rental property business. Flexible deals allow you to overpay or underpay when you want. This flexibility can be useful when dealing with tenants because sometimes even the most reliable ones can forget to pay their rent on time or the property could lie empty for a couple of months in between tenancies. If you paid slightly more than you needed to during those months when the rent was on time or the property occupied, these overpayments count towards the total you owe, allowing you to pay less when the property is empty or when your tenants are struggling to pay the rent one month. The advantage of overpaying and then underpaying is that you aren't penalised for flexibility.

Alternatively, you can take a payment break and make no monthly mortgage repayments at all for a certain period of time – as long as you have built up your credit with overpayments when times were better.

Most flexible deals have interest calculated on a daily basis, which is a real bonus because it means you aren't paying over the odds as you are with monthly or annual calculations.

Remortgaging to a better deal

Once you've carefully chosen your buy-to-let mortgage, that shouldn't be the end of the financial decisions you have to make. Even if you opted for a fixed rate deal for three or five years, after that time, your mortgage reverts to the lender's standard variable rate (SVR), which will inevitably be considerably higher. Likewise, once landlords with discount mortgages come to the end of the offer period, they find themselves on their lender's much higher SVR.

If you are on your lender's SVR, you are almost certainly making higher monthly mortgage repayments than you need to. When this happens, it's time to remortgage to a better deal.

Remortgaging is when you switch from your current deal to another provided by the same lender or another lender if yours can't offer you a better deal. The first step to remortgaging is to approach your current lender and ask whether they can offer you a lower rate. Remind them that you are a loyal customer. If you have more than one rental property mortgaged with them, remind them of that fact, too. If your current lender can't offer you a cheaper deal, shop around, using a mortgage broker if necessary.

Switching to another buy-to-let mortgage could save you hundreds of pounds a year in interest. An increasing number of landlords are cottoning on to the fact that remortgaging is a relatively painless, straightforward way to save cash and help them grow their business. Many landlords take advantage of any increase in the equity in their property to release this cash when they remortgage to put down as a deposit on another rental property.

The process of remortgaging is fairly straightforward. Once you have chosen the deal you want, approach the lender and fill out an application form. Your property will have to be surveyed again, and you'll have to pay legal fees, but some lenders refund these on certain remortgage deals. You may have to pay a penalty for switching however, and a fee on the new mortgage so do the sums, and work out whether it is financially viable before taking the plunge.

Releasing equity

One way of raising finance to buy a rental property is to release money from your own home. With property appreciating so much in value, many homeowners find they are sitting on tens of thousands of pounds worth of equity in their homes. One way of buying rental property is to remortgage your own home to release some of this equity and put it towards the cost of a rental property.

The more the merrier

While you might think that the more properties you take on, the greater the risk, in fact the opposite is the case. As your property portfolio grows, your risks are reduced. For example, if you own ten rental properties and have problems with one of your tenants who is late paying her rent, more than likely things will be running smoothly with your other nine properties, let to good, reliable tenants who pay on time. The bad tenant is just a tiny percentage of the whole and seems like less of a big deal when you look at the bigger picture.

Owning more than one rental property is also useful when it comes to calculating your income on your tax return. Your property portfolio is considered as a single whole, rather than as a number of individual properties, so if you made losses on one rental property you can balance them against the gains made on another one when filling in your self-assessment tax return. Landlords can significantly reduce their tax bill and minimise their losses at the same time by doing this.

Don't run before you can walk. A large property portfolio may be your dream but a slow start is the best strategy to employ. Familiarise yourself with how the system works, what to look for in a property, and how to deal with tenants before taking on another rental property. And never forget to do your research carefully before buying another rental property – no matter how experienced you think you have become.

Renting Out in Order to Buy Again

Let-to-buy is growing in popularity. In let-to-buy, homeowners decide that instead of buying another property to rent out, they'd quite like to move somewhere else and rent out their existing home instead. You may want to do this if you have spent a lot of time and effort doing your current property up, and while you and your family may have outgrown it, you think it would make an excellent rental property.

If let-to-buy is your plan, you must notify your mortgage lender and inform them that you want to switch your mortgage over to a buy-to-let loan. (Most landlords then take out a "regular" mortgage to buy the property they are going to live in similar to the one they had on their first property.)

The mortgage lender is not the only company you have to notify. Insurers often have different policies for rental properties, so don't assume that your current insurance company will continue to offer the same buildings cover on your home as before. You may subsequently find that the insurer refuses to pay out in the event of a claim. It is far better to come clean and make sure you are adequately covered.

Not everyone will want to live in a home decorated or furnished to your individual taste. In addition, being dispassionate about a property is harder if you've lived there for many years and spent a lot of time and effort doing it up. Tenants might want something quite different, so if you want to be successful in letting your former home, try to look at it from their point of view.

Using a Mortgage Broker

If you really want to make life simple and ensure you get the best mortgage or remortgage deal, your best bet is to employ the services of a good independent mortgage broker. These brokers have a good grasp of the market and know about the best deals available. You may have to pay a fee for their expertise, but if you save money on mortgage interest repayments, such a service can more than pay for itself in the long run. About three-quarters of landlords use a broker, according to Arla, and many of these are highly experienced landlords.

A landlord who uses a mortgage broker knows that the best mortgage deal can make the difference between running a profitable rental business and not. A broker spends all of her time sourcing deals, helping clients find the best mortgage, and giving recommendations as to how best to structure your property portfolio. A broker can offer plenty of good advice about the buy-to-let scheme and might be able to point out something you have overlooked or simply not thought about.

Choose your mortgage broker with care. Look for one who is independent, so has access to all the deals on the market, and who specialises in the mortgage market. If you can, use a broker who has been personally recommended to you by a friend or fellow landlord who has experience with their services.

A broker receives either a fee from the landlord and/or a commission paid by the mortgage lender. Be sure to clarify right from the beginning which type of broker you are dealing with – after all, you don't want to be stung with an unexpected bill for hundreds of pounds once the mortgage is finalised.

You'll hear arguments in favour of both type of broker; some clients believe a broker is only truly independent if he receives a fee from the client. Other borrowers would prefer not to stump up a sizeable sum – often around 0.5 per cent of the mortgage – and don't have a problem with the broker receiving commission from the lender whose product he recommends.

Chapter 17

Avoiding Property Taxes

In This Chapter

- Understanding which taxes you have to pay
- Reducing your tax bill
- Planning to reduce future tax liabilities

Death and taxes: the two things in life that are said to be impossible to avoid. And when it comes to investing in property, there are plenty of taxation rules that you need to get to grips with. These are far more complex than those regarding homeownership but they can work in your favour – as long as you have a general understanding of the basic concepts.

While taxes may be unavoidable, you can reduce them in several ways – completely legitimately – when it comes to investing in rental property. In this chapter, we look at the taxes you must pay as a rental property owner and how you can avoid these, saving your hard-earned cash and ensuring your business is as profitable as possible.

Tax is, of course, a taxing subject, and you may find it helpful to have a copy of Tony Levene's *Paying Less Tax 2006/2007 For Dummies* (Wiley) to hand in addition to the information included in this chapter.

Knowing Which Taxes You're Responsible For Paying

As a landlord, it is your responsibility to declare your taxable income to the Inland Revenue. You must notify the Revenue within three months of setting yourself up as a landlord or face a £100 fine. Once you have informed the Revenue that you are investing in property, you're issued with a self-assessment tax return requiring you to give details of Schedule A income. This is all your income generated from property, as opposed to Schedule E, for example, which is income from employment. As long as gross receipts in any tax year are less than £15,000, you don't have to go into details of your incomings and outgoings. All you have to do is provide figures for your total income, expenses, and profit.

You must submit your tax return by 30 September if you want the tax office to calculate what you owe for the previous tax year. If you are happy to make the calculation yourself, you have until the following 31 January to submit your return and pay any tax you owe. Failure to do so results in an automatic £100 fine. The interest and penalties increase the longer you fail to submit your completed return and pay the tax you owe.

Each April, the Inland Revenue automatically issues you with another tax return for the following tax year. But instead of paying a lump sum every 31 January in arrears for the previous tax year, you start paying in six-monthly intervals on account, if you had to pay more than £500 the previous year. Payments on account are based on last year's profits, so if you paid £5,000 in tax last year, you would pay £2,500 on 31 January and another £2,500 on 31 July after the tax year. If, when you submit your tax return the following 31 January, it turns out that you have paid more on account than you actually owe in tax, the Inland Revenue sends you a cheque for the difference. If you owe more, you are obliged to send a cheque for the shortfall to the Revenue.

The Revenue can make random enquiries of any taxpayer and undertake specific investigations if it is suspicious of any figures you supply. Protect yourself by maintaining accurate records and keeping all receipts, bank statements, and invoices for at least six years.

Tax requirements change frequently, so be sure to check with your tax adviser before taking any action. Using a chartered accountant or tax specialist to prepare your tax returns if you have investment property makes life a lot easier.

For more details about the tax aspects of renting out property, the Inland Revenue's Web site is well worth a look at `www.hmrc.gov.uk`.

Avoiding Income Tax

The main tax you must pay is on your income. When calculating what tax you owe, the Inland Revenue takes all sorts of income into account, including your wages, bonuses and commission, rents, dividends, and interest. This income is taxed at various rates up to 40 per cent.

Landlords have to pay income tax on any profits they make from their rental property. But you can reduce the tax you pay – completely legitimately – by deducting all operating expenses from rental income. Operating expenses that can be deducted include:

- Cost of maintenance and repairs.
- Management fees.
- Advertising costs.
- Accountancy and legal fees (although not those incurred on the sale or purchase of property).
- Service charge and ground rent (where applicable).
- Travelling expenses.
- Insurance.
- Interest paid on mortgage debt and other finance costs.

The initial cost of buying the rental property is a *capital outlay*, not an allowable expense. Sometimes there's a very fine line between capital outlay and expenses that are allowable deductions from income so the situation can become confusing. For example, if your rental property is in a lettable state when you buy it and you give it a lick of paint, such redecoration costs are allowed against rents received. However, if the property was dilapidated when you bought it so you got it cheap but then had to spend several thousand pounds on renovations, you wouldn't be able to claim the cost of these against the rent.

Many capital expenses will be deductible at a later date – when you come to sell the property (see 'Avoiding CGT' later in this chapter). Be sure to keep receipts for when the time comes.

Many landlords opt for interest-only mortgages. There are two advantages in doing this. The first is that monthly payments are lower than on a repayment mortgage – where some of the capital is repaid each month along with the interest – although you will need to pay the capital back at the end of the mortgage term (you can always sell the property to do this). The other advantage of an interest-only deal is that the total monthly amount can be offset against the rental income for income tax purposes. If you opt for a buy-to-let mortgage on a repayment basis you can deduct only the interest portion from the rental income when calculating how much tax is due: it is a more complex calculation and you will have to pay tax on the repayment part. See Chapter 16 for more information on interest-only and repayment mortgages.

If you let more than one property, these are treated as a single property business for tax purposes. The advantage of this is that if you make profits on one property and losses on another, these will cancel each other out. It is also much easier to complete your tax return as you do one for all your properties and are spared the effort of filling in one for each property.

Tax on deposit money

You don't have to pay tax on deposits you receive from tenants until these deposits become income. When received, the deposits are a liability that must be paid back to the tenants at a later time, after deductions are made for damage to the property and your furniture, or cleaning. However, after your tenant vacates the property and you withhold a portion of the deposit, it may be classified as income. Essentially, the deposit isn't taxable as long as you have an expense for the same amount as the deduction. For example, if you deduct £300 from a tenant's deposit in order to paint the rental property, and actually hire a decorator for £300, then you don't owe any tax on that £300 you retained. But if you deducted £300 and then did the work yourself for £100, strictly speaking you owe tax on the £200 difference, which is classified as income.

Allowances on furnished property

If your rental property is furnished, you can claim a deduction for the net cost of replacing a particular item of furniture or furnishings. However, you cannot claim for the cost of the original purchase of the item.

Alternatively, you can opt for an annual allowance for wear and tear, which is offset against your income. This allowance is 10 per cent of your annual rental income after deducting charges or services that would normally be borne by a tenant but are actually being borne by the landlord, such as council tax (see the following section for more on council tax).

You must choose whether you want to opt for a deduction for a specific item or an annual wear and tear allowance. Once you've made your decision you must stick with it; the Inland Revenue does not allow you to chop and change between the two.

Avoiding Capital Gains Tax

Capital gains is income generated when possessions, including property (which is not your main residence), are sold for a profit. As a landlord, you won't have to pay capital gains tax (CGT) until you actually come to sell your property.

Every person has a CGT allowance – £8,800 in 2006-07 tax year – so any profits above this amount are taxed. Each person has their own annual allowance so if you own a property jointly with a spouse, you can subtract a total of £17,600 from the profits you make before any tax is due.

There are other allowances and expenses which can be deducted from this profit, thereby reducing the CGT you have to pay. For example, you can legitimately set against tax all the costs incurred in the purchase of the property, such as:

- Stamp Duty Land Tax.
- Legal fees.
- Cost of capital improvements – renovating and furnishing the rental property.
- Accountancy fees.

When calculating the CGT you owe, inflation also plays a part. This is known as *taper relief* and is based on how long you have owned the property. The longer you own the property, the less you are taxed on any profit you make from the sale because the indexed gain is tapered. There is no taper for the first two years, but after that, the taxable gain is discounted by 5 per cent per year up to a maximum of 40 per cent for properties owned for 10 years or more.

CGT is calculated at the same rate as income tax. So if you are a higher rate taxpayer, CGT is paid at a flat rate of 40 per cent. If you are a basic rate taxpayer, what remains of your lower and basic rate tax bands is used up (£32,000) in total, with tax on any remaining amount at the higher rate of 40 per cent.

For example, if you bought a property for £200,000 and sold it for £300,000, your profit would be £100,000. You then subtract your annual allowance – £8,800 – leaving a profit of £91,200. Say the cost of purchasing the property amounted to £15,000, this leaves you with a taxable profit of £76,200. Assuming you pay CGT at 40 per cent, this will leave a tax bill of £30,480.

CGT can be incredibly complicated and very expensive if you aren't sure what you are entitled to and what allowances you can offset against income. It is well worth getting an accountant or tax adviser to advise you before you come to sell one of your rental properties.

Steering Clear of Council Tax

Council tax is paid to the local authority under whose jurisdiction your property comes under. Under the Local Government Finance Act 1992, the tenant is obliged to pay this tax for living in the property. When the property is empty or between tenants, the landlord is responsible for footing the bill.

Council tax is calculated on the basis of the property's value, with all properties divided into bands, according to their value. The amount of tax due depends on the band the rental property is placed in, with more expensive properties liable for higher council tax bills than cheaper properties. Certain properties are exempt from council tax, including those empty for more than six months and those let to full-time students.

Council tax is charged on a daily basis, so your tenants are liable for it from the day they move into the rental property until the day they move out. Ensure that when tenants move in that they contact the local authority and get the council tax bill put into their names, so that you don't continue to be liable. You may want to write this letter and send it yourself to ensure it gets done.

If the property is empty, you may be liable for the council tax, depending on whether or not it is furnished. If the property is furnished and empty, you get a discount on the full amount; the size of this depends on the local authority. If the property is unfurnished and empty, no council tax is paid for the first six months. After this time, if the property is still empty, you have to pay the discounted charge – whether the property is furnished or not.

While tenants are responsible for council tax in most rental properties, this is not the case when a house is in multiple occupation (HMO). Check out Chapter 8 for more details on properties which are defined as being HMOs. If the property is a HMO, the owner is responsible for paying the council tax rather than the tenants. For council tax purposes, the definition of multiple occupation includes any dwelling inhabited by persons who do not constitute a single household, all of whom have the right to occupy only part of the house. Working out whether people sharing a house constitute a single household or not can be difficult. If in doubt, include a provision in the tenancy agreement allowing you to increase the rent by the amount of any council tax you might end up paying on the rental property.

Minimising Stamp Duty Land Tax

Stamp duty is payable when you purchase a property costing more than £125,000. It is payable at a rate of:

- 1 per cent on properties costing between £125,000 and £250,000
- 3 per cent on properties costing more than £250,000 and less than £500,000
- 4 per cent on properties costing more than £500,000

The tax is not progressive, which means that if you buy a property costing £550,000 you pay 4 per cent on the entire amount, rather than just the amount above £500,000. Thus, the bill will be £22,000 rather than £10,800.

There are ways in which you can minimise your stamp duty bill. Properties sold in certain 'disadvantaged areas' costing less than £150,000 don't incur stamp duty.

If you are making an offer on a property it is also worth considering the impact of stamp duty on the transaction. If the property costs £250,005, for example, you will pay 3 per cent tax on the entire amount. If you paid £249,095 for the property however, you would pay just 1 per cent tax on the entire amount. Think carefully before making your offer; it is always worth checking whether the vendor will accept a lower price.

Advanced Tax Avoidance Tips

The best way of ensuring you don't pay more tax than is absolutely necessary is to plan aheadSeeking professional advice is worthwhile long before you reach the stage where you have to pay tax to ensure you don't miss any opportunities. If you leave it too late, it may cost you.

Share and share alike: Owning property with someone else

Owning property jointly with one or more other people can have a positive impact on your tax bill. However, the extent of the savings you make depends on how you are related to the person you are buying with. Below, we look at the tax advantages of joint ownership, as well as the specific advantages of buying with a spouse or civil partner.

Joint ownership

There are a number of tax reliefs and bands that every person is entitled to. So when you buy a property with one or more people, you have double, triple, or even more the value of these.

For example, everyone has a personal allowance; an annual CGT exemption; a lower and basic-rate tax band; as well as a nil-rate band for inheritance tax purposes. So if you are a higher-rate taxpayer and buy a property with a basic-rate taxpayer, it is assumed that you own it 50:50. So instead of 40 per cent tax payable on the total profit, half the profits will be subject to tax at a rate of 22 per cent.

It is not just income tax where joint ownership can result in savings. When you sell the rental property, each person has their own annual CGT allowance so both count towards any profit made. Thus, if each person has an annual CGT allowance of £8,800, £17,600 can be deducted from profits before any tax is payable.

Several tax reliefs and bands don't necessarily make it advantageous to purchase property with another person. Stamp duty is still payable in full, for example, no matter how many of you are buying the property together, although of course you should be able to split the cost between you.

You can save income tax by ensuring the property is in joint names or even in the sole name of person with the lower overall income. If one of you pays tax at 40 per cent and the other 22 per cent, it makes sense for at least half (if not all) of the property is in the lower taxpayer's name so less tax is due. If you don't decide this initially at the time of purchase it is possible to transfer a share later on – by consulting a solicitor – but it makes sense to plan ahead and do this from the start.

Buying with a spouse or civil partner

Spouses and civil partners who buy property together can benefit from the same advantages as those of joint owners. But the main additional advantage of being married or having a registered civil partnership is that you can transfer assets between the two of you without incurring CGT or other charges. In some instances, an outright transfer of the whole property to your spouse – if they don't work or pay less tax than you – may be beneficial. But if you have bought with someone who isn't a spouse or civil partner, tax must be paid.

Thinking about inheritance tax

Many people don't realise that inheritance tax (IHT) is payable on their estate after their death. This is because IHT is no longer a tax on the rich: any estate worth more than £285,000 (2006-07 tax year) is liable, as the threshold hasn't kept in line with house price growth. IHT can create quite a dent in what you leave your beneficiaries as it is payable at a rate of 40 per cent. But with a bit of forward planning it is possible to avoid paying this tax – or at least reduce the amount you pay.

If your estate passes to your spouse or civil partner, there is no IHT to pay. But this is not particularly tax-efficient. Each person has a nil-rate band, so it is worth utilising both of these to reduce the tax payable. For example, if a husband leaves his share of the property to his wife on his death, she pays no IHT. But when she dies and leaves the property to their children, only her nil-rate band can be utilised (meaning the first £285,000 is tax-free). However, if he had given his share direct to the children, they could have utilised his nil-rate band (meaning the first £285,000 would be tax-free and then when their mother died, the first £285,000 of her share would also be tax-free). Therefore, they inherit £570,000 in total before they have to pay any tax.

Writing a will – and keeping it updated

The most important step you can take is to make a tax-efficient will. This sets out who gets what when you die. Make sure you take into account both your own nil-rate band and your partner's when doing any IHT planning.

Writing a will is fairly straightforward; contact a solicitor (look in the Yellow Pages for details of one near you) to do this. For more on wills, grab a copy of Julian Knight's *Wills, Probate & Inheritance Tax For Dummies* (Wiley).

Giving it away

If your estate exceeds the nil-rate band it may be necessary to give some of your belongings away during your lifetime – rather than waiting until you die. You can give away as much as you wish, without paying any tax, as long as you live for seven years after making the gift. Keep a record of such gifts and ensure it is in a place where it is easy to find.

Establishing a trust

A trust is a legal arrangement enabling you to give away assets, such as property, in a tax-efficient and controlled way for the benefit of nominated individuals. It can be set up during your lifetime or on your death, as stated in your will.

Many people use a discretionary trust to hold property for the benefit of stated people, such as their spouse, children and other relatives. Trustees have control over the funds but you can direct them as to when beneficiaries can get their hands on the assets.

Many tax benefits can be derived from a trust but make sure you understand exactly what you are getting into. Seek advice from a trust specialist.

Chapter 18

Using a Company to Hold Your Property

In This Chapter

- Recognising the advantages of using a company to purchase property
- Avoiding the pitfalls
- Setting up a company

Many landlords want to know whether they should use a company to purchase their property or buy it as an individual or via a partnership. This isn't as straightforward a question as it seems. Many factors need to be taken into account; otherwise you could find you are making a huge mistake by choosing one option over another.

The tax regime for companies is very different to that for individuals or partnerships. This chapter examines the pros and cons of using a company so that you understand what's involved. We also give help on setting up a company – if you decide it's the right course of action for you – and details on how to place property you already own into a company.

Understanding the Pros of Using a Company

Using a company to purchase property rather than as an individual or via a partnership has several advantages. Much depends on your investment strategy, ambitions, and how long you intend to hold onto the properties for. The main advantages are explained in more detail in the following sections.

For more information on your setting up as a company, and on your tax responsibilities, pick up a copy of Tony Levene's *Paying Less Tax 2006/2007 For Dummies* (Wiley), and Colin Barrow's *Starting a Business For Dummies* (Wiley).

Beneficial tax regime

The main reason landlords use a company to purchase property is to save tax. A limited company pays corporation tax on all its profits, including income and capital gains. Corporation tax isn't paid on the first £10,000 of a company's profits; after this, it is charged at lower rates than higher-rate income tax. The maximum effective corporation tax rate is 30 per cent, compared with 40 per cent for a higher-rate taxpayer holding property outside a company.

Companies choose their own year-end accounting date, unlike individuals who must use the end of the tax year (5 April). Companies also work out their own tax liability and must pay any tax owed to the Inland Revenue within nine months of their financial year end. Interest is charged at a commercial rate on late payments.

The corporation tax self-assessment form must be filed to the Revenue within 12 months of the company's financial year-end or you are liable for penalties.

Deciding to use a company to purchase property simply on the basis of corporation tax rates may turn out to be extremely short sighted. Look at the bigger picture and avoid making a snap decision.

Limited liability

One of the biggest worries facing landlords is what might happen if a tenant sues after having an accident in their rental property. For example, if a tenant falls down the stairs, which are later found to be faulty. If the tenant sues the landlord, the cost could be prohibitive. It may result in the landlord having to sell the rental property, or even their own home, to raise the compensation payable to the tenant.

The advantage of a limited company is that it is a separate legal entity, responsible for its own debts and other liabilities. Your liability is strictly limited to your direct investment in the company: you are not personally responsible for any liabilities, debts or charges for which the business is liable. So if your tenant does fall down the stairs, the limit of your liability is the amount you have invested in the company. The tenant can't come after any of your assets that are held outside the company, such as your own home. If you buy property as a sole proprietor or via a partnership there is no protection for your own assets or your partner's, and all your assets are potentially at risk.

Flexible ownership

Property held outside a company is generally in the names of two or three people at most. If you are the sole owner of a property, transferring ownership to others is complicated. But if a company owns the property getting more investors involved is easier. Many people start their business small but then want to involve family members or others later on. A company structure makes this far easier to achieve.

If you want to pass a property onto a family member, a capital gains tax (CGT) is paid if the property is held outside a company. But if the property is inside a limited company, that family member can subscribe for some shares. The ownership can then pass from you to someone else tax-free, because the value of the transfer is held over for CGT purposes.

A limited company can also be advantageous in retirement. You may decide you want to stop working but want the business to keep going. Using a company structure means you can retain ownership as a shareholder but still pass on the day-to-day management to someone else.

Status

Creating the right impression is a vital part of business and a company sounds more professional than a business in your own name. Putting 'Limited' after your name, it tends to make people think you are perhaps a bigger organisation and more professional than a one-man band. This may be helpful in encouraging potential tenants to rent one of your properties or persuading investors to take a stake in your company.

Spotting the Cons of Using a Company

Using a company to hold your rental property isn't all plain sailing – otherwise, all landlords would do this instead of owning it as an individual or via a partnership. The company framework tends to mean increased bureaucracy, paperwork, and administration compared with holding property outside a company.

Considering whether the financial savings are sufficient to compensate for the time running a company inevitably takes up is vital. Although corporation tax rates appear highly attractive compared to personal tax rates, these may be outweighed in the longer term by the difficulty in extracting gains from the company. If you sell property you own outside a company, once you have paid any CGT you owe, the remaining cash is yours. You also get an annual exemption for CGT purposes, so are not liable for tax on the whole amount – which isn't the case if you sell property owned by a company. But if you sell property owned through a company, corporation tax is payable on any gain.

There is no *taper relief* (which reduces CGT) for capital gains purposes either if it is held in a company. For individuals, the longer you hold an asset, the more taper relief you get, reducing the CGT you owe.

If you, or any member of your family, are planning on using any of the properties held by the company for personal use, severe tax consequences could arise. Compare this with the CGT benefits of personal use when investing in property directly.

Obtaining relief for certain administrative expenses, such as using your home as an office or motor expenses, may also be more difficult when investing through a company.

Setting Up a Property Company

Setting up a company is fairly straightforward and probably easier than you might think. Companies House (`www.companieshouse.gov.uk`) can advise on the basics of registering, but can't give detailed advice. Most solicitors and accountants can set up a company on your behalf, with some providing off-the-shelf companies. Alternatively, you can use a company formation agent, who will advise you and carry out the process for you. Look in your local Yellow Pages or on the Internet for details of these.

You could handle the registration process yourself but it is worth seeking professional advice to ensure you don't make any mistakes.

Before you can begin operating as a limited company, you must register with Companies House or the Companies Registry for Northern Ireland, depending on where you live. You will need:

- **A Memorandum of Association:** This gives details of the company's name, location and states what the company will do, such as borrow money, buy or sell land and property, and rent out property. It also sets out the framework for the share structure.
- **Articles of Association:** This describes how the company will be run, shareholders' rights and the power of the directors of the company.

- **Form 10 (Statement of the First Directors, Secretary and Registered Office):** This details the company's registered office, as well as names and addresses of the directors and company secretary.
- **Form 12 (Declaration of Compliance with the Requirements of the Companies Act):** This states that the company meets all the legal requirements of incorporation.

For downloadable forms relating to company registration in England and Wales, go to the Companies House web site at `www.companieshouse.gov.uk` or if you're in Northern Ireland, the web site of the Department of Enterprise, Trade and Industry Online at `www.detini.gov.uk`.

Private or public?

You must decide whether you want your company to be private limited company or a public limited company (PLC). Most small businesses opt to become a private limited company because they have no intention of being quoted on the stock market.

PLCs also require share capital of at least £50,000, while such companies must also have two shareholders, two directors, and a qualified company secretary. If you opt for a private company, you must appoint at least one director and a company secretary. The same person can't undertake both roles.

Choosing a name

It may sound a simple enough task but you can't call your company the same name as another company. You may also want to avoid names that are similar to those of existing companies. It may be worth getting 'Property' somewhere in the title so that prospective tenants and investors know exactly what the company does.

The company will need a registered office address, where the name of the company should be prominently displayed. The name should also be displayed on your stationary, letters, receipts, invoices, and cheques.

Registering to pay tax

Once you have registered your company, Companies House passes on your details to the Inland Revenue. But you must ensure that you also contact your local Revenue office to let them know that your company exists. If you don't you may be fined.

The Revenue sends you form CT41G. This must be completed and returned in order to get the company into the Corporation Tax system. You must do this within three months of starting your business activities or penalties are imposed. You must also register the company as an employer for PAYE purposes or for VAT, if either is applicable.

Placing Existing Property into a New Company

While you may have set up a company to buy property in the future, you may already have property that you would like to transfer over. The problem is that as you already own the property you are trying to place in your company, you could potentially be liable for a huge CGT bill if you transfer it over. Careful timing and the use of annual exemptions and taper relief might make it possible to do the transfers without having to pay any, or much in the way of, tax. Seek specialist tax advice to ensure you don't pay more tax than you need to.

If the property has been your main residence at any time in the previous three years it may usually be transferred tax-free into a property investment company.

While certain reliefs minimise potential CGT bills incurred when transferring property you already own into a company, avoiding a hefty tax bill entirely is difficult. In most cases you should keep the company for future investments and leave your existing properties as they are.

Chapter 19

Financial Management and Recordkeeping

In This Chapter

- Setting up a filing system to keep track of your paperwork
- Hanging on to the records you need for the right amount of time
- Taking advantage of computer software to help you with your accounting

If you ask a group of landlords what their least favourite part of the job is, you'll probably hear 'the paperwork' more than any other response. Most owners don't mind the hands-on aspects of managing their properties, like cleaning or painting; many of them even enjoy it. And meeting prospective tenants and showing the property is fun compared to recording when the rent is paid, sending out late notices, and writing out cheques to pay the bills. But the financial management aspects of accounting for all the funds you receive and expend are critical elements of running your rental housing venture. In this chapter, we show you how to do it.

Organising Your Files

If you have an aversion to keeping track of documents, then managing your own rental properties may not be for you. If you own rental property, you need to prepare many important written records and keep them ready for prompt retrieval. Every landlord must have a basic filing system with separate records kept for each rental property.

If you own one or even a few rental properties, your filing system can be a simple box file with dividers, available at any office supply shop. If you own more properties and your box file is overflowing, moving up to a filing cabinet (preferably one that is lockable) makes sense.

The property ownership file

From the moment you take your first steps towards purchasing an investment property, begin storing your paperwork in a property ownership file. Keep all the important documents relating to the property in this file, including purchase offers and contracts, structural surveys, mortgage loan, insurance policies, pest control reports, and correspondence. Also keep a photocopy of your deeds in the property file and place the original in a fireproof safe or bank safety deposit box.

Separate files for each rental property

Each of your rental properties should have its own file with separate folders for income items, as well as a separate folder for each of the property's expenses. Keep copies of all receipts in the expense folders so that when you come to file your tax return, you can easily locate the information you need.

We recommend keeping a master maintenance file for the records and receipts for all maintenance and capital improvements of each rental property. Doing so gives you a history of the physical condition of each rental property throughout your ownership of it.

Tenant files

In addition to having a file for expenses and income, create a tenant file for each rental property containing all the important documents for each specific tenant, including his rental application, tenancy agreement, and all other legal notices, tenant maintenance requests, and correspondence. Always keep the original of each document and provide the tenant with a photocopy.

You may opt to keep many of these files on your computer, but for owners of only a few rental properties, a manual system is fine.

Use a system for recording all significant tenant complaints and maintenance requests. This will provide a valuable paper trail if a dispute ever arises regarding your conduct as a landlord in properly maintaining the premises. Failing to have good records could very well result in a court dispute being determined solely on your word against your tenant's word – and the odds aren't good under such circumstances.

When your tenants move out, attach a copy of their Deposit Itemisation report (of which more details can be found in Chapter 13) and bind the entire tenant file together. Transfer it to a separate file for all former tenants, filed alphabetically by rental property.

Insurance file

Insurance is such an important issue that you should have a master insurance file that contains current policies for all types of insurance cover on all your rental properties (you can find out more about insurance in Chapter 15). This file should also have a calendar on which you can track the expiration or renewal dates for each policy and ensure that you have requested competitive bids well in advance of the policy expiration date. Keeping accurate records of any incident reports or claims made on your insurance policy is critical as well.

Maintaining Property Records

Maintaining complete and accurate records of all transactions is extremely important in the world of property management. An inventory, for example, is vitally important to avoid disputes with tenants when they come to move out of the property; you can use the inventory to account for any deductions in their deposit. If a dispute between you and your tenant does end up in court, having documents outlining the understanding between the parties makes life a lot easier. If you can't provide the required records, your tenant will have a stronger case than he or she otherwise would have.

But maintaining proper records is also important because you have to report your income and expenses for each rental property on your annual self-assessment tax return to determine whether you've made a profit. The Inland Revenue requires all landlords to substantiate all income and expenses by maintaining proper records, including detailed receipts of all transactions. You don't want to be in a situation where you can't support the accuracy of your tax return, particularly if the Revenue asks to see the evidence. Chapter 17 explains what a landlord needs to know about the Inland Revenue and other taxes.

The following tips should help you to keep on top of your records:

- Document your income in a notebook and keep all bank deposit slips and statements. Rental property expenses, even if you write a business cheque, should have a written receipt to fully document the expenditure.

The Inland Revenue may not accept a cheque as proof of a deductible property expense unless you have a detailed receipt to back it up.

- Develop and assign a one- or two-character code for each property you own (if you have several rental properties) and mark each receipt accordingly. When you have information for several properties on a single receipt, make photocopies and store the receipts in the folders you've set up for your respective properties. This way, you can provide evidence of the expense for each property instead of having to wade through all your folders looking for the information you need.
- Keep all receipts, bank statements, and invoices concerning your rental property for at least six years in case the Inland Revenue decides to conduct an investigation. For taxation purposes, you need to maintain records regarding the purchase and capital improvements made during your ownership for as long as you own the property. Certain rental property records such as those concerning injuries to children should be maintained forever.

If you are using your car to visit your rental property, make sure you keep a detailed written log of all your mileage. Your mileage is a deductible business expense as long as it is directly related to your rental property and you have accurate records to document the mileage. This simple log should indicate the date, destination, purpose, and total number of miles travelled. You may be surprised at the number of miles you travel each year in your rental activities – and the deductible expense can be substantial.

Taking Care of Business: Rental Property Accounting

The Inland Revenue does not require you to keep a separate bank account for each rental property that you own, but you do need to keep your rental property activities separate from your personal transactions.

If you only have a few rental properties, you may be able to keep track of your tenants' rent payments in your head. But don't rely on your memory. Always track each rental payment in writing. The best policy is to provide a receipt whenever possible, regardless of the method of payment.

Be sure to accurately record the payment of a tenant's deposit. These funds are typically not considered income; instead, they are a future liability that is owed back to the tenant if the tenant honours the terms and conditions of the tenancy agreement. The deposit may become income at a later date, if you apply any portion of it to cover delinquent rent, cleaning, repairs, or other charges. (See Chapter 17 for details about when the deposit changes from a future liability to income.)

If you manage your own property and do your own accounting, it's important to actually review and analyse your finances in the same manner as a professional property manager would. You may think that you know everything you need to know about your rental property, and setting aside your finances until the end of the tax year may seem harmless, but financial management (and an understanding of your current financial situation) is an important skill for any landlord to master.

Creating a budget and managing your cash flow

Every landlord should have a *budget*. A budget is a detailed estimate of the future income and expenses of a property for a certain time period, usually one year. A budget allows you to anticipate and track the expected income and expenses for your rental property. Many landlords neglect to allocate and hold back enough money for projected expenses, so when the time comes to make a repair, for example, they don't have the money set aside to cover it. But if you set up a budget, you'll be better able to anticipate your expenses.

Although the budget for a small family rental property is fairly simple, a proper budget is essential if you own several properties, which require more careful planning. That planning includes a thorough review of past expenses and the current condition of the property. Trends in expenses, such as utilities, can also be important when estimating the future cash flow of a rental property, so be sure you don't overlook them.

Many landlords rely on cash flow from their rental properties not only to cover their expenses, but also to supplement their personal income. But you need to have a built-in reserve fund set aside before you start taking out any rental income funds for personal reasons, particularly if you're a small-time landlord. Maintain a reserve balance large enough to pay your mortgage and all the basic property expenses for *at least* one month without relying on any rental income.

Set up a bank account in which you set aside money for anticipated major capital improvements. For example, you may own a rental property that will need a new roof in the next five years. Rather than see your cash flow wiped out for several months when the time comes to pay for that new roof, begin setting aside small amounts of money into a capital reserve account over several years.

Don't forget to allocate funds to cover bi-annual and annual expenses such as council tax (if you pay it) and potential income tax due on your rental property net income. You can read about these and other outgoings in Chapter 17.

Using computers for financial management

Most landlords begin investing in property with a small house or flat. At this level, the accounting is extremely simple, and you can do it manually with pen and paper in a simple spiral notebook. But when you expand to a property portfolio comprising several rental flats or houses, you need to look for better and more efficient systems that are geared to the specific needs of rental property bookkeeping. Consider using a computer and a spreadsheet or general accounting software. Doing so can make your life a lot easier because, once set up, using a computerised system makes it quicker to record the information you need and simpler to review it.

Many basic software spreadsheets (such as Microsoft Excel) should handle your needs if you own a handful of rental properties. But you might want to opt for more specialised software, such as a general business accounting package. Good software providing this service are the entry-level Quicken and the more advanced QuickBooks or Peachtree Accounting. This software can handle and streamline all the basic accounting requirements of a landlord managing several rental properties. You can customise the financial reporting offered by software to meet your needs. Monthly reports often contain income and expense information compared to the monthly budget, as well as year-to-date numbers.

While this software is useful, keep in mind that it lacks specific rental-housing industry information and reporting that are invaluable to effective property management.

If you want more help managing and organising your rental properties, *Property Intellect* (Wild Rabbit Software) is an easy software package to use. This includes inventories, space for details of your rental properties, and options to add in automatic tenancy agreement generation and inventory taking. *Landlords Property Tax Manager* (Property Tax Portal) is another powerful software package enabling you to manage your properties, tenants, finances, and even calculate your tax liability.

The US has a much wider range of professional rental accounting software programs for landlords. These programs are aimed at those with scores of rental properties. Recommended programs include *Tenant Pro for Windows* and *Yardi Professional* (yes, we know – this one sounds more like a hitman than a computer program). They typically offer the following:

- Complete accounting (general ledger, accounts receivable, accounts payable with cheque writing, budgeting, and financial reporting)
- Tenant management, including many standard rental management forms
- Tenant service requests, timetabling maintenance work, and reminder notes
- Additional services such as tenant screening and utility billing

As you can imagine, American landlords find these packages very useful. But as they are designed for landlords with at least 100 rental properties, they aren't really necessary for the majority of UK property managers.

Most UK landlords who don't use manual accounting will probably opt for more basic accounting software to ease the process of running your rental property business. Before picking this software, gather as much information as possible. Be sure to talk to actual users of the product, preferably people who have comparable rental properties and similar accounting needs. Determine what features the software offers, how easy it is to operate, the computer hardware requirements, the availability and cost of technical support, and the strength and reputation of the company backing the product. Try to get hold of a demo or trial version of the software that you can use before you buy, just to make sure it's what you want. Or at least ask your landlord friends to give you a quick demo of how the package works.

Hiring a professional number-cruncher

Although rental property accounting is fairly straightforward, you may not have the time or inclination to do it yourself. If you aren't prepared to handle your own accounting and record keeping, hire an accountant to handle it for you. Alternatively, try to find a lettings agent who's willing to just perform rental property accounting services for a fee. Your local phone book is a good place to begin your search.

When you use an agent you typically receive several important accounting reports within a couple of weeks after the end of each accounting month. If you review these reports regularly, you can get a lot of information. These reports can provide you with a good understanding of your rental investments and give you the opportunity to enquire about or suggest changes in operations.

Part VI
Only for the Daring

"I'm sorry, Mr Waldini, cats are included in the no-pets rule even if you do keep them under control."

In this part . . .

When you're looking to increase your cash flow (and who isn't?), and after you have a little landlording experience under your belt, you may want to try your hand at some less common endeavours, like working with housing associations or tenants on Housing Benefit. Although these programmes sometimes get a bad press, they're often a great way to get a reliable source of rental income. Finally, you may want to think about appealing to niche markets – people with special needs that your property may be perfect for. In this part, we guide you through each of these areas so that you can figure out whether they're right for you and use them to your advantage – with few worries.

Chapter 20

Government Programmes

In This Chapter

- Taking on tenants claiming Housing Benefit
- Working with housing associations

Housing is generally the largest single expense for most families and certain parts of the UK, particularly London and the South East, are facing a very severe affordable housing crisis. Many key workers on low wages, such as nurses and teachers, can't afford living accommodation near the hospitals and schools in which they work because property prices have rocketed. This situation is forcing shift-workers to live many miles away from their workplace and to commute some distance to get home late at night when they finish their shifts.

But while buying property is out of the question for many low-income families, even rented accommodation can be expensive. Stumping up at least a month's rent in advance and the equivalent of another month's rent for the deposit is beyond the means of many. Others on low incomes have to rely on Housing Benefit – a means-tested benefit – to pay their rent.

With such a shortage of decent, affordable rental housing, low-income tenants have a very difficult time finding somewhere to live. To make matters worse, many landlords and managing agents have a firm policy that they won't accept rental applicants who rely upon subsidies to assist with their rent payments.

In this chapter, we review some of the benefits and concerns for landlords presented by tenants who rely on rent subsidies such as Housing Benefit. If you're not sure whether accepting tenants in receipt of benefit or in need of the assistance of a housing association is for you, read on.

Housing Benefit

Many landlords and managing agents absolutely refuse to accept tenants who qualify for benefits administered by the Department for Work and Pensions (DWP), such as Housing Benefit – a means-tested payment available to tenants who cannot pay their rent, and administered by the local council. Tenants on benefit seem to rank alongside students, people with pets, and smokers in terms of desirability as far as many landlords are concerned. As a landlord, your main priority is that your tenants pay their rent on time every month and look after your rental property. Indeed, your tenant screening process (see Chapter 8 for more information on this process) is important in establishing whether the prospective tenant is likely to pay the rent. So the idea of accepting tenants who obviously can't afford the rent – because if they could they wouldn't qualify for Housing Benefit – might seem to be contradicting everything we have been telling you in this book.

People fall on hard times. And given that hundreds of thousands of households in England and Wales are currently receiving Housing Benefit, you could be missing out on a large source of potential tenants if you refuse to consider these applicants. Not all properties are suitable, however: a large six-bedroom rental property in an affluent area is unlikely to be suitable for tenants on benefit. But smaller properties in inner city areas, or less palatial properties, are ideal. As long as you insist that certain criteria are met before letting your rental property to a tenant in receipt of benefit, you should be able to minimise the possible risks involved.

Housing Benefit can be paid directly to the landlord by direct debit if the tenant is agreeable. We suggest that you absolutely insist on this and include a term in your tenancy agreement that the tenant agrees to the benefit being paid direct to you.

Landlords should bear in mind that rent officers have wide powers to limit the amount of rent charged. This policy is designed to stop unscrupulous landlords from charging what they like, knowing that the tenant's rent is met, at least in part, by Housing Benefit. The tenant receives a rent allowance on a weekly basis so that he can pay the landlord. This benefit may not necessarily be as much as the full rent in order to avoid excessively large rents and properties. The tenant is obliged to make up the shortfall out of his own funds. If the benefit only covers part of the rent, ensure your tenants also set up a direct debit to pay you the shortfall every month.

A tenant who can afford to pay the rent without needing Housing Benefit can still pay late every month or completely forget to pay it. Just because on paper she can afford your rent doesn't automatically make her any more reliable than a tenant in receipt of benefit. A tenant on Housing Benefit could prove more reliable as long as you take the steps mentioned previously to ensure that the money goes straight to your bank account each week.

The disadvantage of Housing Benefit being paid directly to you is that if an overpayment of benefit is made because the claimant forgot to tell the local authority of a change in his or her circumstances and then does a runner, you have to pay the difference back. Insert a clause in the tenancy agreement stating that you can hold on to the tenant's deposit until it's clear that an overpayment hasn't been made. But be aware that if you also have to use the deposit to pay for damage to the property, you may not have enough to cover the rent you're owed.

Ask Housing Benefit tenants for a guarantor. The guarantor should be a homeowner in full-time employment who's willing to guarantee the rent in case the tenant defaults. Also ensure that a proper deposit is paid when the tenant moves into the rental property. Don't let yourself feel sorry for a prospective tenant who says he'd love to pay you a deposit but simply can't afford to. Such tenants should be given a very wide berth.

Housing Associations

A housing association is a non-profit making body that provides affordable accommodation. They have been around for a long time and now there are over 2,000 housing associations in England alone, managing 1.45 million homes and at least twice that many people.

So how does this affect private landlords like you? Well, how does guaranteed rent at a market rate for a set number of years sound to you? Housing associations, desperate to get more properties on their books, are making such offers to private landlords in order to provide a roof over the heads of those who can't afford rented accommodation, or temporary housing to people who need it for one reason or another. Such an offer proves attractive to many landlords, particularly those who may be having trouble renting their properties. Not only that, but a golden hello of a few thousand pounds when you sign the agreement is a welcome bonus. *And* you get someone else to manage your property for you, visiting frequently to keep an eye on the property and carry out any necessary repairs.

How they work

Housing authorities guarantee that the rental property will be let for a choice of three to five continuous years at the current market rate. And rents tend to be competitive because there is a shortage of property. You make over the property to the housing association, which handles rent collection, although you may still be responsible for repairs and maintenance. The housing association makes regular checks on the property to make sure it is being well maintained. If the tenant defaults on the rent, the housing association even handles the eviction. You get someone else to manage your property and don't even have to pay management fees – or commission. At the end of the lease, you get guaranteed vacant possession.

While you may be nervous letting your property to tenants in receipt of Housing Benefit, keep in mind that if you do so through a housing association your risks are greatly reduced. You get your rent every month, even if the tenant defaults on the rent.

If you're interested in such a scheme, you have plenty of housing associations to choose from. In London, for example, such schemes are available in several boroughs, providing housing for more than 50,000 homeless people. The Notting Hill Housing Group is a good example of a pro-active housing association. It is one of the largest housing associations in the UK with a turnover of £86.5 million and assets of approximately £3 billion. Its remit stretches well beyond its headquarters in west London, and it is constantly looking for properties in north London (Camden), north-west London (Ealing), east London (Newham), south London (Wandsworth), south-west London (Kensington & Chelsea), and Westminster in central London. It even accepts properties outside of these areas as demand is constantly changing.

Which properties are eligible

Not all properties are accepted by housing associations. Bedsits, houses in multiple occupation, studio flats, or those above shops are not accepted. As a general rule, houses and flats must have one bedroom or more, but different types of property tend to be popular in certain areas: In Camden, for example, two-, three-, and four-bedroom flats and houses are required. But in Ealing and Newham, bigger properties with five or six bedrooms are also sought. Whatever size of rental property you have to offer, the property usually has to be furnished to qualify.

Pursuing this option

If you're interested in the scheme, contact your local housing association. You can find its number in your Yellow Pages or you can try looking on the National Housing Federation Website at `www.housing.org.uk`.

When you call, a negotiator talks you through the scheme and answers any questions you may have about it. Once you have decided to go ahead, you need to fill out a lease application form and send it back with a cheque for the survey fee. This fee costs in the region of £125. The housing association's surveyor then visits your rental property and prepares a full assessment.

If the surveyor decides that upgrades are necessary before the property can be let, you're responsible for paying for these. Usual upgrades include safety items such as the installation of smoke detectors, window locks on ground floors and basement flats, and fire-resistant doors in kitchens – all general safety precautions for rented accommodation anyway. You must also arrange a gas safety check by a CORGI-registered plumber (see Chapter 4 for more details) and an electricity safety check by an electrical contractor registered with the National Inspection Council for Electrical Installation Contracting (NICEIC). A service contract for the hot water and central heating is also required.

Once the work is completed, the surveyor makes another inspection. If the property is accepted its condition is recorded in detail at the start of the lease. The housing association then asks the local authority to provide a tenant to live in your rental property and your lease starts from the day the tenant moves in. Your guaranteed rent is paid directly into your bank account every month until the end of the agreement. You don't have to do anything else – the housing association takes care of everything.

If you want to be completely hands off when it comes to renting out your property, getting your local housing association to handle the management of your property is the answer to stress-free landlording. And with so much demand for rental property, and with the majority of landlords not knowing about such schemes, you have a very strong chance of your property being taken on.

Chapter 21

Working in Niche Markets: Students, Pets, and Smokers

In This Chapter

- Re-examining your thoughts on pets
- Handling student tenants
- Offering smoking and non-smoking rental properties

Sometimes thinking outside the box and looking for angles that other landlords overlook or are not willing to pursue makes sense. You may own property in a soft rental market, or maybe you just want to find a market niche where your rental properties can outperform other rental properties.

This chapter explores several of the niche rental markets that you can use to your benefit – everything from students to non-smokers to tenants with pets. These niche markets may or may not be right for you. But make sure you consider whether you could dip into one or more of these markets and increase your cash flow in the process.

Taking Another Look at Your Pet Policy

In today's rental market, one of the most effective strategies to keep your rental properties occupied with stable, paying tenants is to allow pets. Although many landlords immediately reject this idea, the reality is that the rental options are extremely limited for many tenants with pets – which means that if you're one of the few who accepts pets, you'll immediately increase the demand for your rental property.

Even 'no pet' properties must accommodate tenants who have animals, such as guide dogs if they are prescribed by a tenant's GP under the Disability Discrimination Act.

Allowing pets under certain conditions can result in much higher rental income and fewer vacancies. For example, accepting pets can be successful if you:

- **Have a rental property that is suitable for pets.** Some rental properties are particularly well suited for tenants who have pets. An older rental property, or one with certain features such as a fenced garden, wooden floors (as opposed to carpets), and blinds (as opposed to curtains) would be a good candidate for tenants with pets.
- **Verify through references and an interview that your tenant is a responsible pet owner.** Be sure to verify all references and ask specific questions about the pet. Conducting an actual interview with the pet present in order to determine its temperament is a good idea. Be sure to properly complete the pet or animal agreement addendum to your tenancy agreement and get the tenant to agree to your terms. Don't allow any animal with dangerous or potentially dangerous tendencies, and take a photo of the pet for your tenant file.
- **Implement and enforce stringent pet policies and rules.** For your pet policy to run smoothly, you need detailed rules, including a limit on the number of animals in the rental property. You also need to have clear policies about pet and tenant behaviour. For example, you'll want to forbid tenants from flushing cat litter down the toilet (otherwise, you'll end up with blocked drains). Make sure that you put limits on what you consider as an acceptable pet; consider making exotic animals, such as snakes or tarantulas, off-limits.
- **Require an extra deposit for tenants with pets.** Because so few rental properties accept tenants with pets, those landlords who do are able to charge higher rent and collect much larger deposits from tenants with pets. Most responsible pet owners don't baulk at a reasonable monthly rental rate premium or an increased deposit of a couple of hundred pounds. Avoid using the labels *pet rent* or *pet deposit;* instead, try to keep the language generic. A pet deposit, for example, may limit your use of those funds to damage that you can prove was caused by the pet. Your goal is to ensure that the rental rate and larger deposit provide adequate compensation and protection against any or *all* damage to the rental property resulting in increased costs of cleaning or repair.

Renting to Students: Is It Really Like the Young Ones?

It doesn't have to be – honest! Many landlords have the same strong feelings against renting to students as they do about accepting pets or tenants on Housing Benefit. The major problem, however, is that (except for the Disability Discrimination Act exemption) you can legally have a "no pet" policy, but you can't discriminate against students if they meet your tenant screening criteria.

Nowadays, an increasing number of landlords are specifically targeting student tenants. The growing number of students and demand for properties for them to rent while they're at university or college makes rental property in university towns an attractive option.

With students relying on student loans to see them through their studies, many accept debt as a matter of course and are unprepared to skimp on accommodation and live in a hovel. Instead, they want to rent a reasonable property. And many well-heeled students are around as well, with parents more than happy to cough up a bit more for decent accommodation while their children are studying.

Getting a rental property in a university town

Some landlords with rental properties in university towns bought their property in the first place because they had children studying at university and needed accommodation in the area. You may want to consider this option. Buying property for your own child to live in is often cheaper than renting, particularly if you buy a property with a couple of spare rooms that you can rent out to your offspring's friends. The rent you receive can cover your mortgage repayments, and, because you aren't paying rent for your child to live in someone else's property, you may find that this strategy can work out very well financially. In addition, finding tenants while your child is studying at university shouldn't be a problem because your child will undoubtedly have a steady stream of friends looking for decent accommodation.

Before joining the thousands of parents buying a property for their child to live in, bear a couple of things in mind:

- **How your child will cope with being the managing agent for your property and, in effect, his friends' landlord.** You may think that things are less likely to go wrong with your son living in your rental property with a couple of mates. But he could find laying down the law and insisting on certain rules and behaviour difficult if he's dealing with his friends. And he might not want this responsibility anyway.
- **What you're going to do with the property after your child graduates.** Property should be bought with a long-term view in mind – and a three- or four-year university course is not the long haul. A ten-year view is the most sensible approach to take, so you should be prepared to keep the property once your son or daughter has graduated and may no longer want to live in there. After your child leaves your rental property, you'll have to manage the property yourself or pay a letting agent to do it for you. The university may be able to help you find some student tenants, but you still need to employ someone to manage the property if you don't live nearby or don't want the hassle.

Many universities and colleges have accommodation officers who are constantly looking for suitable properties for students to rent. If you approach one of these and let them know you are interested in renting to students, they can help find you suitable tenants. And if you have any problems with rent collection, they are also a useful port of call.

If you're buying in a university town, which perhaps you don't know very well, the same rules apply as when you buy any rental property in an area you are not familiar with. Get to know the area as best you can by driving round to get a feel for it and checking out whether local letting agents seem to be busy. Find out what rent you can realistically charge and whether there is a good source of tenants. Ask the local university whether they can help with finding student tenants and what guarantees they offer if something goes wrong.

Challenges to prepare for

One of the most common problems associated with renting to students is the fact that students have special needs regarding the length of their tenancy. Terms can be anything from 10 weeks to three months long, and there are three terms every year. Most students have a month off at Christmas and Easter, plus four months or so in the summer. Many students plan to stay in a property for one academic year. If your tenancy agreement (explained in Chapter 5) is six months long, this won't be long enough – while 12 months is likely to be too long. If you only offer a 12-month tenancy agreement, you may end up with student tenants who default on their agreements and leave straight after the end of the summer term.

The best strategy is to offer a six-month tenancy agreement, which can run for a further six months if both sides are agreeable. Every student tenant must pay a deposit equal to at least one month's rent before moving in and must sign a tenancy agreement making them joint and severally liable for the rent. This ensures that if one of them defaults on the rent, or does a runner, the others are liable for the shortfall. Reiterating this fact should minimise misunderstandings and help ensure that your student tenants stay put and pay up.

The other primary concern with renting to students is their behaviour. Make sure that you implement strict policies and rules concerning noise. Make sure you consistently require a larger deposit on rental properties let to students or insist that parents act as guarantor. Also (as discussed in Chapter 10) you should insist that each student sets up a direct debit from his or her bank account so you receive the full amount of the rent each month without having to chase up your tenants.

If you have rental properties that attract prospective student tenants, be sure to adopt policies that allow you to take advantage of this large target market while minimising the downside.

Smoking or No Smoking? Tapping into Potential Markets

People tend to feel very strongly about smoking. Those who smoke want to be able to smoke in peace and quiet and in the comfort of their own home. Those who don't smoke, and wish others wouldn't, don't want to have to put up with the smell, let alone be exposed to second-hand smoke.

Both the smoker and the non-smoker represent potential – albeit opposing – niche markets. As a landlord, you have to decide whether you want to tap into either (or both) of these markets. The following sections explain how.

Catering to smokers

When you flick through the rental ads in your local newspaper, one requirement stands out time and time again, along with 'no pets' and 'no DSS'. Many landlords won't rent their properties to smokers, and 'no smokers' is therefore a common detail in many rental adverts. Many landlords also include a clause in the tenancy agreement stating that smoking is not allowed in the rental property – by tenants or their guests.

There are several good business reasons to consider banning smoking in your rental properties. Most landlords have seen the additional damage caused by smokers, including damage from burns, the need to thoroughly clean the carpets, curtains, and all surfaces, in addition to possibly having to redecorate the entire property to remove the smoke that has permeated it, once the smoking tenants move out. If your tenants don't smoke, your insurance premiums are also likely to be less.

But having said that, with so many landlords banning smoking, grateful smokers are likely to pay more for a property where they are accepted. Given that you may have to redecorate when they move out, you could feasibly ask for higher rent and a higher deposit. If you're prepared to do more extensive turnaround work in between tenancies than you would with non-smokers, you may find a rental opportunity for you here, particularly if the rental market is going through a soft patch and good, non-smoking tenants are thin on the ground.

Smoking can be a serious addiction, and it isn't feasible for you to demand that your tenants give up if they are heavy smokers. However, it is reasonable to request a bigger deposit from a smoker.

Designating your rental properties no smoking

The flip side to the coin is that non-smokers often prefer to rent a flat in a building where smoking is partially or completely restricted in communal areas, such as hallways, stairwells, and lifts. If you own a rental property in such a building, or are really opposed to smoking yourself, you could market your flat as a non-smoking one and hope to attract tenants looking for a smoke-free environment. The 1998 Government White Paper, *Smoking Kills*, stated that 70 per cent of the UK population doesn't smoke. It also highlighted the health risks of passive smoking – inhaling other people's tobacco smoke. By targeting non-smokers, you could be tapping into a potentially rich source of prospective tenants.

The advantage of non-smokers is that your property is likely to require less work to bring it up to scratch for the next tenant.

As with any major policy change, be sure to implement a conversion to a no smoking rental property upon tenant turnover or only after giving proper notice. You can't simply impose this policy upon your smoking tenants without giving them enough notice.

Part VII
The Part of Tens

"Now according to this, you have had problems getting rented accommodation because of your very large family."

In this part . . .

This wouldn't be a *For Dummies* book without the Part of Tens. Here you'll find short bursts of information on everything from why you should buy rental property in the first place, to how to rent a vacancy when you do, to increasing your cash flow. So if you're looking for a lot of information, but you don't have much time, you've come to the right part.

Chapter 22

Ten Reasons to Become a Rental Property Owner

In This Chapter

- Understanding the benefits to owning rental property
- Working out whether owning rental property is right for you

Owning rental property isn't for everyone. So if you're just starting to think about investing in property and letting it out to tenants, in this chapter we offer ten great reasons to take the plunge.

You Can Diversify Your Investments

If you already have significant assets in unit and investment trusts, bonds or gilts, and equities, you can diversify your investments and spread your risk by buying rental property. Owning your own home is a first step toward diversification, but owning investment properties is a prudent strategy to protect your assets from volatility in certain areas of the economy.

You Don't Need Much Money to Start

Many people think that property is an investment only for the wealthy. In fact, a lack of money is often cited as the number one factor preventing people from investing in property. But property is a tangible asset that you can typically purchase for a deposit of as little as 15 per cent of the asking price. Buy-to-let mortgages are readily available at very competitive rates (see Chapter 16). Alternatively, if you have built up a lot of equity in your home, you could release some of this and use it to buy a rental property outright, rather than take on another mortgage to buy one.

It Can Be a Second Income

Many of the greatest rags-to-riches stories are based on property investors who started from scratch. The majority of residential rental property is owned by working people of modest means from all backgrounds and ages, who sought viable opportunities to supplement their current income or career. Property investing can begin as a part-time job and offer a second income.

You Gain Tax Advantages

Plenty of tax breaks are available when it comes to investing in rental property. The Inland Revenue has many unique taxation advantages for property (see Chapter 17 for more about these). You can benefit by deducting expenses and claim an annual wear and tear allowance on furnishings. Owning and operating rental property is a business, and the Inland Revenue encourages it by allowing deductions against your rental income. That means you can deduct all operating expenses, including the cost of advertising your property, maintenance and repairs, insurance, and your expenses for visiting the property.

As with all taxation matters, be sure you understand the basic concepts of property taxation issues, but rely on an accountant or solicitor for advice on details, procedures, and tax laws. Tax codes change from year to year, so discussing your personal tax situation with your accountant on at least an annual basis is always a good idea.

Property Holds Its Value

Property has proven to be one of the most popular investments around, because house prices tend to appreciate over time. Rental property has become very popular because, while the capital value of the property is increasing, you also get a rental income at the same time to cover the mortgage and other costs associated with being a landlord.

Property is cyclical. Many businesses have their ups and downs, and property is no exception. However, property usually rebounds and grows in value after a market slump. Historically, many solid property investments have depreciated for a period of time, but then they have grown again in value. Property appreciates when demand is great – more than can be met by the housing supply. In the long run, property has been an established performer and offers a solid foundation for your financial future.

You Get Leverage

Property *leverage* is the use of mortgage financing to purchase an investment property with only a small cash deposit, with the expectation that appreciation and inflation will create a disproportionately high return on the original cash investment upon sale. The key to successfully using leverage is having a mortgage interest rate *lower* than the return on your property investment.

Here's a simplified example. A buyer purchases a £100,000 rental home with a £20,000 cash deposit and applies for an £80,000 loan at interest of five per cent. If the property appreciates and sells in three years for a net of £120,000, the owner will have earned £20,000 (a 100 per cent return) on their money. This is called *positive leverage.* Conversely, high interest rates and flat property prices with no increases in cash flow results in *negative leverage,* and undercapitalised investors may lose their property.

It Beats Inflation

Inflation is the loss of buying power as prices rise. Most investments, such as bonds, equities, and unit and investment trusts, provide some return but have trouble keeping up with the rate of inflation. Thus, investors in these assets often find that they are actually losing purchasing power over time. However, property has some unique advantages that make it a formidable tool in the battle against inflation. When you purchase rental property with a fixed rate mortgage, the price and financing cost of the property is fixed. Certain operating costs such as utility bills, if you (and not the tenant) pay them, are bound to increase; however, landlords usually increase the amount of rent charged to offset the increased operating costs. Of course, temporary softness or downturns in the rental market may delay rent increases in the short run, but historically, property cash flows have been able to maintain the owner's purchasing power in the long run.

You Get a Positive Cash Flow

Landlords know that the right investment property generates sufficient rental income to cover the mortgage and all operating expenses of the property. And after the tax advantages of depreciation, property generally provides positive cash flow. This may not always be true in the first few years of ownership, but positive cash flow is a real benefit for many investors. Of course, after the mortgage has been paid, the positive cash flow can be very significant.

It's an Alternative to a Pension

Pensions may be the traditional way to save for retirement, but they have gradually fallen out of favour with the British public. Several factors have contributed to this, including poor performance as a result of the disappointing performance of the stock market in the early 2000s, and the bad press caused by the troubles of the Equitable Life pension group. As well as these problems, the pensions industry hasn't been helped by the fact that an increasing number of employers are closing their final salary pension schemes to new employees. Planning for your own retirement is becoming an unavoidable fact of life.

Property is proving to be an excellent alternative to a pension, because you have more control over your investment. You decide what to buy, how much to invest, and how you manage it. You also decide when to sell up and get your hands on your money, subject to the market at that particular time. It is all a far cry from waiting until you are 50 (55 from 2010) before you can get your hands on the cash, which is what you have to do with a pension.

An increasing number of retirement experts are recommending that, when funding your old age, you spread your risk by investing in pensions, individual savings accounts, and property. In the long run, this strategy gives you far greater control over your finances and saves you from putting all your eggs in one basket.

It Can Make You Wealthy in the Long Run

Property investment is one of the best methods to fulfil the dream of retiring wealthy. This worthy goal requires a diversified investment strategy, with assets that can be purchased with leverage, generate cash flow, appreciate consistently over time, and maintain their purchasing power in an inflationary environment. Like most investments, the earlier you begin your property investment career, the better your results. Buying and holding the right rental properties for 20 to 30 years is an ideal way to hedge inflation, take advantage of unique tax benefits, and build wealth for retirement.

Chapter 23

Ten Ways to Get and Keep Full Occupancy in Your Property

In This Chapter

- Staying ahead of the competition
- Keeping the interests of your prospective tenants in mind

Every day that a rental property sits empty is a loss of revenue that you can never fully recover. Even if you get a higher rent when you eventually let the property, the lost rent due to that void period is usually gone for good. In this chapter, we give you ten specific tips or tools to help you rent your empty property straightaway.

Maintain Kerb Appeal

When you're letting rental properties, the prospective tenant's first impression is determined by the exterior kerb appeal of the property when he approaches it. If your rental property doesn't look clean and attractive on the outside, the tenant will often never even wait to see the inside! Your chances of renting out your property and getting a competitive amount of rent from a stable and financially reliable tenant is just about nil when your property doesn't have good kerb appeal. You can't always dramatically improve the architectural look of your rental property, but you can usually control the kerb appeal of the garden and overall appearance from the street.

Familiarity is the enemy of landlords; when you're familiar with your property, you may have trouble looking at it with an independent and critical eye. Drive up to your property and continually ask yourself what catches your eye and what looks tacky or poorly maintained. You may really have to focus, but you are likely to find several items that need immediate attention. Deal with them now.

Keep the Property in Rent-Ready Condition

Although you may eventually find a tenant who is willing to accept your rental property before it's ready to rent, you can almost guarantee that the property will be returned to you in even worse condition when that tenant moves out. Of course, the tenant will then argue with you if you try to make any deductions from his deposit, and the courts will probably side with the tenant because the property wasn't clean in the first place. Spare yourself the agony and aim to have a rent-ready property that is clean and free of defects.

You need to distinguish your rental property from the others out there. So although your property may have certain factors or issues that are negatives beyond your control, the professionally maintained, clean, bright, and airy appearance of your rental property is a noticeable difference that appeals to the best prospective tenants.

Establish a Competitive Rent

If you don't have vacancies on a regular basis and you're in a rental market where rents are fluctuating, ensuring that you're charging the right amount of rent can be a real challenge. Be sure to do your homework and carefully review the local rental market for properties that are truly comparable. If you set your rent too low, you may get several suitable applicants but you won't maximise your rental income. If the rent is too high, you'll suffer lost rental income that is tough or impossible to ever recover, even if you ultimately succeed in getting an above-market rent. The key is to set your rent at or slightly below market rent for your area.

Offer Prospective Tenants a Rent Guarantee

Most prospective tenants are concerned about the rent. Although they may feel comfortable with the amount of rent you are currently charging, virtually all tenants are concerned about your ability to unilaterally increase their rent. Of course, a long-term tenancy agreement, which is what tenants are usually after, isn't in your best interests. With such an agreement, you can't increase the rent, and you may also have trouble evicting a problem tenant.

If you know that you have no intention of raising your new tenant's rent in the near future, offer the prospective tenant a rent guarantee for a set period of time. This guarantee allays the tenant's fears of being hit with an unreasonable rent increase soon after moving in; at the same time, it doesn't lock you into a long-term tenancy agreement that requires expensive and aggravating court action in the event that you want to remove the tenant from your rental property.

Stay Ahead of the Technology Curve

Every day, access to technology becomes more important, so ensuring that your property has more than one telephone line (so that your tenant can access the Internet and use the phone at the same time) can be a great way to distinguish your property from the competition.

Offer Referral Fees

Often your current tenants or the neighbours to your rental property can be the best source for finding your next tenant. They may work or go to college with someone who's looking for a new place to rent. Or maybe they have social, recreational, or religious activities with people who need a new place to live. So let them know that you have a vacancy coming up and that you want to reward them for taking the time to refer a prospective tenant to you. Referral fees can be an extremely cost-effective source of suitable tenants. Another benefit is that most people don't personally refer a potential tenant whom they don't respect and trust. Referral fees are a way for people to make some money and have a hand in picking their own neighbours!

Accept Pets

Although many landlords have very firm policies against accepting pets, they are missing out on a significant number of potential tenants who might be near perfect in every other way. With the legal requirement to accept those pets that disabled tenants rely upon under the Disability Discrimination Act, many landlords find that their ability to enforce 'no pet' policies is already diminished anyway.

So if you can't beat 'em, why not join 'em? If you establish sound pet policies, collect a larger deposit, and meet both the tenant and the pet, you often find that you have an excellent, stable tenant for many years to come.

Offer Move-In Gifts or Upgrades

The word *free* is one of our favourite words – and one of the most powerful sales tools ever! If you want to let your empty property today, seriously consider offering your prospective tenant a move-in gift or an upgrade to the rental property. Remember that every day your rental property sits empty, you lose money that you'll never see again, so you may as well sweeten the pot!

You can offer a move-in gift that immediately belongs to the tenant, or you can offer an upgrade to the rental property that stays when the tenant leaves. For example, a bottle of champagne and a couple of cheap champagne flutes is a nice gesture for tenants to welcome them into their new home – and the gesture doesn't cost you the earth. Alternatively, if you're planning to replace the carpet, consider giving your incoming tenants the option to choose among their favourite neutral carpet colours.

Contact Big Companies or Corporations

In big cities, demand for rental houses and flats can be high, especially if company employees are relocating into the area. In particular, many companies and corporations have an extremely difficult time finding rental properties in cities for families of executives who need a small family home with a garden and plenty of storage for a short period of time. Corporations are often willing to pay significantly above the going market rent – sometimes 20 to 50 per cent – for properties with tenancy agreements ranging from a few weeks to a few months. If the rent is enough to meet your outgoings, shorter tenancy agreements can be worth the additional tenant turnover. However, short-let properties must be fully furnished and decorated to a higher standard than ordinary rental properties. The property should also be ready for tenants to move in straightaway.

Some companies or corporations may want to rent your property for several years with the provision that they can move in different occupants. Make sure that you have very firm house rules and a reasonable limit on the frequency of tenant turnover. In addition, require a detailed inspection every time a new tenant moves in.

Accept Housing Benefit

As we discuss in Chapter 21, you can increase the number of potential tenants by considering those who are in receipt of Housing Benefit, a means-tested social security benefit for tenants who can't meet their rental payments in full. Many landlords tend to shun such tenants and refuse to rent property to them. However, some landlords specialise in taking such tenants. The advantage to accepting tenants who receive Housing Benefit is that the rent is often paid in full, so you can be reasonably sure that it will be paid regularly. To make sure, and as long as the tenant agrees, you can require that the Housing Benefit be paid directly to you. If you decide to go down this route, include a clause in your tenancy agreement stating this arrangement. The only disadvantage is that rent is paid four weeks in arrears rather than in advance.

Chapter 24

Ten Ways to Increase Cash Flow

In This Chapter

- Finding ways to bring in more cash
- Working out how to reduce your expenses

Maximising your cash flow is one of the most important goals of owning rental property, because cash flow essentially represents profit. Cash flow can be *positive,* which means you receive income from your rental property, or *negative,* which means you must put in cash to meet your expenses. Even if your cash flow is currently positive, you may be able to improve or increase it.

Increase the Rent

Raising the rent is one of the easiest ways to increase your cash flow. Most landlords fail to keep their rents up to market levels because they're worried that they'll lose good tenants. Some owners are just too nice, or they become personally involved with their tenants and can't operate their rental properties like a business. Minimising turnover is one of the most important concepts of rental property management, but it shouldn't be at the expense of lost rental income because the rent you charge is significantly below the going rate.

Most tenants realise that the cost of operating and properly maintaining rental properties is continuously rising, and they'll accept a reasonable increase once a year. Ensuring that the increases are reasonable means you can increase your cash flow without significant tenant turnover.

Decrease Your Operating Expenses

Reducing your operating expenses can lead to a direct increase in your cash flow or profit. Of course, you can only reduce your expenses by a certain amount. If you become too zealous in trying to save money, you may find that you're compromising the way you manage your rental property – and that will only hurt your rental business in the long run. So each year, prepare a simple budget for the 12 months ahead and look at every single one of your expenses. Some items, such as a thorough survey before you decide whether you are going to purchase the property, are beyond your control and shouldn't be skimped on. Other expenses, such as replacing worn carpets or curtains, can get out of hand and eat into your profits if you replace them too frequently or go for very expensive brands. Remember that you're running a business, and this involves saving money where possible – without cutting corners. Save cash by buying carpets and curtains in bulk, and in neutral colours, so that you can use them in all your rental properties. While the cheapest quality will turn out to be false economy in the long run, there's little point in wasting fine Axminster carpets on tenants who are unlikely to care for them as well as you would.

Reduce Your Turnover

Turnover is one of the most costly problems for landlords with small rental properties. And no matter what you do, your tenants will move out eventually. So turnover is inevitable. But if you can keep your tenants for longer periods of time, you can greatly reduce your operating expenses while maintaining steady rental income. If you take the time to properly screen and select your tenants (as explained in Chapter 8), and look for someone who intends to stay for a long time, you're usually rewarded. Treating your tenants with respect and responding promptly to their reasonable requests often leads to longer tenancies as well.

Remortgage Your Rental Property

The interest you pay each month on your mortgage is generally one of the largest single expenses you have. Saving costs here will have an impact on your profits. Most landlords acquire their investment properties using a buy-to-let mortgage and have to stump up a sizeable deposit of around 20 to 30 per cent as part of the deal (see Chapter 16 for more details on mortgages). Remortgaging is simply taking out another loan to replace the one you currently have on your rental property; the new loan should be on more favourable terms.

Taking out a fixed or discount rate on a buy-to-let mortgage when buying a rental property is common; when this offer comes to an end, the loan reverts to the lender's standard variable rate, which is inevitably higher. If you're in this position, think about remortgaging to a lower rate of interest. One of the primary goals and benefits of remortgaging without changing the length of the term of the loan or the amount borrowed is to obtain a lower interest rate and lower monthly payments. The lower the monthly payments, the greater your cash flow.

Upgrade Your Rental Property

Apart from just raising the rent, one of the quickest ways to increase your cash flow is to upgrade or renovate your rental properties. Rental properties can become stale and dated and not very competitive when their kerb appeal falters compared to the newer rental properties in your area. Installing new carpets and painting the walls a lighter, brighter colour can really make a difference. A new microwave or walk-in power shower can also make your property more attractive to prospective tenants. Spending a bit of extra cash in the short term can help you increase your cash flow through higher rent in the longer term.

Pre-Let to Minimise Void Periods

Ask for permission to inspect the rental property as soon as the tenant gives notice that she's leaving. Then you can prepare a list of the work you need to do to the property to get it up to a rent-ready condition and schedule all of the work for the two to three days straight after the tenant moves out. In the meantime, you can advertise the rental property and, upon giving the current occupant proper notice (see Chapter 7), show it to interested prospective tenants while the current tenant is still living in the property. By following this strategy, you can line up new tenants before the existing one has moved out. And the new tenant can move in within a week of the former tenant's departure, decreasing your loss of rent and increasing your cash flow.

Buy Freehold Rather than Leasehold

When you purchase a flat in the UK, you most likely buy the leasehold rather than the freehold. As the leaseholder, you have the right to live in, or rent out, the property for a set number of years, after which time the property reverts back to the freeholder. (See Chapter 3 to find out more about the difference between these.)

During the lease, the landlord is responsible for paying the freeholder an annual service charge and ground rent, which pushes up costs. Service charges start at about £250 a year for an ex-council flat, rising to several thousand pounds for a flat in a smart mansion block with 24-hour porter. Ground rent is about £50 to £100 per year.

Service charges can fluctuate from year to year, so budgeting for them can be hard. Try to get a good estimate as to how much these fees are likely to be by obtaining the accounts for the past three years from the freeholder or his managing agent, along with estimates for future service charges. Such charges eat into your profits, so even if you manage to pass them onto the tenant in the form of higher rent, you still end up paying in the long run. To avoid service charges, buy a freehold property.

Avoid Gas Appliances

If your rental property has gas appliances, you're required by law to employ a CORGI-registered engineer to carry out an annual gas safety check. She must provide you with a certificate confirming that this check has been done and you must pass a copy of this onto your tenant. Faulty gas appliances can be extremely dangerous, and carbon monoxide poisoning kills many people living in rented accommodation every year (see Chapter 15 for safety issues related to gas appliances). Landlords who don't have the necessary certificate can face a fine and even a jail sentence. Obviously, getting the gas supply checked and paying a professional to do it costs time and money. Although it might not seem like a lot, if you have 20 rental properties requiring an annual gas safety check, the amount soon adds up. Many landlords understandably don't want the hassle of gas, so they opt for electric cookers and storage heaters instead.

Do Your Own Repairs

Even the best maintained rental properties require basic maintenance from time to time. This maintenance can be expensive if you have to call out a carpenter, plasterer, plumber, or electrician every time something needs doing. You can save money by doing as much as you can yourself. If you are good at DIY, tackling projects yourself shouldn't be a problem – the only issue might be whether you have enough time to do the work when it needs doing. If you aren't very handy around the home, you can learn how to carry out simple repairs and maintenance from books, evening classes, or from working with someone who is experienced in DIY.

Manage Your Rental Properties Yourself

A managing agent undoubtedly saves landlords time and hassle. But you have to pay up to 15 per cent of your annual rent for a full management service. Agents argue – reasonably – that this fee is more than justified, given the amount of work they do. Also, many landlords simply don't want to be involved in the day-to-day running of their rental properties and are happy to pay someone else to do it. But managing your properties yourself saves money, as long as you check the references of prospective tenants with care. Some landlords prefer the cut and thrust of managing their rental properties, handling existing tenants and finding new ones. They also enjoy the maintenance aspect. By all means do it yourself – if you have the time to do so and are prepared to put up with phone calls from your tenants at all hours of the day or night. Otherwise, employ someone else to manage your rental properties; doing so costs more money, but allows you to get on with your life and is less hassle.

Appendix

Resources

Professional and Trade Organisations

Association of Residential Letting Agents (Arla): Arla is the professional and regulatory body for letting agents in the UK, originally set up in 1981 to promote standards in the residential lettings market. Over 1,200 member offices are located throughout the UK. Landlords who decide to use a letting agent to manage their rental properties have the reassurance that Arla agents have demonstrated a thorough knowledge of their profession and conduct their business according to current best management practice. Arla's Web site (www.arla.co.uk) also offers plenty of useful information for landlords. Arla publishes a buy-to-let guide, available from Arla agents or by contacting Arla via phone (0845 345 5752).

Citizens Advice Bureaux: Landlords after free, confidential, and impartial advice could do worse than to contact their nearest CAB at www.citizensadvice.org.uk.

Council of Mortgage Lenders (CML): The CML is the representative voice for the residential mortgage lending industry. It publishes a couple of free leaflets on buy-to-let, including questions you should ask yourself before deciding to take the plunge. You can access this information via the CML Web site at www.cml.org.uk.

The Law Society: The Law Society provides advice on choosing and using a solicitor. For information, contact the Society by phone (020 7242 1222) or visit its Web site at www.lawsociety.org.uk.

National Approved Letting Scheme (NALS): The NALS is an accreditation scheme for letting and management agents. Because agents who meet NALS criteria agree to meet defined standards of customer service, both landlords and tenants who use them can have peace of mind. NALS agents are insured (to protect clients' money). In addition, landlords who have a complaint about a NALS-registered agent can express their grievances through the NALS customer complaints procedure. To find a NALS-registered agent, visit the Web site at www.nalscheme.co.uk.

National Federation of Residential Landlords (NFRL): There are some 40 affiliated private landlord associations throughout the UK (for your nearest one, check out the NFRL's Web site at www.nfrl.co.uk). Around 10,000 affiliated member landlords belong to these groups, which support and promote working with local authorities, universities, and tenant groups. You can reach the NFRL by phone at 0845 456 0357.

National Association of Estate Agents (NAEA): The NAEA has become the leading professional body for residential estate agents in the UK over the past 40 years. It represents estate agents and property professionals and aims to improve professionalism and accountability in the industry. There are over 10,000 NAEA members nationwide. If you use a NAEA member when you buy, sell, or let a rental property, you can be assured of certain standards. Members are bound by a Code of Practice and adhere to professional Rules of Conduct. For more information, call 01926 496800 or visit NAEA online at www.naea.co.uk.

Royal Institution of Chartered Surveyors (RICS): The RICS is a global professional body representing, regulating, and promoting chartered surveyors. If you are looking for a surveyor, contact the RICS for your nearest member. You can reach them via phone (0870 333 1600) between 8:30 am and 5:30 pm, Monday to Friday. You can also visit the RICS Web site at www.rics.org.uk.

National Landlords' Association (NLA): The NLA represents small-time landlords who own just one or two rental properties. This accounts for around 90 per cent of all landlords. The NLA is a good source of free advice and useful leaflets. Membership starts at £65 a year. For information, you can phone 0870 241 0471 or visit www.landlords.org.uk.

Government Organisations

Department for Work and Pensions (DWP): The DWP is a useful resource for landlords requiring more advice and information about taking on tenants in receipt of Council Tax Benefit and Housing Benefit. For information, visit the DWP Web site at www.dwp.gov.uk.

Inland Revenue: The Inland Revenue publishes several leaflets that are helpful for landlords. You can download these leaflets from the Inland Revenue Web site (www.hmrc.gov.uk) or call its orderline at 08459 000 404, from 8 am to 10 pm, 7 days a week.

For individual advice, contact your local Inland Revenue office. For the phone number, look in the Yellow Pages.

Office of the Deputy Prime Minister: You can find plenty of advice for landlords, including information on fair rents and how rent assessment committees work. Also available is useful advice on how to deal with the tenant's deposit and housing benefit. Landlords will also find plenty of information on houses in multiple occupation and the latest Green Papers and other up-to-date research into the private rental market. For information, go the Office of the Deputy Prime Minister Web site at www.housing.opdm.gov.uk.

Further Information

Landlordzone (www.landlordzone.co.uk) is an excellent independent Web site offering all sorts of information for novice and experienced landlords. Landlords get free access to information, resources, and contacts that they are likely to find useful. As well as the latest rental property news, landlords can also find a guide to letting, advice on how to verify prospective tenants and how to manage the tenancy, and information on landlord insurance. All the latest information on safety regulations is also included, along with details of landlords' obligations. If landlords only look at one Web site, it should be this one, as it's a great one-stop shop.

Mortgage Brokers

John Charcol has a buy-to-let section on its comprehensive Web site, with a free online calculator enabling you to find out what sort of buy-to-let mortgage you can expect to get. Landlords can also find out how much they would save by remortgaging an existing rental property. After you fill out all the relevant fields, the online calculator tells you what loans are suitable for you, and you can apply online. If you want more advice and information, you can contact John Charcol over the phone or arrange a face-to-face meeting with a broker. If you apply online, you don't have to pay any broker fees, but John Charcol charges a fee if you speak to a broker.

You can contact John Charcol via phone (0800 718191) or Web site (www.charcol.co.uk).

London & Country: The fee-free independent mortgage broker offers advice both on finding a buy-to-let mortgage for a new rental property and on remortgaging an existing rental property. You can contact London & Country via phone (0800 9530304) and Web site (www.lcplc.co.uk).

Savills Private Finance (SPF): SPF specialises in larger mortgages, charging clients a fee for advice and arranging a buy-to-let deal for them. You can contact SPF via phone (0870 900 7762) or Web site (www.spf.co.uk).

Credit Reference Agencies

Equifax PLC: Credit File Advice Centre
PO Box 1140
Bradford, BD1 5US

Phone: 08705 143700
Web site: www.equifax.co.uk

Experian Ltd: Consumer Help Service
PO Box 8000
Nottingham, NG1 5GX

Phone: 0870 241 6212
Web site: www.experian.co.uk

Callcredit PLC: Consumer Services Team
PO Box 491
Leeds, LS3 1WZ

Phone: 0870 060 1414
Web site: www.callcredit.plc.uk

Index

• A •

• D •

• E •

• G •

• H •

• I •

• J •

• K •

• L •

• M •

• N •

• O •

• P •

• R •

• T •

• U •

• V •

• W •

Notes

Notes

Notes

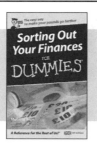

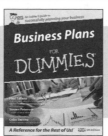

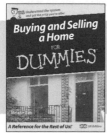

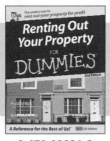

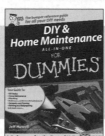

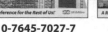

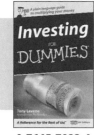

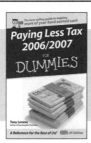

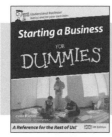

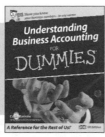

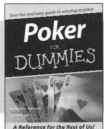

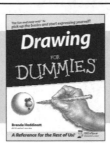

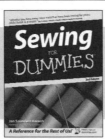

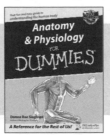

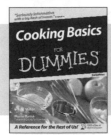

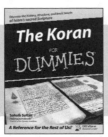

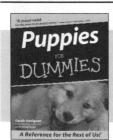

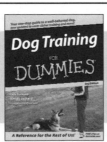

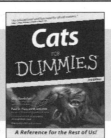

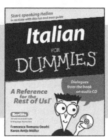

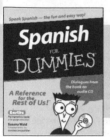

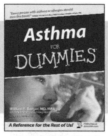

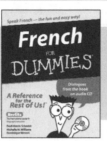

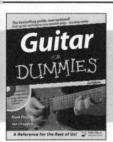

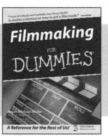

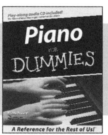

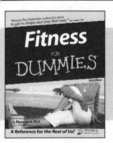

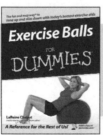

FOR DUMMIES®

Helping you expand your horizons and achieve your potential

INTERNET

0-7645-8996-2

0-7645-8334-4

0-7645-7327-6

Also available:

eBay.co.uk For Dummies (0-7645-7059-5)

Dreamweaver 8 For Dummies (0-7645-9649-7)

Web Design For Dummies (0-471-78117-7)

Everyday Internet All-in-One Desk Reference For Dummies (0-7645-8875-3)

Creating Web Pages All-in-One Desk Reference For Dummies (0-7645-4345-8)

DIGITAL MEDIA

0-7645-9802-3

0-471-74739-4

0-7645-9803-1

Also available:

Digital Photos, Movies, & Music GigaBook For Dummies (0-7645-7414-0)

Photoshop CS2 For Dummies (0-7645-9571-7)

Podcasting For Dummies (0-471-74898-6)

Blogging For Dummies (0-471-77084-1)

Digital Photography All-in-One Desk Reference For Dummies (0-7645-7328-4)

Windows XP Digital Music For Dummies (0-7645-7599-6)

COMPUTER BASICS

0-7645-8958-X

0-7645-7555-4

0-7645-7326-8

Also available:

Office XP 9 in 1 Desk Reference For Dummies (0-7645-0819-9)

PCs All-in-One Desk Reference For Dummies (0-471-77082-5)

Pocket PC For Dummies (0-7645-1640-X)

Upgrading & Fixing PCs For Dummies (0-7645-1665-5)

Windows XP All-in-One Desk Reference For Dummies (0-7645-7463-9)

Macs For Dummies (0-7645-5656-8)

Available wherever books are sold. For more information or to order direct go to www.wileyeurope.com or call 0800 243407 (Non UK call +44 1243 843296)

9035_p4

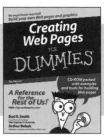

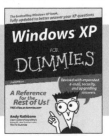